Kant's Doctrine of Virtue

OXFORD GUIDES TO PHILOSOPHY

Oxford Guides to Philosophy presents concise introductions to the most important primary texts in the history of philosophy. Written by top scholars, the volumes in the series are designed to present up-to-date scholarship in an accessible manner, in order to guide readers through these challenging texts.

Anscombe's Intention: A Guide
John Schwenkler

Kant's Doctrine of Virtue: A Guide
Mark Timmons

Kant's Doctrine of Virtue

A Guide

MARK TIMMONS

OXFORD
UNIVERSITY PRESS

Oxford University Press is a department of the University of Oxford. It furthers
the University's objective of excellence in research, scholarship, and education
by publishing worldwide. Oxford is a registered trade mark of Oxford University
Press in the UK and certain other countries.

Published in the United States of America by Oxford University Press
198 Madison Avenue, New York, NY 10016, United States of America.

Library of Congress Cataloging-in-Publication Data
Names: Timmons, Mark, 1951– author.
Title: Kant's Doctrine of virtue : a guide / Mark Timmons.
Description: New York, NY : Oxford University Press, [2021] |
Includes bibliographical references and index.
Identifiers: LCCN 2020052410 (print) | LCCN 2020052411 (ebook) |
ISBN 9780190939229 (hardback) | ISBN 9780190939236 (paperback) |
ISBN 9780190939250 (epub)
Subjects: LCSH: Kant, Immanuel, 1724–1804. Metaphysische Anfangsgründe der
Tugendlehre. | Kant, Immanuel, 1724–1804—Criticism and interpretation. |
Virtue. | Ethics. | Metaphysics.
Classification: LCC B2785.5.Z7 T56 2021 (print) |
LCC B2785.5.Z7 (ebook) | DDC 170—dc23
LC record available at https://lccn.loc.gov/2020052410
LC ebook record available at https://lccn.loc.gov/2020052411

DOI: 10.1093/oso/9780190939229.001.0001

1 3 5 7 9 8 6 4 2

Paperback printed by Marquis, Canada
Hardback printed by Bridgeport National Bindery, Inc., United States of America

For Betsy

Contents

Preface

This book, included in the Oxford Guides series, is a concise guide to Kant's last publication in ethics, Part II of the 1797 *The Metaphysics of Morals, The Doctrine of Virtue*. *The Metaphysics of Morals* comes after the two foundational works, the 1785 *Groundwork of the Metaphysics of Morals* and the 1788 *Critique of Practical Reason* and represents Kant's exposition and defense of his normative doctrine of morals. Part I, *The Doctrine of Right*, contains Kant's legal and political philosophy, while Part II is his ethical theory. *The Doctrine of Virtue* is relatively short, only 116 pages as it appears in volume VI of the Academy edition of Kant's works. Because it is short and yet intended to cover the science of ethics (on Kant's understanding of "science"), it moves rapidly over much ground, challenging any reader's understanding of it. *The Metaphysics of Morals* includes a general introduction that is crucial for understanding the entire book. In it, Kant explains what a metaphysics of morals is, relates the idea of moral law to the faculties of the human mind, reviews core concepts that figure in such a metaphysics, and explains the basis of the division between its two parts. Given, then, its importance for understanding *The Doctrine of Virtue*, this guide also includes chapters devoted to it.

I have written the guide to be read alongside Kant's text. My hope is that it will help readers navigate the complexity of Kant's thought, due in part to his rich philosophical vocabulary expressing concepts he needed to employ to articulate his thought. To help readers with this vocabulary, I have included a *Guide to Terminology*. Throughout I make occasional contact with some of the ever-expanding secondary literature on Kant's ethics. However, given the aim of the series, I have largely refrained from explicitly engaging this literature. I do, though, point readers to select secondary works in the Further Reading sections at the end of each chapter. In the book's conclusion I review elements of Kant's doctrine of virtue, calling attention to its features that distinguish it from others and briefly indicate its continuing influence on normative ethics.

Acknowledgments

Thanks to the following students who read an early draft of this book that I used along with teaching *The Doctrine of Virtue* in my fall 2018 graduate seminar on Kant's ethics: Gavriel Aryah, Josh Cangelosi, Cristos Chuffe, Max Kramer, Robert Lazo, Andrew Lichter, Shuai Liu, Xihe Ouyang, Susan Puls, Will Schumacher, Jacquelyn Sideris, Robert Wallace, Justin Westbrook, and Ke Zhang. A special thanks to Santiago ("Santi") de Jesus Sanchez Borboa, who contributed substantially to the seminar and for the many helpful conversations we've had about parts of this book.

I made many improvements throughout the book thanks to Adam Cureton's thoughtful comments and suggestions on the book's penultimate draft, saving me from some mistakes and encouraging me to elaborate certain themes and arguments.

Robert Audi read and commented on the penultimate manuscript and offered many helpful suggestions for improving the book's content.

Over the years I have greatly benefitted from discussions with my colleague Houston Smit on many of the topics covered in this book.

Thanks finally to Peter Ohlin, editor at Oxford University Press, and to my co-editors of this series, Becko Copenhaver and Chris Shields, for their help and encouragement.

Abbreviations for Kant's Works

All references to Kant's work include the volume number (in roman numerals) followed by the page number of the German Academy edition of Kant's works: *Immanuel Kants gesmmelte Schriften*, edited by the Königlich Preußischen Akademie der Wissenschaften (Berlin: Walter de Gruyter, 1900–).

The Academy edition page numbers are included in the margins of most English language translations, including the Cambridge Edition series of the Works of Immanuel Kant listed here. The following abbreviations are used throughout.

Anth	*Anthropology from a Pragmatic Point of View*, trans. R. B. Louden (2006)
CJ	*Critique of the Power of Judgment,* trans. P. Guyer and E. Matthews (2000)
Col	*Moral Philosophy from the Lectures of Professor Kant, Winter Semester 1784–85*, Georg Ludwig Collins, ed., included in *Lectures on Ethics*, trans. P. Heath (1997)
CprR	*Critique of Practical Reason*, trans. M. J. Gregor (1996)
CpuR	*Critique of Pure Reason*, trans. P. Guyer and A. Wood (1998)
DR	*Doctrine of Right*, part I of the *Metaphysics of Morals*, trans. M. J. Gregor (1996)
DrMM	*Drafts for the Metaphysics of Morals*, trans. K. R. Westphal in F. Rauscher, ed., *Lectures and Drafts on Practical Philosophy* (2016)
DV	*Doctrine of Virtue*, Part II of the *Metaphysics of Morals*, trans. J. Timmermann and J. Grenberg (forthcoming).
EMH	*Essay on the Maladies of the Head*, trans. R. B. Louden (2007)
G	*Groundwork of the Metaphysics of Morals*, trans. M. J. Gregor and J. Timmermann (2011)
JL	*Jäsche Logic*, trans. J. M. Young (1992)
LA	*Lectures on Anthropology*, trans. R. B. Clewis, R. B. Louden, C. F. Munzel, and A. W. Wood (2012)

LM   *Lectures on Metaphysics*, trans. K. Ameriks and
          S. Naragon (1997)
MFNS   *Metaphysical Foundations of Natural Science*, trans.
          M. Friedman (2004)
MM   Introduction to *The Metaphysics of Morals*, trans. M. J.
          Gregor (1996)
MPT   "On the Miscarriage of All Philosophical Trials," trans. A. W.
          Wood (1996)
NF   *Notes and Fragments*, trans. C. Bowman, P. Guyer, and
          F. Rauscher (2005)
Ped   *Lectures on Pedagogy*, trans. R. B. Louden (2006)
R   *Religion within the Boundaries of Mere Reason*, trans. G. di
          Giovanni (revised edition, 2018)
TP   "On the Common Saying: That May Be Correct in Theory, But
          It Is of No Use in Practice," trans. M. J. Gregor (1996)
Vig   *Notes on the Lectures of Mr. Kant on the Metaphysics of Morals*,
          begun October 14, 1793, Johann Friedrich Vigilantius, ed.,
          included in *Lectures on Ethics*, trans. P. Heath (1997)

Note on Translations

For *The Doctrine of Virtue* (DV), I am using the new English translation by Jens Timmermann and Jeanine Grenberg that includes the German and English side by side.

James W. Ellington's *Ethical Philosophy* by Hackett Publishing Co., besides his translation of DV, also includes translation of the general introduction to *The Metaphysics of Morals*, which I cover in Part II of this guide. (This book also includes translations of Kant's *Groundwork* and the essay "On a Supposed Right to Lie.")

PART I
BACKGROUND

1

Life and Work

Immanuel Kant was born in 1724 in Königsberg, the capital of East Prussia, a bustling harbor city located on the Baltic Sea, where he spent most of his life.[1] His parents were devout Pietists, a form of Protestantism that emphasized "independent Bible study, personal devotion, the priesthood of the laity, and a practical faith issuing in acts of charity."[2] About his parents Kant wrote in a letter: "my two parents (from the class of tradesmen) were perfectly honest, morally decent, and orderly. . . . Moreover, they gave me an education that could not have been better when considered from the moral point of view."[3]

He entered the University of Königsberg in 1740 at the age of seventeen, where he studied philosophy and natural science. His father died in 1746, and without finances to continue his studies Kant earned money as a private tutor, returning to the university in 1754, completing his degree the following year. It was not until 1770 at the age of forty-six that Kant finally obtained a professorship of logic and metaphysics at the University of Königsberg, where he taught until his retirement in 1797. After becoming ill in October 1803, Kant died on February 12, 1804, just shy of his eightieth birthday.

Some of Kant's earliest writings address topics in physical science, including the 1755 *General History and Theory of the Heavens*, in which he speculated that the solar system could have evolved entirely by mechanical means, and so without divine intervention. This same idea was later put forth independently in 1796 by French philosopher Pierre-Simon Laplace (1749–1827), and has become known as the Kant-Laplace nebular hypothesis. The decade of Kant's life in the 1770s

---

[1] Before World War II, Prussia was part of Germany; after the war, it was divided between Poland and the Soviet Union. Kant's city of birth is now Kaliningrad, Russia.

[2] Kuehn 2001: 34.

[3] Quoted in Kuehn 2001: 31.

Kant's Doctrine of Virtue. Mark Timmons, Oxford University Press (2021). © Oxford University Press.
DOI: 10.1093/oso/9780190939229.003.0001

is known as his "silent years" during which he published very little while working out elements of his mature philosophy, culminating in his 1781 *Critique of Pure Reason*, followed by the *Critique of Practical Reason* in 1788, and finally, the *Critique of the Power of Judgment* in 1790. These three books (often referred to, respectively, as the first, second, and third *Critiques*) comprise the major works of Kant's so-called critical philosophy, which, roughly speaking, involves an examination of the character and limits of fundamental human mental faculties as a basis for explaining the possibility of a true metaphysics of both nature and morals. The first *Critique* investigates the nature and limits of human theoretical cognition—cognition of what is—arguing against traditional "dogmatic metaphysics" that sought cognition of a supersensible realm of being. The second *Critique* is Kant's second of three major works in moral philosophy, about which more in a moment. The third *Critique* provides an account of judgments of aesthetic taste and an examination of the role of teleological thinking in regulating the scientific investigation of the natural world.

Kant wrote three works of moral philosophy, beginning with the 1785 *Groundwork of the Metaphysics of Morals*, followed by the second *Critique*, and finally, toward the end of his life, the 1797 *The Metaphysics of Morals*. The relatively short but exceedingly dense *Groundwork* provides a foundation for a comprehensive normative moral theory by articulating and then establishing the supreme principle of morality, which Kant referred to as "the categorical imperative." The second *Critique* represents a systematic investigation of the foundation of morality that Kant traces to our nature as beings with free will. He also explains how God and immortality of the soul figure in a complete account of morality. (More on this in the next chapter.) Both are primarily works in metaethics—investigating the nature and possibility of morality.[4] *The Metaphysics of Morals* by contrast represents Kant's normative moral theory in which he sets forth and justifies a system of duties. Part I of the book, *The Doctrine of Right* (DR), presents the elements of his legal and political philosophy and features duties,

---

[4] However, they also include some elements of Kant's normative ethics, including an articulation of the supreme principle of morality that he later employs in deriving a system of moral principles in DV.

compliance with which is susceptible to legitimate coercion from the state or other people. In Part II, *The Doctrine of Virtue* (DV), the focus of our study, Kant turns to that part of moral philosophy—the ethics— concerning duties not properly subject to such coercion. These two parts comprise Kant's doctrine of morals: his normative theory of law, politics, and ethics. For Kant, a philosophical doctrine of morals can only be a metaphysics of morals.

1.1 Situating Kant's moral philosophy

It is helpful to situate the development of Kant's moral philosophy against two traditions: the seventeenth- and eighteenth-century debate among British philosophers between rationalists and sentimentalists over the foundation of morality, as well as the works of select German philosophers who fell into one of these two camps. Very roughly speaking, the British rationalists, including Ralph Cudworth (1617– 1688), Samuel Clarke (1675–1729), and others, held that it is possible to know fundamental ethical principles on the sole basis of reason, and thus know them a priori without needing to conduct scientific experiments, use our five senses, or otherwise experience them. They drew an analogy between moral and mathematical judgments.[5] In op- position to this view, the British sentimentalists, including Anthony Ashley Cooper, the third Earl of Shaftesbury (1671–1713), Francis Hutcheson (1694–1746) and David Hume (1711–1776), held that moral judgments are analogous to judgments of beauty in that senti- ment (feeling) is the basis for both. For instance, based on his analysis of moral thought, David Hume famously concluded, "Morality, there- fore, is more properly felt than judg'd of" (1739: 470).

Early in his career, Kant expressed sympathy toward the British sen- timentalist school, writing in an announcement for a course he was to teach in winter semester 1765–66, "The attempts of *Shaftesbury, Hutcheson,* and *Hume* although incomplete and defective, have

[5] In Germany during Kant's time, a perfectionist version of rationalism was defended by Christian Wolff (1679–1754) and others, largely inspired by the earlier work of Leibniz (1646–1716).

nonetheless penetrated furthest in the search for the fundamental principle of morality."[6] However, two decades later, and by the time Kant writes the 1785 *Groundwork*, he has developed a distinctive form of rationalism, differing significantly from his rationalist predecessors.

1.2 History and significance of *The Doctrine of Virtue*

As early as 1767, Kant wrote to a former student (Johann Gottfried Herder) that he hoped to complete work on a metaphysics of morals in the following year. However, writing the book was delayed by various things, including Kant's felt need to first complete other philosophical projects, including the *Groundwork* and the second *Critique*. According to one scholar,[7] it is likely that Kant did not begin the actual writing of *The Metaphysics of Morals* until 1795. Its eventual publication was delayed for thirty years after mentioning the project to Herder.

DV is critical for understanding Kant's moral philosophy for several reasons. *First*, it presents a side of his moral philosophy—a normative ethical theory set forth systematically—not found in the two earlier works in moral philosophy. One gets a glimpse of this system from the *Groundwork*'s four sample applications of the supreme principle of morality to the cases of suicide, false promises, helping others, and self-perfection. However, in DV we find a fully worked out system of midlevel duties and associated virtues divided into duties to oneself and duties to others, each of these divisions further subdivided. *Second*, as a treatise about virtue it focuses on one's inner moral life—one's attitudes and motivations in complying with duty and thus with moral character. This aspect of the book combats the impression one might get from the *Groundwork* and second *Critique* that Kant's moral philosophy is overly abstract and does not connect with ordinary moral experience and concrete moral problems. *Third*, DV also discusses topics not treated in other works, including Kant's distinctive

---

[6] This announcement is contained in volume 2, pages 311–12 of the Academy edition of Kant's works.

[7] Kuehn 2010.

conceptions of conscience and moral friendship. A complete moral philosophy addresses metaethical questions about the foundation of morality, as well as general normative questions about what one ought to do and what sort of person to be. In addressing these latter questions, DV (together with [DR]) represent the completion of Kant's moral philosophy.

DV is also not a work of mere historical significance. It is a contribution to normative ethical theory, especially as it compares to other approaches, including forms of consequentialism, contemporary virtue ethics, natural law theory, the ethics of prima facie duty, and religious ethics. These comparisons will emerge as we proceed and are briefly summarized in the book's conclusion as well as how Kant's ethics is relevant to contemporary moral problems

1.3 Reading Kant

As many readers know, reading Kant is challenging, and understanding his writings is often a slow and painstaking process. Part of the challenge is mastering Kant's technical vocabulary, which, as I mentioned in the Preface, he needed to express his complex thought. I hope this book, including the Guide to Terminology, helps overcome this challenge and others. I have just been touting some of DV's virtues, however, it has certain shortcomings as a philosophical treatise. It moves rapidly over many topics, some of its arguments are unclear, others are unconvincing, while sometimes we don't find arguments for claims that need support. Perhaps these shortcomings are due to the fact the Kant wrote the book toward the end of his life when he might not have been at the height of his mental powers. Still, I stand by my positive remarks about the book's importance, which I hope to partly if not fully vindicate with this guide.

1.4 Why the general introduction?

Let me emphasize the importance of the general introduction to the entire *Metaphysics of Morals* and explain why I spend time covering it.

In it, Kant explains what a metaphysics of morals is and why there must be one. Reading DV without this background would likely be puzzling, since contemporary philosophy treats metaphysics as exclusively concerned with the most fundamental constituents of what is and not what we are required to do and the kind of person to be. Normative ethical theory that deals with these issues is thus not taken to be part of metaphysics. Yet, Kant has his own conception of the field of metaphysics which concerns the nature and possibility of synthetic a priori cognition, including cognition of basic moral principles, material covered in chapter 3. Furthermore, Kant's normative ethical theory presupposes familiarity with the concepts and doctrines that Kant only summarizes in the general introduction. This includes how moral laws are related to basic mental faculties of human beings (the focus of chapter 4) and articulation of such basic ethical concepts as obligation, duty, and moral worth, the focus of chapter 5. Kant's treatment of these topics in the general introduction is dense and requires elaboration to be adequately understood; hence, the need for three chapters devoted to it.

1.5 Looking ahead

This guide, written so that it can be read along with Kant's text, has five parts:

> Part I: Background (this chapter and the next). Chapter 2 acquaints some readers and reminds others of some basic theses of Kant's metaphysics and epistemology as a lead-in to his mature moral philosophy. It includes remarks about the roles of freedom, God, and immortality of the soul in Kant's ethical theorizing. Of importance for our study is Kant's distinction between human beings as members of the sensible (phenomenal) world and human beings as members of an intelligible (noumenal) world.
>
> Part II: General Introduction to *The Metaphysics of Morals* (chapters 3–5). Although *The Doctrine of Virtue* (DV) is the focus of this study, as I've just explained, material from the general introduction to the entire *Metaphysics of Morals* (MM) is crucial background for understanding DV.

Part III: Introduction to *The Doctrine of Virtue* (chapters 6–9). Besides the general introduction to MM, Kant wrote dedicated introductions to *The Doctrine of Right* and *The Doctrine of Virtue*. The introduction to DV comprises eighteen sections and includes material that Kant thought essential for understanding his theory of virtue, to which I have devoted four chapters.

Part IV: The Doctrine of Elements (chapters 10–15). The Elements is where Kant spells out and defends his system of duties of virtue that constitutes his normative ethical theory. Here we find various divisions, the most fundamental between duties to oneself and duties to others. Kant fittingly concludes his discussion of duties to others with remarks about friendship.

Part V: The Doctrine of Methods of Ethics and Conclusion (chapter 16). Finally, the Methods concerns moral education and the practice of virtue, outlining the practical import of Kant's normative ethical theory. The conclusion explains why ethics, as a science, does not include religion as a doctrine of duties to God.

Concluding Reflections on Kant's *Doctrine of Virtue*. This brief chapter calls attention to some of the more salient features of Kant's ethical theory, comparing it to others, and suggesting topics for further study.

In his years as a teacher, Kant taught ethics close to thirty times. What survives from some of those courses are student notes. A set of notes from a course offered winter semester 1784–85 is attributed to Georg Collins and is referred to as the Collins notes. Another set (the Vigilantius notes) is attributed to Johann Vigilantius, a lawyer and friend of Kant's whose notes are from a course on the metaphysics of morals Kant taught in 1793–94. Compared to Kant's *Metaphysics of Morals*, the student lecture notes sometimes contain far richer discussions of many of the topics covered in Kant's own writings than in his published works. This is particularly true of the various duties and associated virtues that comprise Kant's normative ethical theory. Besides the *Groundwork* and second *Critique*, two other important sources for understanding Kant's theory of virtue are his 1793 *Religion within the Boundaries of Mere Reason* and the 1798 *Anthropology from a Pragmatic Point of View*. These works and some others will figure in my exposition and elaboration of Kant's doctrine of virtue in the chapters to follow.

Further reading

- For a concise overview of Kant's life and work, see Guyer 2021.
- Kuehn 2001 is an extensive, authoritative biography.

2

Philosophical Background

Kant's ethical theory is embedded in his epistemology and metaphysics. Before beginning our study of his ethics, then, we should acquaint ourselves with some of these views, relating them to key elements of Kant's ethics—freedom, the moral law, and the highest good.

2.1 The nature and limits of human theoretical cognition

Kant's 1781 masterpiece, *The Critique of Pure Reason* (CpuR), contains a detailed account of the nature and limits of human theoretical cognition. This account claims to provide a priori principles that are inherent in our capacity for such cognition. Theoretical cognition (explained further in the next chapter) is cognition of *what is*. By appeal to these a priori principles, Kant argues that we can have theoretical cognition only of things making up the natural world. Our theoretical cognition of things is limited to properties they have, and the changes they undergo, insofar as they are subject to the laws that govern and explain what goes on in nature. All theoretical cognition of things comes about, on Kant's account, through the distinct operations of two fundamental capacities: sensibility and understanding.

Sensibility, which includes the five senses of sight, hearing, touch, taste, and smell, is the capacity to receive representations through the way in which one is affected by things.[1] Every sensibility has a "form" in which representations that are presented to us must be ordered to provide experience. Our sensibility has two forms: space and time. Space is the form of our outer sense through which we order things outside

---

[1] Sensibility for Kant also includes imagination.

Kant's Doctrine of Virtue. Mark Timmons, Oxford University Press (2021). © Oxford University Press.
DOI: 10.1093/oso/9780190939229.003.0002

us. Time is the form of our inner sense whereby the representations we are presented with are temporally ordered. Through the operation of understanding, one subsumes what is given in sensibility under basic concepts including <cause> and <effect> yielding experience of objects. In his masterwork, Kant explains the operations of sensibility and understanding and how, together, they produce theoretical cognition of things. These details are not our concern. The important point for now is that the forms of space and time are contributed by us which, together with how we are affected by the senses, yields experience. Our theoretical cognition based on such experience is therefore limited to things as they *appear* to us and not as they are in themselves. Thus, Kant distinguishes *appearances* from *things in themselves*—arguably, a metaphysical distinction. Let us consider this further.

It is common to distinguish what merely appears to be the case from what really is the case—between appearance and reality. For example, as one drives along a highway, there appears to be a pool of water ahead on the road, but it turns out that (in reality) there is no water, it is only, as we say, an appearance of water—a mirage. Importantly, Kant's contrast between appearances and things in themselves is *not* the same as the appearance/reality distinction just mentioned. For Kant, theoretical cognition yields knowledge of an objectively existing world of objects and their properties. However, it is knowledge of the world as it appears to human beings given their form of sensibility. It is possible, according to Kant, for there to be creatures that have a completely different sensibility or no sensibility at all (as in God's purely discursive understanding) and so do not experience objects as situated in space and time, despite the fact that we are not able to imagine what such experiences would be like. Kant uses various terms in referring to the world as we experience it, including: 'phenomenal world' and 'sensible world.' For Kant all appearances as elements of the sensible world (events, objects, and their properties) are subject to causal explanation—in particular, that every event in time is the inevitable causal result of previous events together with the laws of nature that relate them.

In limiting our theoretical cognition of things to objects (events, properties) of experiences possible for us, and denying any theoretical cognition of things as they are in themselves, Kant stresses that we can and must indeed be able to *think* of the things that appear to us as things in themselves belonging to 'the noumenal world.' Inhabitants of the noumenal world, insofar as we think of them, are 'supersensible objects.' Some concepts, including those of freedom, soul, and God, are concepts of what is supersensible. Because such objects (if they exist) cannot be objects of human experience, no (human) theoretical cognition of the nature of freedom, souls, or God is possible. However, according to Kant, since the concepts of these things do not involve any sort of incoherence, it is conceptually possible that there are things that these concepts refer to. Thus, human beings can consistently think such things, even if they cannot theoretically cognize them. Yet, all three concepts play an important role in Kant's moral philosophy. Let us see how.

2.2 Freedom, the moral law, and the highest good

The phenomenal/noumenal distinction applies to human beings. As members of the phenomenal, sensible world (as *homo phenomena*), one's choices and actions are causally determined. Kant puts the point dramatically, writing that if one had enough insight into someone's mind, together with knowledge of relevant causal laws, one "could calculate a human being's conduct for the future with as much certainty as a lunar or solar eclipse" (CprR 5:99). Yet, as members of the noumenal "intelligible world" (as *homo noumena*), human beings have the power to choose and act without being causally determined by laws of nature. This is Kant's negative conception of freedom of the will. Kant's positive conception, or what he refers to as *autonomy of the will*, involves being subject to the law of freedom—the moral law.[2] His notions of negative and positive freedom and their relation to the moral law are discussed in more detail in chapter 4. (Of course, how to reconcile causal determinism with freedom of choice poses a difficult challenge

---

[2] Autonomy of the will is contrasted with "heteronomy of the will," which refers to exercises of one's faculty of choice based on nonmoral reasons grounded in one's sensible nature—reasons Kant refers to as ones of self-love.

which Kant dealt with at some length. Kant's attempted reconciliation of determinism and free will need not detain us, given our focus on Kant's normative ethical theory.)

As already explained, freedom (as autonomy) refers to something that cannot be an object of sense experience, nor does one need to postulate it in order to causally explain human actions as events in the sensible world; freedom of the will, then, is not something that can be experientially cognized. However, Kant claims that we can affirm our freedom of the will because (*i*) it is a presupposition of being subject to moral requirements (and thus subject to the moral law), and (*ii*) we are able to confirm that we are subject to moral requirements. Metaphysically speaking, then, freedom (autonomy) grounds being subject to the moral law and its requirements. Epistemologically speaking, one can affirm that one is free by affirming that one is subject to the moral law and its requirements.

What about souls and God? Here, again, although Kant denies that human beings can cognize and thus gain theoretical knowledge about the nature of such "supersensible" things, he argues that one can affirm their reality as necessary presuppositions of morality. To fully explain this would require delving into Kant's conception of the foundation of morality, taking us beyond the scope of the present study. However, the basic idea is that the moral law requires that there be some "object" of morality, understood as a possible *highest, most complete good.*[3] For Kant, this good has two components: virtue and happiness. Virtue involves a commitment to morality (a good will) and the acquired strength to comply with this commitment. It also makes one deserving of happiness, so that the highest good for an individual is being as virtuous as possible together with being happy in proportion to one's level of virtue *because* of one's virtue.

How, then, is Kant's conception of the highest, most complete good related to souls and to God? Virtue in its highest form is, for Kant, an ideal of complete perfection that human beings, as mortal beings, are morally required to strive toward. However, as Kant remarks, "virtue is always progressing" (DV 6:409), and thereby something one can never

---

[3] Kant's various arguments for the necessity of the highest good are nicely summarized in Laurence R. Pasternack 2014: chaps. 1 and 2.

fully achieve as a mortal being. Since realization of the highest, most complete good must be possible, one is entitled to postulate having an immortal soul that survives one's physical death, allowing one to progress toward the ideal. Furthermore, since being virtuous does not on its own guarantee happiness in proportion to the level of one's virtuousness, one must postulate the existence of God to ensure that virtue is rewarded with an appropriate level of happiness. Thus, conceiving the possibility of the highest, most complete good requires postulating immortality of the soul and the existence of God. Because postulating immortality and God is based on moral considerations, Kant refers to them as "practical postulates" that we must, as moral beings, assume or have faith in even though we cannot know that they are true.

Thus, while freedom is a necessary presupposition of being subject to the requirements of morality, i.e. the moral law, immortality and God must be postulated to conceive the possibility of the highest, most complete good. Kant's doctrines of the relation between the moral law and autonomy, and the significance of highest good and its relation to the practical postulates, are set forth in his 1788 *Critique of Practical Reason*. In chapter 4, Kant's conceptions of the moral law and autonomy will be further elaborated. And virtue, of course, will occupy center stage once we reach *The Doctrine of Virtue*.

2.3 Concluding reflections

This chapter has described in a *very* bare-bones manner some of Kant's epistemological and related metaphysical views, and how they connect to aspects of his moral philosophy. Let us conclude with a few remarks about Kant's "two-world" metaphysics and associated epistemological views as they bear on his moral philosophy. Regarding the metaphysics, when we examine *The Doctrine of Virtue* we will see how Kant's distinction between human beings as both *homo phenomena* and *homo noumena* figures in his ethical theory at various points. However, Kant's conception of virtue and the system of duties of virtue featured in DV—his normative ethical theory—is arguably not dependent on his general metaphysical view. One could reject Kant's two-world metaphysics and yet embrace key elements of his normative ethical theory, a common theme among contemporary Kantians. (There is a centuries-old debate over whether Kant's phenomena/noumena distinction literally commits Kant to two worlds, or whether the distinction is one of two perspectives on a single world. Although in the text I refer to two worlds, I remain officially neutral over which interpretation is correct.)

Regarding epistemology, while theoretical cognition concerns questions about what *is*, practical cognition concerns what *ought to be*, including what one ought to do. As we have seen, Kant's epistemology of theoretical cognition involves the skeptical claim that human beings are unable to cognize things that are not part of the spatiotemporal (sensible) world (or based on the pure forms of our sensibility, which for Kant includes mathematics). However, practical cognition of moral obligation does not involve skepticism of the sort we find in his theory of theoretical cognition. One of Kant's fundamental tenets regarding the foundation of morality is that its supreme principle is knowable a priori; as supreme it provides a foundation for the duties of ethics. Kant's project in DV, as we shall see, is to derive and thus justify a system of duties and associated virtues from this principle. This is Kant's "grounding project" in DV. It represents a "foundationalist conception" of such grounding—the categorical imperative is the foundation, and the system derivable from this single principle is the superstructure.

Note finally, that were Kant to follow the sentimentalists and claim that moral obligation is grounded in *human* sentiments, he could only conclude that moral obligation applies to human beings, or perhaps to beings subject to similar sentiments. Indeed, sentimentalist (empiricist) views, according to Kant, cannot really make sense of the commonsense notions of obligation and duty; they lack the resources to account for the categorical nature of moral requirements that have their source in pure reason. Kant, as noted in the previous chapter, is a moral *rationalist*. And one of the most fundamental tenets of his moral philosophy is that the moral law is a law for all *rational* beings, whether they are human beings, and whether they have a sensible nature like ours. As we proceed, we will learn more about Kant's moral rationalism.

We are now ready to begin our study of Kant's ethical theory, beginning with chapters on the general introduction to *The Metaphysics of Morals*, which precedes its two main parts: *The Doctrine of Right* and *The Doctrine of Virtue*.

Further Reading

- For a concise discussion of Kant's attempt to reconcile determinism with freedom of the will, see Wood 1984. For a detailed discussion see Allison 1990, chaps. 1–4. Noteworthy is that Kant's attempted reconciliation is not a version of free will compatibilism as such views are understood in contemporary philosophy.
- Kant's doctrines of the relation between autonomy and the moral law, the highest good, and the postulates of immortality and God are developed in his *Critique of Practical Reason*. Besides Allison 1990, Beck 1960, and the 2010 collection by Reath and Timmermann are helpful guides to this work of Kant's.

PART II

GENERAL INTRODUCTION TO *THE METAPHYSICS OF MORALS*

3

On the Idea of and Necessity for a Metaphysics of Morals

General Introduction, Section I

As mentioned previously, *The Metaphysics of Morals* has two principal parts: *Metaphysical First Principles of the Doctrine of Right* (DR) and *Metaphysical First Principles of the Doctrine of Virtue* (DV), each including its own introduction. However, in addition, the entire work features a general introduction, divided into four sections. In the first section, Kant explains what a metaphysics of morals is and why it is necessary. In the three remaining sections, he turns to matters that are fundamental to understanding moral theorizing, including the relation between morality and the faculty of desire, concepts preliminary to the study of moral philosophy, and finally the basis for the division between DR and DV. Because, as mentioned in chapter 1, Kant's introduction is extremely compact in its presentation of key ideas, yet crucial for understanding his moral philosophy, I have devoted this chapter to Section I, the next chapter to Section II, and the one following that to III and IV. It will not be possible or necessary to comment on everything in these sections; coverage is selective, with an eye on what is essential for understanding *The Doctrine of Virtue*.

Kant explains the idea of and necessity for a metaphysics of morals by situating it within his conception of the field of philosophy, which he divides into its pure and empirical parts. This division is the basis for distinguishing a pure doctrine of morals from an empirical practical anthropology—the two main parts of moral philosophy, according to

Kant's Doctrine of Virtue. Mark Timmons, Oxford University Press (2021). © Oxford University Press.
DOI: 10.1093/oso/9780190939229.003.0003

Kant. Guiding our investigation into these matters are the following questions:

- What is Kant's understanding of metaphysics and its place within the field of philosophy?
- What is a metaphysics of morals and in what sense is it necessary for understanding morality?
- What role does anthropology play in a doctrine of morals?

To address these questions, we must first explain the following distinctions that figure centrally in Kant's conception of philosophy:

- Theoretical versus practical cognition,
- Empirical ("a posteriori") versus rational ("a priori") sources of cognition, and
- Analytic versus synthetic propositions.

Explaining these distinctions will occupy us in the first three sections before we move on in 4 to summarize Kant's conception of philosophy and the place of metaphysics in it. In section 5, we tackle Section I of the general introduction, addressing our three guiding questions as well as Kant's conception of morality as a system of categorical imperatives. The final section first summarizes this chapter and then reflects on certain questions about Kant's conception of morality. (To avoid confusion between references to sections in this guide and numbered sections in Kant's texts, I capitalize "Section" thus when referring to specific sections in the latter.)

3.1 Cognition: theoretical and practical

A fundamental notion in Kant's philosophy is that of *cognition*.[1] Generally speaking, cognition is the representation of an object or a state of affairs of which there are two main species: theoretical and

---

[1] Kant also recognizes a distinct category of speculative cognition, which need not concern us. See JL 9:86–7.

practical. In his *Logic*, he describes the difference in terms of what they express. Practical cognitions, which take the form of imperatives, express "a possible free action, whereby a certain end is to be made real . . . theoretical cognitions are ones that express not what ought to be but rather what is, hence they have as their object *not an acting* but rather a *being*" (JL 9:86).[2] In short, theoretical cognition purports to represent what is the case, while practical cognition purports to represent what ought to be the case as a result of an exercise of free choice.

3.2 Two sources of cognition

For the time being, let us focus just on theoretical cognition in order to explain the a posteriori/a priori and analytic/synthetic distinctions.

A posteriori (empirical) cognition

There are two fundamental sources of theoretical cognition: cognition from an empirical or a posteriori source and cognition from a rational or a priori source. Much human cognition in which one judges some proposition to be true is grounded in sense experience (including introspection). One comes to cognize particular matters of fact on the basis of sense experience, which provide grounds for making judgments about the objects of one's experience. One is then able to form empirical generalizations based on what one learns from experience. Such empirically based cognition is called "a posteriori," and applies to cognition involving sense experience and the knowledge gained thereby. Cognition about the natural world acquired through such sciences as physics, chemistry, and biology is also gained on the basis of sense experience, employing experimentation proper to these sciences. (Of course, testimony from others is another source of a posteriori cognition.) Furthermore, the kinds of truths one can come to know based only

---

[2] In this same passage, Kant also recognizes certain theoretical cognitions as practical so long as imperatives can be derived from them.

on sense experience (including scientific truth) are *contingently true* propositions—true in virtue of how the world happens to be. An example of a contingent scientific truth is: The Earth revolves around the Sun. And, of course, cognition leading to knowledge of this proposition is a matter of scientific investigation based ultimately on sense experience. A posteriori cognition, then, is also referred to as *empirical* cognition. By contrast, there is rational, a priori cognition.

A priori (rational) cognition

Some propositions are both strictly universal and necessary. They are strictly universal in that they state truths about *all* members of a class of objects or events and rule out the possibility of exceptions. By ruling out possible exceptions they are *necessarily* true. Strict universality and necessity are characteristics of propositions that are cognizable a priori. One way of describing a priori cognition is to say that it is acquired "*absolutely* independently of all [sense] experience" (CpuR B3), unlike a posteriori (empirical) cognition.[3] But this is only a negative characterization. Since the range of a priori cognition includes as its subject matter pure mathematics, the metaphysics of nature, and the metaphysics of morals, providing a positive characterization is complicated. Suffice it to say for now that cognition of metaphysical truths have their source in "pure" reason.[4] Rather than piling on further descriptions, it is best to work with examples, which brings us to the analytic/synthetic distinction.

---

[3] Cognitions whose source is "absolutely independent" in this way are contrasted with so-called a priori cognitions that are only independent of some particular experience but nevertheless dependent on experiential cognitions, as when one judges, on the basis of an empirical generalization, that undermining the foundation of one's house will cause it to collapse, without having to see it happen. (This is Kant's example in CpuR B2–3). He also distinguishes pure from impure a priori cognitions, the former containing only non-empirical (pure) concepts, the latter allowing a mix (ibid.).

[4] For an illuminating interpretation of Kant's conception of the a priori, see Smit 2009.

Analytic versus synthetic propositions

Propositions are the contents of cognitions, and for Kant there are two importantly different kinds of proposition cognizable by reason alone, independently of appeals to sense experience. Some are *analytic*. Consider the proposition that all bachelors are unmarried. Understanding the meaning of 'bachelor' enables one to cognize a priori the proposition that all bachelors are unmarried, and necessarily so. The truth of this proposition is a matter of the very meanings of the terms they contain (and the concepts those terms express). Kant sometimes describes analytic truths in terms of "containment." Analytic propositions are ones in which the predicate term (e.g. 'unmarried') "is contained in" the subject term ("bachelor"). This metaphor connects with the label, 'analytic', because it is by analysis of the concept <bachelor>—making explicit what this concept includes—that one grasps the necessary truth about bachelors being unmarried without having to go out and observe any bachelors. (Propositions that are false solely as a matter of the meanings of the terms contained in them are referred to as contradictory propositions, e.g. some bachelors are married.)

Notice that for Kant all cognition of analytic truths is a priori, so the category of analytic a posteriori is empty. Granted, one can come to know generalizations on the basis of experience, but these still lack the kind of universality and necessity characteristic of necessary truths. And granted, one can accept a necessary truth on the basis of testimony and thus cognize it empirically. However, if the proposition is a necessary truth, first-hand knowledge of it requires cognizing it a priori.

Unlike analytic propositions, the truth of synthetic propositions is not just a matter of the meanings of their constituent terms and associated concepts. Rather, their truth depends on whether they correspond to facts that they purport to be about. The label 'synthetic' is appropriate because when thinking or considering a synthetic proposition, one is *bringing together* concepts that are not analytically related (one contained in the other) to form a judgment. This bringing together of concepts involves an act of synthesis, to use Kant's own terminology. According to Kant, although some synthetic propositions are contingently true, others are necessarily true. As lately explained, contingently true synthetic propositions (contingent truths) can only be known through sense experience; they are thus knowable only a posteriori. The philosophically interesting category is the synthetic a priori.

Synthetic a priori propositions

One of the fundamental tenets of Kant's entire body of work is that some synthetic propositions can only be properly cognized a priori. It is explaining *how* such cognition is possible that is of central concern in Kant's philosophy. In the *Critique of Pure Reason*, he famously argues that the causal principle—that every event *must* have a cause—is a synthetic a priori proposition. He makes similar remarks about fundamental moral principles; they are synthetic truths that can only be originally cognized a priori. We will return to this very important thesis about fundamental ethical truths in the next section. In the meantime, we can follow Kant in referring to a priori cognition as "rational cognition"—cognition grounded in reason alone. The contrast between empirical and rational cognition provides a basis for distinguishing empirical from pure philosophy, which we will come to in a moment.

3.3 Practical cognition

As noted before, practical cognitions concern what ought to be brought about as a result of an exercise of free will. Because they *direct* one to do or not to do something, they can be expressed as imperatives (commands). Kant applies the analytic/synthetic distinction to imperatives and claims that the supreme principle of morality—the categorical imperative—is a synthetic proposition that can only be cognized a priori. One major task in Kant's foundational works in ethics is to justify this supreme principle by showing that it binds all finite rational beings, including human beings. Many questions immediately arise, including how the analytic/synthetic distinction can be sensibly applied to imperatives that do not have truth values. "Shut the door!" can be complied with or not, it can be appropriate that someone issues it (or not). But what sense does it make to say it is true? Since this volume is not about Kant's foundational views, we need not get into this issue.[5] In any case, as we shall see in chapter 9, the analytic/synthetic, a priori/a posteriori distinctions do come up in Kant's doctrine of virtue—specifically in how he distinguishes the doctrine of virtue from the doctrine of right and in the "deduction" (justification) of the supreme principle of the doctrine of virtue. With this battery of distinctions in mind, we turn now to Kant's conception of philosophy and the place of a metaphysics of morals within it.

3.4 The field of philosophy

Kant's divisions within the field of philosophy concern differences in the *aims*, *subject matter*, and *source* of philosophical inquiry. Regarding aims, one main division is between philosophy as a system and philosophy as a critique. Philosophy as a *system* involves setting forth an organized body of principles and propositions that are knowable a priori. In one place Kant puts this by saying "philosophy is the system of rational cognition through concepts" (CJ 20:195). Philosophy as critique "investigates the faculty of reason in respect of all its pure a priori knowledge" (CpuR A841/B869). More specifically, and as this quote indicates, the point of such a critique is to determine what can and cannot be cognized by reason alone, that is, what can be cognized a priori. Kant's 1781 *Critique of Pure Reason* investigates reason in its theoretical employment, while the 1788 *Critique of Practical Reason* investigates reason in its practical employment. Since the metaphysics of morals is a species of philosophy as a system, let us focus on it, putting philosophy as critique to the side.

   To be a system and not a mere aggregate of synthetic a priori principles and propositions, a philosophy must exhibit a scheme of organization. Kant distinguishes *formal* philosophy—that is, logic—which abstracts from all subject matter and provides rules for thinking, from

---

[5] See Timmons 1992 [2017a] for one attempt to understand how the analytic/synthetic distinction applies to Kant's conception of imperatives.

material philosophy, which does have subject matter. Material philosophy is either about nature and its laws (the world as we experience it) or about the use of one's freedom and its laws (what we ought to do). The former is referred to as philosophy of nature, the latter as philosophy of morals.[6] He also refers to these two types of material philosophy as *theoretical* and *practical*, respectively. Both branches constitute a science[7] whose primary aim is to set forth in a systematic manner those universal and necessary truths that can only be cognized a priori and which express the fundamental truths pertaining to their respective *subject matters*. However, Kant makes a further distinction within the philosophies of nature and freedom, namely, between their pure, rational parts on one hand, and their empirical parts on the other. This distinction pertains to the *source* of cognitions that figure in philosophy as a system. In the *Groundwork*, Kant remarks that "All philosophy in so far as it is based on grounds of experience can be called *empirical*; that which presents its doctrines soley from a priori principles [is called, M.T.] *pure* philosophy" (G 4:388). "Pure philosophy," then, concerns synthetic principles and propositions that can only be known a priori.[8]

The pure parts of philosophy, featuring propositions cognizable a priori, represent Kant's conception of metaphysics.[9] Kant's own description of metaphysics is that it is "a system of a priori cognition from concepts alone" (MM 6:216). Thus, Kant's official view about the pure part of moral philosophy is that it comprises only those synthetic principles and propositions of morality that are knowable a priori (in addition to propositions about the content of moral and related concepts, which are analytic). In contrast, empirical moral philosophy

---

[6] What about nonmoral practical propositions, e.g. those that express rules of good housekeeping, or rules of etiquette, or counsels of prudence: are they part of practical philosophy? No, says Kant, because their contents are theoretical, having to do with causal connections in the natural world between goals of action and the means for producing them. See CJ 5:171–173.

[7] According to how Kant is using the term 'science' (*Wissenschaft*), "Every doctrine, if it is to be a system, i.e., a whole of cognition ordered according to principles, is called science" (MFNS 4:467).

[8] Kant also applies the pure/empirical distinction to concepts and to motives ("incentives"), which we may put to the side for present purposes.

[9] In some passages, Kant includes critique as a part of metaphysics. See CpuR A841/B869.

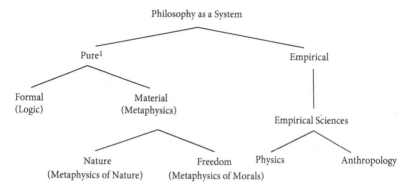

Diagram 3.1 Kant's divisions of philosophy as a system.

is composed of principles and propositions only cognizable on the basis of experience, and so knowledge of them is a posteriori (empirical knowledge). (More on this claim as it pertains to morality in the following section.) Diagram 3.1 summarizes how Kant conceives the branches of philosophy as a system (at least in some passages).[10]

Further divisions include the doctrine of right and the doctrine of virtue, which fit under metaphysics of morals and which receive full attention in chapter 5 when we examine Section IV of the general introduction.

A note on different editions

It should be noted that different editions of Kant's *Metaphysics of Morals* feature different orderings of the four sections of the general introduction. The book was originally published in two installments. DR was published in January 1797 followed by DV in August that same year. It is widely thought that the publication of DR, which

---

[10] There are passages in Kant's writings where he says that in a strict sense of the term, 'philosophy' has no empirical part, but rather must appeal to empirical considerations in its application of synthetic a priori principles that constitute philosophy in the strict sense of the term. See, for example, CpuR A850/B878. In the passage just quoted, Kant is being more inclusive in what he considers a part of philosophy.

included the general introduction, did not fully comply with Kant's intended ordering of the four sections. Some editions have the original ordering, others (including the Cambridge edition I'm using) feature a reordering, believed to be more in accord with Kant's intentions. The difference is that in the reordered editions, Sections I and II from the original are reversed, as are Sections III and IV. This explains why, in the Cambridge edition, the pagination from the standard German edition goes from 6:214 to 6:218 in Section I, but then Section II picks up with 6:211 and goes to 6:214; similarly with Sections III and IV.

3.5 The idea of and necessity for a metaphysics of morals

In light of the various semantic and epistemological distinctions and how they figure in Kant's conception of the field of philosophy, let us now focus directly on Section I of the general introduction, where Kant explains the very idea of a metaphysics of morals, why it is needed, and how it is related to the empirical part of moral philosophy—moral anthropology.

The idea

As just noted, metaphysics for Kant—the kind he approved of—has two branches: the metaphysics of nature and the metaphysics of morals.[11] A metaphysics of nature, as Kant explains at the start of Section I, comprises a system of a priori principles providing a secure foundation for physics and natural science generally.[12] A metaphysics of morals concerns the use of one's freedom of choice and features prescriptive moral laws (principles) that specify how, through the use of one's freedom, one morally ought to act and the kind of person one morally

---

[11] In the *Critique of Pure Reason,* Kant argued that so-called dogmatic metaphysics, which purports to be a science of the supersensible, is pseudoscience.

[12] Kant's metaphysics of nature is developed in his 1786 *Metaphysical Foundations of Natural Science.*

ought to strive to become. In introducing the *idea* of a metaphysics of morals, Kant contrasts a doctrine of morality and its prescriptions that issue from its laws with prescriptions for achieving happiness. Doing so enables him to call attention to the peculiar nature of moral laws, including their source and authority.

In the passages we are considering, Kant describes happiness as "achieving a lasting enjoyment of the true joys of life" (MM 6:215). As he points out, it is only through experience that one learns what will likely bring one joy. And this can differ from person to person, depending on his or her likes and dislikes that give rise to what Kant refers to as "inclinations" (roughly, habitual desires, about which more will be said in the next chapter). Moreover, it is only through experience that one learns how to go about pursuing those things that will bring one true joy. So, anything one learns about securing a "lasting enjoyment" in life, and how to go about achieving it, will be based on experience and thus only learnable a posteriori. In short, when it comes to the pursuit of happiness, there can be no set prescriptions knowable merely based on reason and thus cognizable a priori for what will make us happy or how to go about achieving happiness. Rather, there are only "counsels of prudence," such as being polite and frugal, which likely contribute to one's happiness. As mere counsels, "everyone must be allowed countless exceptions in order to adapt his choice of a way of life to his particular inclinations and his susceptibility to satisfaction" (MM 6:216).

It is different, according to Kant, when it comes to morality. In paragraph 3, Kant remarks that there are prescriptions for behavior that "command for everyone, without taking into account his inclinations, merely because and insofar as he is free and has practical reason" (MM 6:216). These commands have the status of moral *laws*, having the marks of necessity and strict universality—applying necessarily to all rational beings—and are thus certain. As necessary and strictly universal, they can only be cognized a priori, and are "given," as Kant says, "by pure reason alone" (MM 6:217). Their non-empirical a priori source (their purity) together with their certainty means that moral laws are *authoritative* because they ground reasons for action that are superior in their reason-giving force compared to the reasons based in inclination. Kant sometimes puts this (though not in the passages we are considering) by remarking that the laws of morality as they apply to non-holy rational beings, including human beings, ground *unconditionally valid* requirements—*categorical imperatives*. By contrast, so-called hypothetical imperatives that impose requirements on behavior relative to one's inclinations are only conditionally valid and lack categorical authority. In the next chapter, the distinction between categorical and hypothetical imperatives will be explained, and these remarks further elaborated.

This, in *very* rough outline, is Kant's moral rationalism—moral laws and the duties those laws impose are ultimately grounded in reason—which contrasts with all other empirically based moral theories that would attempt to base morality on, for example, feeling, conventions of society, or revelation. Because moral laws are cognizable a priori as well as the fact that their contents are synthetic,[13] means that there can be a genuine metaphysics of morals. However, as we will learn in later chapters, just because the fundamental laws of morality are cognizable a priori, it does not follow that one can determine a priori what they require in circumstances where empirical information is essential for coming to correct moral judgments.

The necessity for

What we've learned so far is that the content of a metaphysics of morals is an organized system of moral laws—laws of freedom—knowable a priori, which provide a foundation for determining one's moral obligations. Kant claims that it is "a *duty* to *have* such a metaphysics, and every human being also has it within himself, though as a rule only in an obscure way" (MM 6:216). Why a duty? And in what sense does every human being have, even if only obscurely, such a metaphysics "within himself"?

The need for a metaphysics of morals in the context of doing moral philosophy, and (more importantly) for purposes of moral education, is that the only way to secure the certainty and authority of fundamental

---

[13] At least those featured in DV are synthetic. In DR, the fundamental principle governing duties of right is analytic.

moral laws is through an investigation into their a priori source as laws of freedom. In the second paragraph in Section I, Kant claims that moral laws "hold as laws only insofar as they can be *seen* to have an a priori basis and to be necessary" (MM 6:215). This is to say that their certainty and authority relies on the possibility of understanding them as grounded in reason. In the preface to the *Groundwork*, Kant stresses the need for a metaphysics of morals partly in order to protect morals from "all sorts of corruption" (G 4:390) to which it is subject if there is unclarity or confusion about the source of fundamental moral laws in reason alone. Additionally, a metaphysics of morals, as Kant conceives it, unifies ethics by explaining midlevel duties (e.g. the wrongness of suicide and lying and the obligations of beneficence and gratitude) by deriving them from a single basic principle of morality.

Kant's reason for claiming that all human beings have a metaphysics of morals within is that "without a priori principles" how could one "believe that he has a giving of universal law within himself?" (MM 6:216). Kant does not elaborate this remark in these passages. Roughly, the idea is that at least upon reflection, one realizes that it is possible to overcome contrary-to-duty inclinations and act from the motive of duty. Doing so involves recognizing the authority of moral laws— that they provide superior reasons for action compared to reasons grounded in inclination—and that one is capable of freely complying with such laws by "oneself giving" such laws. We learn more about inclination versus duty, the authority of the moral law, and about lawgiving in Sections II–IV of the general introduction, so these are ideas we shall discuss as we work through the general introduction.

The role of anthropology

Turning finally to the scope of moral philosophy, pure moral philosophy (metaphysics of morals) is contrasted with *moral anthropology*, "the other member of the division of practical philosophy as a whole" (MM 6:217). While the former features a priori necessary moral laws whose source is pure reason, moral anthropology is an empirical discipline, which includes (but not restricted to) what we now think of as human psychology. In Section I, Kant mentions two ways anthropology is important. *First*, it is only through an empirical study of human nature, including human psychology, which we can learn about the conditions that help or hinder people in complying with moral laws. Thus, moral anthropology is important for moral education of the young and for moral improvement of adults. *Second*, it provides information about human nature needed "in order to *show* in it what can be inferred from universal moral principles" (MM 6:217). As we shall see when we turn to DV, deriving moral laws from the supreme principle of morality—the categorical imperative (CI)—requires reference to facts about human nature. Further, Kant emphasizes that a metaphysics of morals (as pure philosophy) must precede any appeal to moral anthropology. Attempting to base a moral philosophy on anthropology or any empirical doctrine, as lately noted, could never yield moral laws that express authoritative commands for behavior. As Kant remarks, any attempt to provide an empirical basis for morality, as one finds in the empiricist tradition, "would run the risk of the grossest and most pernicious errors" (MM 6:215). Again, in these passages, we find the central idea of Kant's moral rationalism: moral laws and their categorical authority are grounded in reason, not sense experience. The next chapter further develops Kant's brand of moral rationalism by situating it with respect to his theory of action, the elements of which he presents in Section II of the general introduction.

3.6 Summary and concluding reflections

The chapter sought to explain what Kant means by a metaphysics of morals and why he thinks it is necessary that there be one. To sum up, we learned the following:

- For Kant, metaphysics (whether of nature or of morals) is largely composed of synthetic a priori principles that can be cognized and known based on reason alone. Metaphysics is thus "pure" philosophy;[14] philosophy cleansed of anything empirical and instead based entirely in reason itself.

[14] That is, "pure" in the broad sense that identifies a doctrine of pure philosophy with what can be cognized a priori about the subject matter.

- Only by tracing fundamental moral principles to one's faculty of reason as their source, and thus engaging in a metaphysics of morals, can one appreciate the categorical authority of such principles.
- Finally, the empirical part of moral philosophy, moral anthropology, is needed to apply pure moral principles to real world conditions and to inform moral education and guide moral improvement.

In closing, let us further consider Kant's conception of what he takes to be the commonsense idea of moral laws and associated duties as essentially involving requirements on choice and action that are *categorical* and *authoritative*. As explained earlier, they are categorical because they necessarily apply to all rational beings who are subject to duty. And they are authoritative in providing normative reasons for choice and action that are superior to reasons based in one's desires or inclinations as Kant often puts it. (Kant's use of 'categorical' in the context of his moral philosophy includes this notion of normative authority.)

There are three obvious questions to ask about Kant's conception of moral philosophy as featuring categorially authoritative laws. *First*, since Kant conceives of his moral philosophy as capturing the commonsense conception of morality, is he right about this? *Second*, even if moral duties are commonly taken to represent categorically authoritative requirements, are there any? Perhaps common sense is mistaken on this point. *Third*, is Kant right in claiming that only his brand of rationalism can make sense of such requirements? These are questions Kant addresses in his foundational works, the *Groundwork* and *Critique of Practical Reason*. It is beyond the scope of this book to dig into Kant's answers to these questions. However, let us conclude by briefly pondering the first question.

Talk of moral laws and the obligations they impose being categorically authoritative is very abstract. It is intended by Kant to articulate, for purposes of philosophical theorizing, a "common idea of duty and of moral laws" (G 4:389). One way to gain a clearer idea of what Kant has in mind is to contrast morality with other bodies of rules (prescriptions) whose purpose is to guide behavior. Consider the rules of chess. These rules permit and restrict movement of the pieces, but they are entirely conventional. I comply with these rules because, for instance, I enjoy playing and to violate them during play is likely not in my interest, given that I may be caught. Furthermore, those rules only apply to me if I decide to play. It is clear how moral laws (principles, rules) are commonly taken to be different from rules governing a game: (*i*) they are not conventional (at least if one rejects moral relativism as does Kant), (*ii*) they have a binding force that does not depend on whether one happens to be interested in them or in the sort of life governed by them, and (*iii*) one cannot opt out of and thus not be held accountable to moral laws as one can with the rules of chess.

Consider next rules of mere etiquette. These rules are a matter of convention that vary from society to society. Unlike the rules of some game, the rules of etiquette (of a society at a time) are taken to apply to anyone who is a member of the society regardless of their attitude toward those rules. Arguably, one can avoid being bound by rules of etiquette by withdrawing from one's society, and perhaps one can completely avoid them by withdrawing from "polite" society altogether. However, even if such withdrawal is possible so that the rules of etiquette no longer apply to one's behavior, the same is not true of moral laws: they are "inescapable"; they necessarily apply to all rational beings. And, again, this corresponds to the common idea that one cannot opt out of morality. For even if one ignores or otherwise does not care about the requirements of morality, one is still held to them. Finally, it is also commonly believed that moral requirements "override" or perhaps "silence" competing considerations of our own happiness (perhaps not always, but much of the time). Given a choice between intentionally harming others to advance one's own interests and refraining from such harm at the expense of self-interest, it is commonly thought that moral laws against such harm are superior in their reason-giving force compared to reasons of self-interest, and are thus authoritative. In contrast to whatever binding force nonmoral considerations have, whether due to conventions such as the rules of a game or etiquette, and whatever binding force considerations of self-interest (or what Kant calls "self-love") have, I suspect that after reflecting upon the contrast between such considerations and moral requirements, readers will likely resonate with Kant's characterization of the common conception of morality as involving categorically authoritative requirements.

Further reading

- See Gregor 1963, chap. 1 for a helpful discussion of Kant's characterization of a metaphysics of morals, including his confusing and inconsistent use of 'pure' in his taxonomy of the field of philosophy.
- Louden 2000, chap. 1 is helpful for understanding the relation of the empirical side of Kant's ethical theory to the pure, non-empirical side.
- Philippa Foot's 1972 is must reading on the issue of the kind of categorical authority associated with Kant's ethics.

4

Mental Faculties, the Moral Law, and Human Motivation

General Introduction, Section II

Section II, "On the Relation of the Faculties of the Human Mind to Moral Laws," is an extremely concise overview of some key elements of Kant's theories of mind and action as they relate to morality and human motivation. The focus of the Section is the faculty of desire: its nature and function, which includes its relation to feeling, cognition, and freedom of choice. Here, Kant also introduces the notions of maxim and imperative that figure in his theory of nonmoral and moral action—essential (as we shall see in later chapters) for understanding his conception of virtue.

Because Kant's presentation of the ideas in this Section is very compressed, I will be selective in addressing just these questions:

- What is Kant's conception of the faculty of desire and its relation to the faculties of feeling and cognition?
- What is the significance of Kant's distinction between *will* and *choice* and their relation to human freedom?
- How does Kant conceive the two types of practical principle—maxims and imperatives—that are fundamental to this theory of action?
- Crucial to Kant's doctrine of virtue is his conception of human moral motivation. What is its structure and how does it differ from human nonmoral motivation?

The following section addresses the first two questions, the remaining questions are treated in the three sections that follow the first. The concluding section makes a few observations about Kant's theory of action.

Kant's Doctrine of Virtue. Mark Timmons, Oxford University Press (2021). © Oxford University Press.
DOI: 10.1093/oso/9780190939229.003.0004

4.1 The faculty of desire

In his *Anthropology from a Pragmatic Point of View*, Kant distinguishes three fundamental mental faculties: cognition, feeling, and desire, examining each in some detail.[1] As the title of Section II indicates, Kant sketches how these three faculties of the human mind are related to each other as they pertain to morality and moral laws. The Section begins with a 'thin' description of the faculty of desire as "the faculty to be, by means of one's representations, the cause of the objects of these representations" (MM 6:211). Using one's cognitive power to represent some future state of affairs that one would like to bring about (the "object" of one's representation)—for example, eating an ice cream cone—and by successfully exercising one's faculty of desire, one brings about that object (eating the ice cream cone). According to Kant's view, desires themselves, as psychological states, are "always connected with" (ibid.) feelings and thereby involve the faculty of feeling. To explain the connection, let us first consider the faculty of feeling. (In order to relate what I say to Kant's text, I will point to specific paragraphs, numbering them from beginning with the Section.)

The capacity to have feelings of pleasure and of displeasure is how Kant characterizes feeling as a fundamental mental faculty. He distinguishes sensuous pleasure and displeasure from intellectual pleasure and displeasure that will be explained momentarily. For now, let us consider sensuous feelings—feelings that arise from sensation. Kant's contrast between feelings and sensations is best illuminated with an example. The sensations (sense perceptions) one has when biting into a ripe red apple include awareness of the qualities of redness and sweetness that one attributes to the apple. Suppose one experiences a feeling of pleasure resulting from its sweet taste. This feeling of pleasure differs from the sensations of redness and sweetness in how it relates to the apple. In paragraph 3, Kant puts this by saying "pleasure or displeasure (in what is red

[1] Each of these faculties includes further subdivisions. For instance, Kant divides the cognitive faculty into the higher active powers of reason, understanding, and judgment from the lower passive powers of sense and imagination. See Anth Book I.

or sweet) expresses nothing at all in the object but simply a relation to the subject" (MM 6:212). In other words, unlike attributing the qualities of redness and sweetness one should not attribute pleasure to the apple. Feelings of course have a phenomenology; there is something it is like to experience pleasure as a result of eating something sweet, or to experience the displeasure or pain of an injury. But, as Kant says, these feelings "cannot be explained more clearly in themselves" (MM 6:212); one illuminates them by describing the role they play in one's psychology—what tends to cause them and what they in turn tend to cause. An experience of pleasure I have on some occasion urges me "to *maintain* my state (to remain in it)," while experiences of displeasure "urge me to *leave* my state (to go out of it)" (Anth. 7:231).

What, then, is the "connection" between desires and feelings? All desires, and more generally all operations of one's faculty of desire, are causally connected with feelings, however, the causal connection can go in one of two directions. First, "sensible" desires arise from experiencing pleasure in something one finds agreeable, and so feelings precede and are causally involved in coming to have such desires. Habitual sensible desires are called "inclinations." However, the causal connection can go the other way: in some cases, feelings can be the effect of desire or more precisely, they can be the effect of the exercise of the faculty of desire. In the case of moral motivation, the operation of pure reason representing an action as a duty affects one's faculty of desire which causally produces an "intellectual pleasure." This point, crucial to Kant's moral philosophy, will be more fully explained in sections 3 and 4, where the concepts being introduced in Section I are illustrated with examples.

In paragraph 6, Kant enriches his conception of the faculty of desire by distinguishing its two essential elements: *will* and *choice*. Suppose one decides to pursue a law degree as a career path. One's decision is based on an exercise of one's reason—reason used for the practical purpose of setting and pursuing an end. So, one reasons about possible career paths by, say, investigating what having each career would be like and whether one would be pleased in having any of them. One also reasons about the means one must take to succeed in realizing such possible ends. In finally deciding to pursue a law career, the considerations one brings to mind in deciding, or as Kant puts it, the "inner determining ground" of one's decision, depends on the use of reason—practical reason. Considering, then, the relation between the faculty of desire and reason (the latter belonging to the faculty of cognition), "the faculty of desire whose inner determining ground, hence even what pleases it, lies within the subject's reason is called the *will*" (MM 6:213).

Of course, in deciding to pursue a law career, one exerts the power of choice—the other component included in the faculty of desire. It is the power of choice that is the locus of one's capacity to act freely. In paragraph 7, Kant foregrounds the kind of freedom of choice fundamental to his conception of morality. He first contrasts human choice with animal choice. Animals have a faculty of desire; their choices involve an inner determining ground involving the inner workings of the animal. But animal choice is not free; rather the doings of an animal are the product of what Kant refers to as "sensible impulses" of the animal. By contrast, humans can act without their actions being solely determined by such impulses.[2] Of course, impulses in the form of inclinations (desires that have become habitual) can *influence* one's choices. However, human choice is not simply a product of impulsive forces as it is for animals; this is the capacity Kant calls "negative freedom." That is, one has a capacity to act independently of various impulses including desires and aversions one has. In contrast, "[t]he positive concept of freedom is that of the ability of pure reason to be of itself practical" (MM 6:214). It is only because human beings as rational agents have positive freedom, or what Kant refers to as autonomy of

---

[2] Here, I am simplifying because Kant's view is that human choice and action can be viewed from two perspectives, as mentioned in chapter 2. From the perspective of human beings as members of the phenomenal world in which all events are causally determined, human choice and action is causally determined. But from the perspective of human beings as members of the noumenal ("intelligible") world, human choice and action is free.

the will, that they are subject to moral requirements and thus morally accountable.

Kant continues in paragraph 7, by relating the positive concept of freedom to maxims and practical laws, types of practical principle discussed in the next section. Kant also refers to the notion of lawgiving that figures importantly in the distinction between the doctrine of right and the doctrine of virtue—the topic of Section IV to be discussed in the next chapter. In paragraph 8, which ends Section II, he draws various distinctions, e.g. juridical versus ethical laws and legality versus morality of actions that will also be discussed in the next chapter.

To summarize (and briefly answer our first two guiding questions): the faculty of desire refers to the capacity for choice and action. It is related to the faculty of feeling because every exercise of the faculty of desire (all choice and action) involves feeling. It is related to the faculty of cognition because determinations of the faculty of desire involve use of one's cognitive power in representing an object or state of affairs one desires to bring about. Reason (belonging to the faculty of cognition) is a source of objective practical principles for choice and action and as such is referred to as practical reason or (in Kant's technical sense) the "will." One's exercise of choice is that through which one freely adopts and acts on maxims. Freedom of choice has both negative and positive dimensions. Negatively, human freedom of choice includes the capacity to act independently of all of one's (sensuous) desires, aversions, and inclinations. Positively, it is the capacity for acting solely out of respect for the moral law. We gain more understanding of these claims by examining Kant's conception of practical principles and his theory of motivation.

4.2 Practical principles: maxims and imperatives

Two of the most important notions in Kant's theory of action are those of maxim and imperative. This section introduces these concepts in a preliminary way, about which more will be said as we proceed in this and following chapters.

Maxims

In the *Critique of Practical Reason,* Kant writes that "Practical principles are propositions that contain a general determination of the will, having under it several practical rules" (CprR 5:19).[3] Kant distinguishes two types of practical principle: maxims and imperatives. A maxim, Kant explains, "is a *subjective* principle of action, a principle which the subject himself makes his rule (how he wills to act)" (MM 6:225). One acts on maxims, which may be thought of as the contents of one's intentions to act (or refrain from acting).

Maxims may vary in their generality. I might have earning a pilot's license as an end or goal, something I thus intend whose content is a general maxim, a *maxim of ends*. A maxim of ends is then a basis for adopting more specific intentions—intentions to take flying lessons and to study for the licensing exam. If a maxim is the content of an intention, then when one acts intentionally, one acts on a maxim. So, for instance, if I intend to show up on a particular day and time to take a flying lesson, I have in effect adopted a maxim of action—to perform a specific series of actions guided, of course, by my maxim of ends. In morally judging one's actions, one must describe the action, and to describe it is to identify what one intends. Thus, in morally judging an action, one identifies the maxim upon which one acted (or is proposing to act). Reference to maxims thus figure in some of Kant's alternative formulations of his supreme principle of morality, which I will refer to as the categorical imperative (CI).

In the quote that began this section, Kant claims that practical principles, including maxims, "contain a general determination of the will," under which there are several practical rules. In that passage from the *Critique of Practical Reason,* Kant does treat maxims as general rules for behavior that a subject adopts. Thus, in the flying lesson example, one's maxim is to do the things needed to earn a pilot's license, while the more specific intentions one adopts, guided by one's maxim of ends to earn a license, count as "several practical rules" falling under it. As I interpret Kant's theory of action, these

---

[3] Thanks to Robert Audi for useful suggestions on the topic of maxims.

subsidiary rules also count as maxims. This fits well with passages where Kant formulates maxims that are specific in content and concern actions one is contemplating performing. For instance, in considering the morality of making a false promise, Kant formulates the subject's maxim as follows:

> **M** "When I believe myself in need of money, I shall borrow money and promise to repay it, even though I know that this will never happen" (G 4:422).

Maxim M includes a description of a prospective action and the circumstances in which one proposes to make a false promise. This maxim displays the form: Whenever _____, I shall _____, where the first blank is for a specification of one's circumstances, and the second of one's action. This formulation leaves out an explicit mention of some further end that subject has that is his reason for needing money.

However, in other cases, Kant does mention an end the subject has in mind in proposing to perform some specific action in a specific set of circumstances. I have distinguished maxims of actions from maxims of ends (as Kant occasionally does), and when Kant mentions an agent's end in a specification of a maxim, he can be viewed as combining in one formula the agent's maxim of action with her maxim of ends. It is the end that she intends to promote by performing an action in some circumstance that provides her with (what she takes to be) a normative reason for performing the action in those circumstances.[4] Were we to elaborate M to include reference to a likely end, we have:

---

[4] For Kant, can there be cases in which one just arbitrarily chooses an end without thinking that one has a normative reason to pursue it? This raises the question of whether Kant is committed to the so-called guise of the good thesis, according to which everything one desires or pursues is taken by that person to be in some way good and thus something that she takes herself to have a normative reason to pursue. In the second *Critique* at 5:59–60, Kant does in fact seem to commit himself to a qualified version of this thesis. For nonmorally motivated action based on desire one does take the object of one's action to be in some way agreeable and thus in some way contributing to one's welfare. One desires something *because* one takes it to contribute to one's own welfare. (Similarly, one is averse toward something because one takes it to be disagreeable.) However, in morally motivated action one is motivated to act accordingly because one conceives that act to be good as such. Thanks to Adam Cureton for prompting this clarification.

M⁺ When I believe myself in need of money, I shall borrow money and promise to repay it, even though I know that this will never happen, in order to pay my rent.

This maxim displays the form: Whenever _____, I shall _____, in order to_____, where the last blank is for a specification of the end one aims to promote by performing the action. In his writings, Kant formulates maxims in more or less detail—sometime mentioning ends, sometime not—depending on which components are important for whatever point he is making. When fully formulated to refer to a prospective action, a maxim in effect addresses the questions: What shall I do? In which circumstances? For what reason? As we go along in exploring Kant's doctrine of virtue, we will return to the topic of maxims.

Imperatives

The other type of practical principle—imperatives—are "objective" principles that specify what one ought or ought not to do. An imperative directs one to act and can be expressed as an ought-claim. Kant identifies two types of objective practical principle: hypothetical and categorical. An imperative is hypothetical when it applies to an agent only on condition that the agent has certain ends that she seeks to realize. Such imperatives, as Kant characterizes them, specify necessary means to ends. So, for instance, if one intends to earn a pilot's license, and if to do so one must log in thirty hours of instructor-assisted flying time, then one is subject to the following hypothetical imperative:

h If you intend to earn a pilot's license, and taking thirty hours of instructor-assisted flying time is necessary to earn the license, then you ought to take the thirty hours (or give up the intention to earn the license).

Kant would say that h is an objective practical principle—it is objectively valid: for anyone who intends to earn a pilot's license, it specifies what one objectively speaking ought to do. It applies to anyone *conditionally* on the person having the desire to earn a pilot's license and then seriously intending to earn one. Note, however, that h takes no account of an agent's epistemic situation—whether she knows or even believes that taking thirty hours of instruction is necessary for earning license. In most cases and for purposes of evaluating the rationality of agents, we require a version that does include reference to an agent's epistemic situation such as:

> h* If you intend to earn a pilot's license, and *know* that taking thirty hours of instructor-assisted flying time is necessary to earn the license, then you ought to take the thirty hours (or give up the intention to earn the license).

Since we are interested in principles that one can use in guiding choice and action, thus suited to one's epistemic condition, let us work with h*. Notice that h*, and the great many principles like it, are based on a formal principle that arguably represents a fundamental principle of practical rationality:

> H If one intends E and knows that doing A is necessary for realizing E, then one ought to do A (or give up E).

One may look upon H as a rationality constraint on one's intentions, given what one knows about means/ends connections. If I know that A is causally necessary for E, and if I intend E, am I not committed on pain of inconsistency to intend A? One might question whether failure to intend A counts as failure to genuinely intend E, in which case H represents a conceptual constraint on intending. In any case, H as a formal principle of practical rationality, together with relevant causal information about means and ends, yields specific principles of practical rationality that are instances of H.

Kant contrasts hypothetical imperatives that only contingently apply to a person with categorical imperatives that apply to persons necessarily. Such imperatives express moral requirements (duties). "A principle that makes certain actions duties is a practical law" (MM

6:225). As we learned in the previous chapter, moral imperatives are necessary in the sense that their application is not dependent on the desires a person happens to have. Of course, whether one is subject to some moral requirement, e.g. that one keep one's promises, depends on whether one has made a promise. But that one is required to keep the promises one has made, and thus that one morally ought to do so, does not depend on one's desires.

There are many categorical imperatives (practical laws) that express moral requirements. Kant claims that all such imperatives—the ones that represent genuine moral requirements—can be derived from a single fundamental principle—*the* CI. He formulates the principle in various ways. According to the *formula of universal law*,

> FUL "Act only in accordance with that maxim through which you can at the same time will that it become a universal law" (G 4:421).

FUL represents a test to determine whether one's action on a maxim (either in retrospect or prospect) is morally permissible. Kant also formulates his supreme principle of morality in other ways. The formula he typically employs in deriving various duties of virtue is the *formula of humanity*,

> FH "So act that you use your humanity, whether in your own person or in the person of any other, always at the same time as an end, never merely as a means" (G 4:429).

Because both formulae play a role in DV, and because one gains an understanding of them by seeing how Kant employs them in arguing for various duties, we can defer considering them until later chapters.

To sum up: maxims are principles that a person may adopt and act on. Because they depend on the individual (the subject), they are "subjective" principles of action. I interpret them representing the contents of certain of a subject's intentions. Presumably, for Kant, all actions as partly constituted by what one intends are actions on a maxim. Imperatives, which can be expressed as ought-claims, represent principles of practical reason. These are objective practical principles. Hypothetical (conditional) imperatives prescribe taking necessary means to one's ends.[5] Many ends one adopts are based on one's desires—desire-based ends. Desire-based ends vary from person to person and thus the hypothetical imperatives that apply to one person may not apply to someone else. Categorical imperatives, by contrast, apply to persons independently of the desires they happen to have. (By 'desire' here, I mean to include inclinations—habitual desires.)

How, then, are imperatives and maxims related to the faculty of desire? Moral laws, as they bear on human action (i.e. categorical imperatives), "proceed from the will, *maxims* from choice" (MM 6:226). That is, adopting maxims and acting on them result from exercising one's power of choice—it is choice that is properly described as free. Moral laws "proceed" from the will, which, as lately noted, Kant identifies with practical reason. The job of practical reason is to legislate; the job of choice is to execute. If categorically binding moral laws have their source in practical reason and maxims come from choice, what about those hypothetical imperatives whose application to an agent is conditional on her desires? Kant does not address this question in the general introduction to MM. Certainly the formal principle of such imperatives—H—represents a constraint of practical reason and so, like moral laws, "proceeds" from the will. However, the contents of specific hypothetical imperatives are based on theoretical means/ends relations.

In this section and the previous one, the aim has been to introduce some of the most general concepts that figure in Kant's theory of action. In the next two sections, the aim is to elaborate this theory by examining his conceptions of both nonmoral motivation and moral motivation. In doing so, we return to some of the early paragraphs of Section II of the introduction, as well as some of the remarks in Section III.

---

[5] Kant, to my knowledge, never discusses hypothetical imperatives that relate sufficient means to one's ends, though arguably any complete theory of action will include them. See Audi 2006: chap. 8, sec. 3 for an illuminating discussion of hypothetical imperatives.

4.3 Nonmoral motivation

For the first time, and with some trepidation, one takes a ride in a hot-air balloon and enjoys it. One anticipates taking pleasure in future balloon rides, and as a result of taking them forms a standing or "habitual" desire—what Kant refers to as an *inclination*—for doing so. One's acquired inclination is now part of what explains having desires for taking balloon rides on particular occasions. Nonhuman animals, too, have desires and inclinations. My two dogs have acquired a standing desire—an inclination—for peanut butter. However, in Kant's technical vocabulary, my dogs do not count as having an *interest* in peanut butter, for interests require the use of understanding. "[A] connection of pleasure with the faculty of desire that the understanding judges to hold as a general rule (though only for the subject) is called an *interest*" (MM 6:213). In the hot-air balloon example, given that one understands the relation between taking such rides and the pleasure one gets from them, one may thereby take an interest in hot-air balloon rides and come to have what Kant refers to as an *interest of inclination*. Interests of this sort are reflected in judging that one has a *reason* for taking such rides—namely, that one derives pleasure from them.

Now consider nonmoral motivation. Again, suppose that one has acquired an interest of inclination in taking hot-air balloon rides— a standing desire—based on experience. Suppose further that one believes that one can enjoy a ride tomorrow afternoon, and thereby forms a specific desire to do so. Assuming that tomorrow afternoon one's desire is active, one chooses to take the ride. All this constitutes a psychological explanation of one's action, which may be diagrammed as follows (see Figure 4.1).

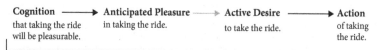

Cognition ⟶ Anticipated Pleasure ⟶ Active Desire ⟶ Action
that taking the ride in taking the ride. to take the ride. of taking
will be pleasurable. the ride.

Interest of Inclination
in hot air balloon rides based
on the fact that one's gets pleasure
from such rides which serves as one's
reason (incentive) for having this
particular interest.

Figure 4.1 Diagram of the structure of a sample case of nonmoral motivation

The connecting arrows indicate causal connection among *token* psychological states (i.e. instances of the psychological types) leading to action. In this example, the causal sequence being illustrated is itself explained by appeal to one's standing interest of inclination. Kant often refers to such cases of nonmoral motivation simply as acting from inclination.[6] Cases of acting from *interests of reason* concern moral motivation, which we take up in the next section. Before doing so, we need to consider Kant's important concept of an *incentive*. We will then be able to complete our characterization of nonmorally motivated action.

Kant does not mention incentives in Section II and does so only once in III. However, in IV reference to them plays a fundamental role in distinguishing the doctrine of right from the doctrine of virtue. The concept is also the subject matter of Chapter III of the second *Critique*, entitled, "On the Incentives of Pure Practical Reason." There, he writes: "From the concept of an incentive arises that of an *interest*, which can never be attributed to any being unless it has reason and which signifies an *incentive* of the will insofar *as it is represented by reason*." (CprR 5:79). He goes on to say, "On the concept of an interest is based that of a maxim" (ibid.). What does Kant mean by "incentive"? And how do incentive, interest, and maxim figure in Kant's theory of action?

Kant writes that "by incentive (*elater animi* [trans. mental spring of action, M.T.]) is understood the subjective determining ground of the will" (CprR 5:72).[7] And since all three concepts—incentive, interest, and maxim—pertain to the use of reason, I understand "subjective determining ground of the will" as referring to a *motivating reason*—a consideration that one takes to be a normative reason for

---

[6] Whether these are entirely discrete psychological states is something I leave open. For instance, one might interpret the state of cognition as including the anticipated pleasure and thus as a single complex psychological state.

[7] I think this remark should be taken as follows. Insofar as one acts on an incentive it is thereby a determining ground of the will. Being a "determining ground" in this way is compatible with freedom of choice: in exercising one's freedom of choice one is said to "freely determine" the will by choosing to act on the incentive. And of course, one can have (and recognize) some consideration as an incentive but choose not to act on it.

choice, the "taking up" of which (can or does) plays a causal role in explaining choice and action. This is to consider an incentive as a psychological state, as indicated by the Latin *elater animi*. However, talk of an incentive can also refer to whatever consideration or fact is a *normative reason* for you (the "object" of the incentive qua motivating psychological state).[8] The fact that by performing a particular action one would thereby suffer harm is a reason to refrain from the action—an incentive not to perform the action (or better, a disincentive). Such a reason would be the "object" of an incentive as a psychological state—its content, i.e. what the psychological state is about or directed toward. Presumably, for Kant, all intentional choice and action is based on one or more incentives—one acts for reasons.

Let's work through an example to illustrate the notion of incentive considered first as a normative reason and then as a motivating state. In contemporary English, referring to something as an incentive typically indicates that the thing in question is something one likely desires to have, and it is being offered in order to get one to do or refrain from doing something. For example, a car dealer may offer a cash bonus for purchasing a vehicle within, say, the next two weeks. This incentive could serve as a reason for someone now in the market for a car to buy in the next two weeks. In Kant's theory of action, reference to incentive is somewhat similar. That is, an incentive is a consideration that one does (or might) take as a *reason* to do or refrain from some course of action—a reason that *favors* the action. Reasons that favor in this way are called "normative reasons." Suppose one is now in the market for an automobile but was thinking of putting off buying one for a month or so. However, the offer of a cash bonus provides one with some reason to purchase one from the dealer in the next couple of weeks; sooner than one originally anticipated. Suppose one goes ahead and makes the purchase in the next two weeks from the dealer offering the bonus and does so to take advantage of the cash savings. Then one's

---

[8] I would add (on behalf of Kant), that for something to be a normative reason *for you*, that reason must be available to you as a motivating reason. In contemporary jargon, this makes Kant an internalist about reasons for action. (What "available" means here, I leave open. It is where the action is.)

reason for buying the car earlier than anticipated was to take advantage of the cash bonus. Reasons for which one acts are called "motivating reasons"—motivating, because of the role they play in explaining action. Thus, in the car-buying case, one has a normative reason to buy early, and acting on that reason makes it one's motivating reason. Of course, one can have a normative reason or a motivational reason for doing something and not act from that reason. (Also, of course, one can *take* some consideration to be a normative reason for action yet be mistaken.)

Going back to the hot-air balloon example, the pleasure one gets from taking such rides is one's incentive (reason) for taking them and is what leads to taking an interest in this activity. Taking such an interest, as Kant says, "signifies an *incentive* of the will insofar *as it is represented by reason*" (CprR 5:79); that is, insofar as it is taken as a normative reason for action. "An interest [then, M.T.] is that by which reason becomes practical, i.e., becomes a cause determining the will" (G 4:460n. *See also* CJ 5:204). Put another way: taking some consideration as a reason for action (taking it to be an incentive) is to take an interest in performing that action. One's incentive for taking a balloon ride on some occasion is one's cognition that doing so would be pleasurable (as featured in figure 4.1).

Earlier, maxims were characterized as a kind of practical principle that one adopts. Such principles are the contents of intentions. Maxims, we learned, figure centrally in Kant's theory of morality. One determines the deontic status of an action (its rightness or wrongness) by appealing to the maxim upon which one acted; by appealing to the content of the intention that partly constitutes the action, making it the type of action it is.[9] How does Kant's conception of maxim relate to our balloon example? It is not explicitly represented in Figure 4.1. The answer is that although there is no explicit reference to maxims in the diagram, it is appropriate to mention them in two places. First, in

---

[9] Talk of deontic status of actions is meant to capture what Kant means when he refers to the "legality" of action. The "morality" of action concerns motivation—whether the action was done from the sole motive of respect for the moral law (duty) or done from self-love and thus whether a fundamental maxim of respect for the law or for promoting self-interest was behind one's action. The legality/morality distinction is explained later in chapter 5, sec. 4.

the upper portion of the diagram, when one acts on one's desire to take a particular hot-air balloon, one is acting on a maxim. It has become one's intention to take *this* ride. If one asks why one has this intention, one can refer to a more general maxim associated with one's interest. Of course, given what was said earlier about formulating maxims, we can combine a maxim of ends with a maxim of action to reveal the agent's full intention: *Whenever there is an appropriate occasion for taking a hot-air balloon ride, I shall do so in order to experience the pleasure of taking such rides.* So, by taking an interest in such rides one comes to adopt a general maxim (intention) of taking such rides when occasions for doing so arise. Therefore, Kant writes: "On the concept of an interest is based that of a maxim" (CprR 5:79).

Finally, Kant holds that the ultimate source of nonmoral motivation is the inclination for one's own happiness, or "self-love," as he often refers to this source of reasons, motivation, and action. In the *Groundwork*, he claims that "all people have already, of themselves, the strongest and deepest inclination to happiness because it is just in this idea that all inclinations unite in one sum" (G 4:399). He claims that having such an end is part of the essence of being human (G 4:415–16). An individual's happiness, according to Kant, just is the satisfaction of one's more specific inclinations over the course of one's life.[10] These more specific inclinations and the feelings and desires that relate to the end of one's own happiness, are "sensuous" psychological states, because they arise from our nature as physical beings. Kant also refers to these as "pathological," though without the implication that they indicate any sort of sickness or disease. Indeed, in his 1793 *Religion within the Boundaries of Mere Reason,* Kant remarks that "*Considered in themselves* natural inclinations are *good,* i.e., not reprehensible, and to want to extirpate them would not only be futile but harmful and blameworthy as well" (R 6:58). Self-love, then, as a fundamental source of reasons, motivation, and action is contrasted with moral reasons,

---

[10] The most revealing description of Kant's conception of happiness is in the first *Critique*: "Happiness is the satisfaction of all our inclinations (*extensive,* with regard to their manifoldness, as well as *intensive,* with regard to degree, and also *protensive,* with regard to duration)" (KrV A806/B834). Thus, there are three dimensions to inclinations as they figure in one's happiness; how to balance them (since there will be trade-offs) Kant never explains.

motivation, and action that have a different fundamental source. This brings us to the topic of moral motivation.

4.4 Moral motivation

Action motivated exclusively by one's recognition that an action is morally required or prohibited is morally motivated action. Kant sometimes puts this by saying that moral motivation is being motivated solely by the thought that some action is one's duty. Moral motivation, compared to nonmoral motivation, has a distinctive etiology and so differs structurally from the latter.[11] Roughly speaking, while nonmorally motivated action, based on inclinations of self-love, is ultimately grounded upon what one takes sensuous pleasure or displeasure in, morally motivated action is ultimately grounded in reason. These two distinct sources comprise Kant's motivational dualism. Let us now consider moral motivation and how it differs structurally from its nonmoral counterpart.

Actions that are morally motivated are products of the faculty of desire through which one exercises one's power of choice. In addition, "Any determination of the faculty of choice proceeds *from* the representation of a possible action *to* the deed through the feeling of pleasure or displeasure, taking an interest in the action or in its effect" (DV 6:399). Therefore, feeling must be involved in all action, moral and nonmoral alike. The quote continues: "the *aesthetic* condition (of the affection of the inner sense) is either *pathological* or a moral feeling" (ibid.). It is the nature and role of moral feeling that is crucial for understanding Kant's distinctive theory of moral motivation. To outline this theory, let us begin with the kind of interest (i.e. that by which one takes an incentive to be a reason for action) involved in moral motivation.

As lately noted, an interest of inclination is contrasted with an *interest of reason*, briefly mentioned in paragraph 4 of Section II. The

---

[11] It also enjoys a distinctive and complex phenomenology—the phenomenology of respect—that is the subject of Chapter III of the second *Critique*. Interesting as it is (see Kriegel and Timmons 2021), for present purposes we can put aside this aspect of moral motivation.

latter is *moral interest* described in the second *Critique* as "a pure sense-free interest of practical reason alone" (CprR 5:79). One can take an interest in the laws of morality, an interest whose source cannot be traced to one's sensuous nature as can an interest of inclination. In taking or having any interest, one is responding to an incentive (a normative reason or at least what one believes to be one) by taking it to be a reason for one to engage choice. Thus, taking a moral interest in the moral law requires that the moral law or, more precisely, the moral requirements grounded in the moral law, provide normative reasons, indeed normatively authoritative reasons, for choice and action. (We saw earlier that for Kant an interest is that by which an incentive—a normative reason for action—is taken up as such.) The engagement of moral interest is reflected in a state of feeling—the feeling of respect for the moral law involved in morally motivated choice and action. For instance, upon reflection, one recognizes that one has a moral obligation to speak the truth; dissembling or lying would be morally wrong. That one has an obligation to speak the truth provides one with an authoritative and sufficient reason to act accordingly. When cognition of this incentive becomes a motivating reason, it engages *moral feeling*, a capacity to be motivated by recognition of an obligation, whose exercise is experienced motivationally as "respect" for the moral law. Moral motivation is motivation solely out of respect for the laws of morality.

Returning now to paragraph 4 of Section II, where interests of inclination and of reason are distinguished, Kant recognizes intellectual pleasures. Interests of inclination result from the pleasures (and displeasures) of sense experience—sensual pleasures (displeasures). Anticipated pleasures based on inclination *precede* desires and resulting choice. However, as lately noted, for Kant, "pleasure or displeasure in an object of desire does not always precede the desire and need not always be regarded as the cause of the desire but can also be regarded as the effect of it" (MM 6:211). That is, some practical feelings—feelings concerning choice and action—are *effects* of an exercise of the faculty of desire. Here, Kant may be referring to the feeling of respect which has a complex phenomenology including aspects analogous to both fear and inclination (G 4:401n). Alternatively, the reference may be to what Kant refers to elsewhere as feelings of "contentment with oneself" that accompanies "consciousness of virtue"

(CprR 5:117); an "intellectual contentment" (ibid.). The contentment in question arises from having a sense of exercising one's capacity to act solely from nonsensuous motives, thus fully expressing one's autonomy of will in having acted virtuously.

Regarding, then, the role of feelings in moral motivation, the feeling of respect figures centrally in the production of actions done solely for the sake of the moral law. There are also feelings of contentment spurred by a sense of having exercised one's autonomy that may arise in cases where it appears that one has acted solely from duty. Notice, however, in cases of moral motivation it is "[r]espect, and not the gratification or enjoyment of happiness" (CprR 5:117) that constitutes genuine moral motivation. If we now assemble the elements of morally motivated action we have been describing, the following structure emerges (see Figure 4.2):

(The dashed line between action and the feeling of contentment signifies that such feelings *may* accompany an instance of morally motivated action.)

Scholars differ over how to understand the psychological role of moral feeling in Kant's theory of action. The diagram represents a token instance of moral feeling as a psychological state caused by one's cognition. However, based on Kant's texts, one might argue that there is only one, albeit complex, psychological state preceding morally motivated action that includes cognition and feeling. Or, again, based on some passages, one might argue that cognition of the moral law is a direct cause of action and that moral feeling is a mere by-product of one's acting from cognition of a moral requirement. I don't believe

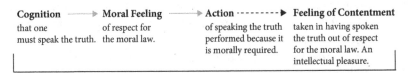

Cognition ⟶ **Moral Feeling** ⟶ **Action** ┈┈┈┈▶ **Feeling of Contentment**

Cognition	Moral Feeling	Action	Feeling of Contentment
that one must speak the truth.	of respect for the moral law.	of speaking the truth performed because it is morally required.	taken in having spoken the truth out of respect for the moral law. An intellectual pleasure.

Interest of Reason
one takes in acting from the CI based on one's recognition of the normative authority of the moral law.

Figure 4.2 Diagram of the structure of morally motivated action

these differences over the precise role of moral feeling in the etiology of morally motivated action matter for our purposes. Going forward and unless indicated otherwise, "moral feeling" as a psychological state that plays a role in moral motivation refers to the feeling of respect. (Moral feeling, as a "natural predisposition"—a capacity to feel respect as well as moral disgust, moral horror, guilt, and shame—will come up when, in part III, we turn to the dedicated introduction to DV.)

Finally, my description of moral motivation did not include reference to maxims. However, as with nonmoral motivation, it is appropriate to mention them in two places. In the upper part of the diagram, when one performs a dutiful action one is acting on a maxim which, if fully elaborated, includes the ultimate motivating reason, respect for the moral law. The feeling of respect one experiences on an occasion of action reflects one's interest of reason; one's so-called moral interest. This interest expresses a general commitment to the moral law—an intention to comply with the requirements of duty from respect for the law. It is thus a higher-order maxim of ends.

Let us now sum up the account of motivation. Kant, as lately noted, is a motivational dualist—there are two fundamentally different sources of reason for action—inclination and duty, as Kant often draws the contrast. The faculty of desire "operates" in concert with feeling. If sensuous feeling leading to desires and inclinations precedes one's interest in some course of action, the resulting actions are instances of nonmoral motivation. If the feeling involved in action has an exclusively intellectual source—in one's cognition of the moral law and either generating or including respect for the law—then the action is morally motivated. Finally, the significance of all this for understanding the doctrine of virtue is that moral motivation is essential to having a good will, which in turn is central to virtue—one's ultimate moral vocation in life. All of this will be spelled out in more detail in the chapters to come.

In the preceding, we have covered most of the material in the first seven paragraphs of the eight-paragraph Section II, with some elaboration of Kant's theory of motivation. Paragraph eight concerns distinctions (juridical vs. ethical laws, external vs. internal use of freedom, and legality vs. morality of actions) that we take up in later chapters.

4.5 Concluding reflections

Here are some questions and perhaps worries that may have occurred to readers. Kant claims we act on maxims whenever we deliberately perform (or refrain from performing) actions. Is his view too intellectualist? Much of what one does, one does spontaneously without any conscious awareness of formulating maxims and then acting on them. So, isn't Kant's view psychologically implausible for overly intellectualizing human action?

This is not a problem for Kant. Maxims, as we've seen, are the contents of intentions and we should distinguish between *prior intentions* that precede action and serve to guide it from *intentions in action*.[12] A prior intention is illustrated by my intention to take hot-air balloon rides when I can. Suppose some afternoon I decide to act on that intention. This decision triggers a series of actions: getting up from my chair, walking to a closet to fetch what I want to wear, putting on the select clothes, et cetera. Each of these actions are intentional doings. But they are spontaneous. I did not form a prior intention specific to each of them. Rather, because they are intentional actions, it is appropriate to recognize an intention *realized in* spontaneously performed actions. And, of course, some intentional spontaneous actions are not preceded by any prior intention. On the spur of the moment, I may spontaneously, yet intentionally, jump up and down. Here we have an action that embeds, as it were, an intention where my reason for jumping up and down is simply that it is what I felt like doing.

Of course, in consciously determining whether an action one has done or proposes to do is morally permissible, one must first describe what that action is. And to do this for purposes of moral evaluation, it is often essential to characterize the circumstances in which the action takes place and the end one aims to promote in so acting. That is, in Kant-speak, one must formulate one's maxim for purposes of reflective

---

[12] See Searle 1984, chap. 3 for discussion of this distinction. As Robert Audi pointed out to me, talk of intentions in action might be taken as attributing too much to consciousness at a time, thus intensifying the worry the distinction in intention is supposes to address. One way to handle this is to hold that the intentions on which one acts spontaneously need not be *consciously* represented to play a role in such action.

moral judgment and decision-making. But given that to formulate one's maxim just is to provide an appropriate description of one's action, doing so is what one would have to do no matter one's moral theory. Kant's notion of a maxim and its role in explaining action does not overintellectualize human action.

Second, one may wonder why Kant takes such great pains to distinguish moral from nonmoral motivation in the way he does, by claiming that moral motivation has a distinctive intellectual source. That is: why suppose there are two sources of motivation when a single-source view is simpler? The answer goes to the heart of Kant's conception of moral obligation and duty, which we take up in the next chapter. In the meantime, here is a short answer. As explained in chapter 3, in theorizing about morality, Kant takes himself to be articulating the presuppositions of ordinary moral thought and discourse. He claims that moral laws, if they are to be genuinely authoritative, must hold in virtue of the nature of rationality, which he connects with autonomy of the will. It is only as agents who are rational and free that moral laws apply to us. So understood, those laws apply to humans independently of those desires and inclinations that ground nonmoral reasons for action. If recognition of moral laws must be motivating, then the source of their motivational power cannot be desires and inclinations; it must be reason itself. Another way to explain this point is by noting that for Kant moral laws are categorical imperatives—categorical in the sense that they apply to human beings independently of desire and inclination. If it were necessarily the case that all human motivation is inclination-based, and based ultimately on considerations of self-love, the implication would be that all rational requirements on action would be hypothetical in nature; none of them would yield *moral requirements*.

The empiricist David Hume argued that "reason can never produce any action, or give rise to volition" and famously concluded that "reason is, and ought only to be the slave of the passions" (*A Treatise of Human Nature* Book II, Part III, Section II). Kant, of course, claims that reason is a source of action and volition. Kant would claim that Hume cannot account for genuine moral obligation, and this is why he wrote (to quote the remark once again) that a view like Hume's "would run the risk of the grossest and most pernicious errors" (MM 6:215).

Kant's brand of ethical rationalism requires his rationalist theory of moral motivation.

Further reading

- For a comprehensive treatment of Kant's theory of action see McCarty 2009.
- See Frierson 2014 for an extended treatment of Kant's empirical psychology

5

Preliminary Concepts and Division for a Metaphysics of Morals

General Introduction, Sections III and IV

We now turn to Sections III and IV of the general introduction.[1] In Section III, "Preliminary Concepts of the Metaphysics of Morals," Kant introduces the basic concepts he employs in the rest of the book. My plan for handling it is to focus only on those concepts that are essential for understanding DV which will occupy us in the first four sections of this chapter. Section 5 is devoted to "On the Division of a Metaphysics of Morals" (Section IV), where Kant explains the main division between *The Doctrine of Right* and *The Doctrine of Virtue*. It is here that Kant invokes the concept of incentive, introduced in the previous chapter, to explain two types of lawgiving that serve as the basis for the division. Section 6 explains Kant's project in *The Doctrine of Right*, an understanding of which helps set the stage for *The Doctrine of Virtue*. In the final section, I briefly summarize what has been covered in chapters 3–5 and briefly comment on Kant's conception of moral requirements and the idea of lawgiving.

5.1 Freedom, practical laws, imperatives, obligation, and duty

In Section III beginning at 6:221 and up through most of 6:223, Kant briefly addresses several questions, including:

- What is the relation between freedom and the moral law?

---

[1] Recall from chapter 3 that in some translations the order of these two sections is reversed.

Kant's Doctrine of Virtue. Mark Timmons, Oxford University Press (2021). © Oxford University Press.
DOI: 10.1093/oso/9780190939229.003.0005

- What are practical laws and why, as they apply to human beings, do they take the form of imperatives?
- How is one to understand the concepts of obligation, duty, and deed that are fundamental in moral philosophy?

Let us take these up in order.

As we learned in chapter 2, for Kant the concept of freedom is transcendent in that it refers to a supersensible capacity that cannot be an object of human experience (though, of course, one can exercise this capacity). It is therefore not possible, according to Kant's epistemology, to have theoretical cognition of one's own freedom. In the previous chapter, we learned that Kant distinguishes negative from positive freedom. To review, negative freedom is one's capacity to choose and act independently of one's choice and action being determined by sensible desires and aversions. Positive freedom (autonomy) involves one's capacity to act solely out of respect for the moral law (from the thought of duty alone). In the opening paragraph of Section III, Kant writes that "freedom proves its reality by practical principles, which are laws of a causality of pure reason for determining choice independently of any empirical conditions (of sensibility generally) and prove a pure will in us, in which moral concepts and laws have their source" (MM 6:221). In short, through one's awareness of those practical principles that are moral laws and whose source is one's own reason, one can affirm one's freedom of choice. (This theme is developed most fully in the *Critique of Practical Reason*, chap. 1, Section I, 5:42–5:50). Later in Section III, Kant writes, "The ground of the possibility of categorical imperatives is this: that they refer to no other property of choice . . . than simply to its *freedom*" (MM 6:222). The ground Kant is referring to is metaphysical and so *being subject* to moral requirements (the moral law) requires that one is free, while *recognizing that one is subject* to the moral law is the epistemological basis for confirming that one is free. (This two-sided relation between the moral law and freedom was briefly mentioned in chapter 2, sec. 2.)

Consider now our second question about the relation of practical law (practical principles that are laws of morality) to imperatives. In chapter 4, the distinction between two types of practical principle—maxims and imperatives—was introduced, as was the distinction between hypothetical (conditional) and categorical (unconditional) imperatives. In paragraph 2 of Section III, Kant says that unconditional practical *laws* are called moral. What is Kant's conception of a practical law and how is it related to unconditional (moral) imperatives?

A practical law in Kant's technical sense "represents an action as necessary but takes no account of whether this action already inheres by an *inner* necessity in the acting subject (as in a holy being) or whether it is contingent (as in the human being)" (MM 6:222). Kant's generic concept of practical law pertains to both finite and nonfinite (holy) beings. A holy being such as God (if in fact God exists)[2] is subject to practical laws, but because God is perfectly rational, God *necessarily* complies with practical laws. Practical laws as they pertain to God (or any perfectly rational being) *describe* how in fact such a being acts. And thus, for such a being, the idea of being subject to a *requirement* represented as a command or imperative is out of place. Practical laws, as they pertain to imperfectly rational beings, *prescribe* how such beings ought to act. The very idea of obligation for Kant entails that of a rational being who is not perfectly rational; a being for whom complying with a practical law is *contingent*. An imperative, Kant writes, "is a rule the representation of which *makes* necessary an action that is subjectively contingent and thus represents that subject as one that must be *constrained* (necessitated) to conform with the rule" (MM 6:222). To be morally necessitated is to be morally constrained— subject to an obligation. So, while the concept of practical law applies to both nonfinite, perfectly rational beings like God and to finite, imperfectly rational beings, including human beings, the relation of moral laws to these two types of rational being differs. It is important, then, to be aware of the moral law/moral imperative distinction when interpreting Kant, although in many passages his mention of the moral law or moral laws refers to moral imperatives.

Turning now to the third bulleted question, Kant distinguishes the concepts of obligation and duty. "*Obligation* [is] "the necessity of a free

---

[2] As we learned in chapter 2, Kant holds that human beings can consistently think the concept of God but denies any theoretical cognition of the existence and nature of such a being. Still, Kant claims we can and must postulate God's existence for the practical purpose of explaining how the highest good (virtue proportionally rewarded by happiness) is possible.

action under a categorical imperative" (MM 6:222). The necessity here refers to *moral* necessity, an unconditional requirement to either do or refrain from doing some action. "*Duty* is that action to which one is bound" (ibid.); such actions are the content or the "matter of obligation" (ibid.). Actions that one is morally obligated to perform (duties of commission) are morally required. Actions that one is morally obligated to refrain from performing (duties of omission) are morally forbidden (or wrong), and actions that are neither required nor forbidden are merely permissible. The supreme principle of morality, *the* categorical imperative (CI), is the basis in Kant's theory for deriving actions that are morally required (morally necessary), morally forbidden, and merely permitted ('merely' in the sense of being neither required nor forbidden). Finally, Kant refers to actions for which one is morally accountable as *deeds*. He puts this by saying they "come under obligatory laws" (MM 6:223), that is, as deeds they are subject to and thus can be evaluated by the laws of morality. Thus, deeds include actions that are duties, those that are contrary to duty, and actions that are merely permitted.

For readers following along in Kant's text, we are two paragraphs shy of 6:224. Before moving forward, let us look back to the latter part of the second paragraph of Section III. There Kant writes that the observance or transgression of a duty is "connected with a pleasure or displeasure of a distinctive kind (moral *feeling*)" (MM 6:221). In the previous chapter we noted that for Kant "any determination of the faculty of choice proceeds *from* the representation of a possible action *to* the deed through a feeling of pleasure or displeasure, taking an interest in the action or in its effect" (DV 6:399). In cases where one knowingly complies with duty for nonmoral reasons, "pathological" feeling *precedes* the representation of the law. In cases where compliance is from the sole motive of duty one experiences moral feeling that *follows from* the representation of the law representing the action as a duty. Feeling is involved in both morally motivated and nonmorally motivated action. What Kant is emphasizing in this paragraph is that feelings have "nothing to do with *basis* of practical laws" (DV 6:221) of morality but only with the mental effect of one's faculty of choice being determined by such laws. In effect, Kant is stressing commitment to his form of moral rationalism: morality (its laws and the capacity to act from them) is based in reason, not feeling.

5.2 Moral personality, humanity, and the human being

The concept of moral personality is fundamental in Kant's understanding of human moral agency. By having moral personality, a human being is morally accountable.[3] At 6:223, Kant writes: "A *person* is a subject whose actions can be *imputed* to him. *Moral* personality is therefore nothing other than the freedom of a rational being under moral laws. . . ." The kind of freedom in question—autonomy—is the capacity to in part act solely out of respect for the moral law. More specifically, the supreme principle of morality (the CI) and the particular categorical imperatives derivable from it have their source in one's lawgiving reason, and this is why, having introduced the notion of moral personality, Kant writes: "a person is subject to no other laws than those he gives to himself (either alone or at least along with others)" (ibid.).[4]

To highlight this point: as we have learned, for Kant, human beings are members of both the sensible spatiotemporal world (*homo phenomena*) and the "intelligible world" (*homo noumena*). In the *Critique of Practical Reason*, Kant explains that what elevates a human being "above himself (as part of the sensible world) . . . is nothing other than *personality*, that is, freedom and independence from the mechanism of the whole of nature, regarded nevertheless as also a capacity of a being subject to special laws—namely, pure practical laws given by his own reason . . ." (CprR 5:87). It is in having this elevated status (as members of an intelligible world) that human beings have *dignity*—according to

---

[3] For Kant so-called psychological personality refers to one's capacity to be conscious of one's identity over time. See CpuR A 362–366.

[4] Kant's talk of "giving" oneself the moral law can be misleading in suggesting that somehow being subject to the moral law is up to the choice of the individual. But this is not Kant's view. The source of the moral law (here understood as the supreme principle of morality) is one's reason and it represents a fixed norm of reason whose binding force does not depend on individual choice. See Kleingeld and Willaschek 2019 for an enlightening discussion of this matter.

which one is not to be treated merely as a means but as an end in itself. One's dignity, then, is expressed in the humanity formulation of the CI, encountered in chapter 4:

> FH: "So act that you use humanity, whether in your own person or in the person of any other, always at the same time as an end, never merely as a means" (G 4:429).

What is important to notice is that here and in other passages humanity is equated with moral personality. For instance, in the introduction to DR, Kant writes:

> In the doctrine of duties a human being can and should be represented in terms of his capacity for freedom, which is wholly supersensible, and so too merely in terms of his *humanity*, his personality independent of physical attributes (*homo noumenon*), as distinguished from the same subject represented as affected by physical attributes, *a human being* (*homo phenomenon*). (DR 6:239).

In other places (as we shall see in chapter 8), Kant distinguishes humanity from both animality and moral personality, where 'humanity' refers more narrowly to the capacity to set ends and act on them, but does not also include the capacity to set and act from moral ends, i.e. from reasons grounded in the CI. So, we find a narrow and a broad use of 'humanity'. Its broad use refers to the capacity to set *and* act from nonmoral ends as well as the capacity to set and act from moral ends. In its narrow sense, it refers just to the capacity to set ends based entirely on nonmoral incentives. Furthermore, the concept of humanity should not be confused with the concept of a human being. The former (in the sense of moral personality) refers to one's rational nature as a member of an intelligible realm, the latter (as indicated in the earlier quote) refers to humans as members of both the sensible and intelligible realms.[5] (Kant's technical distinctions, using for the most part

---

[5] MM 6:434–435 is another place where Kant distinguishes a human being as a mere rational animal (*homo phenomenon*) from a human being considered as a person subject to the moral law (*homo noumenon*).

ordinary language, do pile up and can be confusing. Hopefully consulting the *Guide to Terminology* will help with this.)

5.3 One supreme moral law, many duties

At 6:225, Kant remarks that "The categorical imperative, which as such only affirms what obligation is, is: act upon a maxim that can also hold as a universal law." As we know, reference to *the* categorical imperative (CI) is to Kant's supreme moral law or principle, and here it is formulated in terms of the concept of universal law.[6] As mentioned in the previous chapter, the universal law formula expresses a *test* of an action's moral permissibility. The procedure is to "first consider your actions in terms of their subjective principles," that is, formulate one's maxim, and then "subject it to the test of conceiving yourself as also giving universal law through it." Presumably, to conceive giving universal law "through" one's maxim is to consider whether one can consistently will one's maxim and at the same time will it as a universal law of nature governing the behavior of everyone. If one can consistently will one's maxim while simultaneously willing it as a universal law of nature, then action on the maxim is morally permissible.[7] What determines, for Kant, whether one can consistently will one's maxim as a universal law of nature is a matter of scholarly dispute. I will not pause here to delve into this matter, though this test will come up later in chapter 13 when we consider Kant's argument for the duty of beneficence.

In this same passage at 6:225, after referring to the universal law formula of the CI as a test, Kant goes on to say:

---

[6] While this is a single supreme principle of morality, Kant offers various formulations of it. In addition to the formula of universal law and the formula of humanity, there is the universal law *of nature* formula, the formula of autonomy, and the kingdom of ends formula—all of these presented in Section II of the *Groundwork*. Neither of the last two formulas play a role in DV.

[7] As Kant mentions in the *Groundwork* (G: 4:421) and explains in the second *Critique* (CprR 5:67–71), testing one's maxim by asking whether one can consistently will it as a *law of nature* is a way of allowing the more abstract formula "act only according to that maxim through which you can at the same time will that it become a universal law" (G 4:421) to be applied to actions as part of the natural world. A full explanation of this matter would take us beyond the scope of the present study.

The simplicity of this law in comparison with the great and various consequences that can be drawn from it must seem astonishing at first, as must also its authority to command without appearing to carry any incentive with it. But in wondering at an ability of our reason to determine choice by the mere idea that a maxim qualifies for the *universality* of a practical law, one learns that just these practical (moral) laws first make known a property of choice, namely its freedom, which speculative reason would never have arrived at . . .

In the first sentence, Kant refers to the *simplicity, fecundity,* and *authority* of the moral law. The simplicity is that the test expressed by the universal law formula refers to the conceivability of one's maxim as a universal law—a single feature that Kant thinks is fecund in that it can be used to derive an entire system of duties (its consequences). As explained in the previous chapter in connection with moral motivation, the incentive that the moral law carries with it and which gives it authority just is the law itself which is registered in one's experience as a feeling of respect for the law.

Since there are many duties, one may wonder whether there could be a conflict of duties in that one could be simultaneously subject to more than one duty at a time and not be able to comply with all of them. Kant claims that this is not possible, "since duty and obligation are concepts that express the objective practical *necessity* of certain actions and two rules opposed to each other cannot be necessary at the same time" (MM 6:224). If it is a rule of morality that one should not break one's promises and also a rule of morality that one should help others, and one finds oneself in a situation where to help someone in need, one must break a promise, it cannot be one's duty to both keep the promise and help the one in need. Yet one may be faced with two or more competing *grounds* of obligation. If, for Kant, reference to a ground of obligation is equivalent to *reasons* that serve to morally favor or disfavor some course of action, then we can say that on one hand the fact that someone is in need of help (who one is able to help) is a reason (or ground) that favors helping. On the other hand, the fact that stopping to help would mean breaking a promise is a reason or ground that favors not stopping. "When two such grounds conflict with each other, practical philosophy says, not that the stronger obligation takes precedence ... but that the stronger *ground of obligation* prevails" (MM 6:224).[8] For an action to be the content of an obligation, and hence a duty, *full stop*, is for that action to be favored or called for by the stronger ground of obligation in cases where there are two or more competing grounds of obligation.[9]

How does one determine which of two competing grounds of obligation is the stronger ground or reason? Part of the answer adverts to Kant's distinction between perfect and imperfect duties. Roughly speaking, perfect duties require strict compliance while imperfect duties allow more latitude for compliance. More must be said about this distinction, and we return to it in chapter 7.

5.4 Legality (rightness), morality (moral worth), and merit

Throughout his writings in moral philosophy, Kant distinguishes the "legality" of actions from their "morality." The legality/morality distinction must be handled with care. By the *legality* of an action, Kant is not referring to an action's being permitted or required by some institutional law, including criminal and civil law, although his idea of legality is analogous to this. Rather, an action is, in Kant's sense, legal (or has legality) if it is permitted by the moral law; if it is not forbidden. The *morality* of an action refers both to its being required by the moral law and to the ultimate reason the action is undertaken. If the underlying and sole motivating reason which explains why an agent performed a required action is that she regarded it as morally required, then the action has moral worth. Kant's conception of moral motivation—motivation involved in performing actions that have moral worth—was the focus of section 4 in the previous chapter. There, the incentive of respect for the law as moral feeling was explained as central to Kant's conception of moral motivation—motivation that results in an action having moral worth.

---

[8] On conflicting grounds of obligation, see also Vig 27:493, 508–509, and 537.

[9] That the set of true moral principles must be consistent is, as Adam Cureton reminded me, an aspect of Kant's moral rationalism.

In the *Groundwork*, the legality/morality distinction is illustrated by Kant's example of the shopkeeper. If a shopkeeper deals honestly with his customers and does so out of care for his business, then he complies with his moral duty not to cheat, and so the action has legality, but it lacks morality or moral worth. It is only if a shopkeeper refrains from cheating his customers solely because he recognizes that he has a moral obligation not to cheat that his action has moral worth. Thus, at 6:225, Kant writes: "The conformity of an action with the law of duty is its *legality* . . . the conformity of the maxim of action with a law is the *morality* . . . of the action." (See also CprR 5:81).

Because the morality or moral worth of an action is central to Kant's conception of virtue, this too is something we come back to in a later chapter. However, note here that talk of "respect for the law" as a motive and acting "for the sake of the moral law alone" are being equated in the case of human beings and other imperfectly rational agents. And often when referring to this species of motivation, Kant will refer to an action being done from the sole "motive of duty." Of these ways of referring to moral motivation, talk of *respect* for the law invokes Kant's conception of moral feeling, which he mentions in the second paragraph of Section III. Again, we will consider Kant's doctrine of moral feeling in chapter 8.

In the passage just quoted, Kant refers to acting *in conformity with* duty as the mark of legality of action. Going forward, I will use 'comply' as in 'comply with duty' as a simpler equivalent to Kant's usage.

Finally, moral merit. It is perhaps tempting to equate the morality of an action—its moral worth—with moral merit. However, this is a mistake. Toward the end of Section III, Kant remarks that if "someone does *more* in the way of duty than he can be constrained by law to do, what he does is *meritorious* . . . ; if what he does is just exactly what the [moral, M.T.] law *requires*, he does *what is owed* . . ." (MM 6:227). As noted earlier, Kant distinguishes perfect duty from imperfect duty. Actions that merely comply with one's imperfect duties are generally meritorious,[10] their merit resulting from the fact that in complying with them one goes beyond what "strict" perfect duty requires. Note,

---

[10] Only generally, because helping someone from a malicious motive does not count as meritorious.

too, that merit comes in degrees, while moral worth apparently does not. Either one acts solely from duty or not. There are two parameters that govern degree of merit. At 6:228, near the end of Section III, Kant says that "The greater the natural obstacles (of sensibility) and the less the moral obstacle (of duty), so much more the merit is to be accounted for a *good deed*, as when, for example, at considerable self-sacrifice I rescue a complete stranger from great distress" (MM 6:228). In Kant's example here, one's overcoming an inclination to avoid putting oneself in harm's way (natural obstacle of sensibility) and the fact that one does not (in the case being imagined) have a strict obligation to rescue a complete stranger (a weak moral obstacle in the way of not rescuing) combine to confer great merit on the rescue. Notice that there is no mention of motive. It might be that the rescuer acts from natural sympathetic feeling and is thus not morally motivated. Of course, it might be that the rescuer was *in a sense* motivated by duty in that she acted from the thought that while this specific act is not her strict duty, nevertheless it is an instance of partly fulfilling one's wide imperfect duty of beneficence. Perhaps Kant thought that morally meritorious actions must have this kind of moral motivation behind them. Even so, merit and moral worth are distinct properties of actions.

5.5 Two types of lawgiving and the main division in *The Metaphysics of Morals*

The doctrine of morals comprises two main divisions: the doctrine of right, which concerns duties of right, and the doctrine of virtue, which concerns duties of virtue. (Kant reserves the term 'ethics' for this latter division.) This division is based on Kant's concept of lawgiving and its two kinds: juridical and ethical. What distinguishes them is the type of incentive associated with duty. Kant's use of the German term, *Triebfeder,* is commonly translated into English as 'incentive', and was introduced in the previous chapter when explaining his theory of motivation. There we quoted Kant as saying that "by incentive (*elater animi* [trans. mental spring of action]) is understood the subjective determining ground of the will" (CprR 5:72). For actions that have been performed or will be performed, the subjective determining ground of the will refers to one's motivating reason(s) for performing the action. Kant, we noted, is a motivational dualist. One source of motivation is self-love (broadly conceived) and the other source is morality itself, that is, respect for the moral law. Reference to incentives is how Kant explains the difference between duties of right and duties of virtue and the corresponding division of MM.

Section IV begins with this sentence:

> In all lawgiving (whether it prescribes internal or external actions, and whether it prescribes them a priori by reason alone or by the choice of another) there are two elements: first, a law, which represents an action that is to be done as *objectively* necessary, that is, which makes the action a duty; and second, an incentive, which connects a ground for determining choice to this action *subjectively* with the representation of the law (MM 6:218).

As with many of Kant's long sentences, this one is a mind full. Let's break it down. First, in the parenthetical remark, Kant refers to internal and external actions. An external action is publicly observable behavior that requires outward bodily movement, such as paying a bill, helping someone in need, or running a marathon. By contrast, an internal action is something private that does not require bodily movement, such as the act of deciding to go to law school or vowing to lose weight. In short, external actions involve observable doings while internal actions are private, mental acts.

Lawgiving, we are told, has two elements: a law and an incentive. The law specifies some action to be done (where actions include intentionally refraining from doing something). Laws make an action (or omission) "objectively necessary"; they are required (or forbidden). The second element—the incentive—determines how one's representation of the law (and its specific requirements) is related to human choice. For human beings to be *obligated* to comply with the demands in question, there must be some reason (incentive), the appreciation of which, can motivate one to comply. In contemporary metaethical parlance, Kant holds a version of *ethical internalism*—internal to the very concept of a moral obligation is the idea of there being a reason to comply, the appreciation of which can motivate one to comply.[11] In line with his motivational dualism, Kant distinguishes two types of incentive. It is the type of incentive associated with a duty that distinguishes duties of right (juridical duties) from duties of virtue.

Duties of right pertain to a legal system (statutory law) and what one may legitimately be coerced to do or refrain from doing. One has a moral requirement to obey legitimate statutory laws, and the incentive directly associated with such requirements is grounded in self-love. That is, the threat of punishment and one's aversion to such punishment may serve as an incentive for complying with statutory laws. Kant refers to this type of lawgiving as "juridical lawgiving." He also refers to it as "external lawgiving"—external because the source of the relevant type of incentive is the coercive power of the state, a constraint coming from others that is external to the agent. By contrast, "That lawgiving which makes an action a duty and also makes this duty the incentive is *ethical*" (MM 6:219). This kind of lawgiving connects complying with the moral law with the motive of duty. Kant also refers to ethical lawgiving as "internal lawgiving" because the source of the incentive is *self*-constraint.

In addition to using the "external/internal" terminology to contrast types of constraint that can serve as motivating reasons for action, Kant also applies this terminology to actions that are the content of obligations—the duties one has an obligation to perform. Juridical lawgiving is exclusively concerned with external actions and thus with external duties. One can only be legitimately coerced to perform external actions. Ethical lawgiving is concerned with internal actions and

---

[11] There is a variety of internalist theses in ethics. Mark van Roojen (2015: ch. 4) identifies twelve forms of ethical internalism. What I am attributing to Kant really amounts to two distinguishable forms. To use the terminology of van Roojen, I interpret Kant as committed to a version of moral/reasons existence internalism, according to which in order for one to have a moral obligation to φ, one must have a (sufficient) normative reason to φ. (The existence of a moral obligation to φ entails having a sufficient normative reason to φ.) I am also attributing to Kant reasons/motive existence internalism, according to which in order to have a reason R to perform some action, recognition of R by an agent must be capable of motivating her to perform the action. (The existence of a normative reason R to φ entails that one is capable of being motivated by one's recognition of R to φ. In the case of reasons that ground moral obligations, the existence of such a reason entails that one is capable of being *sufficiently* motivated by one's recognition of that reason.)

thus with internal duties. This is because, as noted earlier, ethics is concerned with setting ends, something that strictly speaking one cannot be coerced into doing according to Kant.[12] However, there are three important clarifications about Kant's way of dividing duties of right from those of ethics mentioned in Section IV.

First, some duties of virtue concern obligations to perform external actions, such as acts of beneficence where one acts to help others. So, ethics includes obligations to both external actions and internal actions. *Second*, some external actions are both duties of right and duties of virtue, and so the division between DR and DV is not fundamentally a matter of a difference in the actions that are duties. Rather, as noted, it is the type of lawgiving that is the basis for distinguishing duties of right from those of virtue.

> So it is an external duty to keep a promise made in a contract; but the command to do this merely because it is a duty, without regard for any other incentive, belongs to *internal* lawgiving alone. So the obligation is assigned to ethics not because the duty is of a particular kind (a particular kind of action to which one is bound)—for there are external duties in ethics as well as in right—but rather because the lawgiving in this case is an internal one and can have no external lawgiver (MM 6:220).

Third, cases may arise in which one cannot be coerced into complying with a duty of right, because, for instance, the party to whom I am obligated to keep a contractual promise is not in a position to coerce me to keep it, and perhaps I am also beyond the reach of state authorities who enforce contract law. In such cases, because the external action in question is a moral obligation, the idea of duty, or respect for the law, can serve as a sufficient incentive to comply. "So while there are many *directly ethical* duties"—duties that *only* admit of internal lawgiving—"internal lawgiving makes the rest of them, one and all, indirectly ethical" (MM 6:221). When one performs a duty— any duty, whether of right or of virtue—from the sole motive of duty

---

[12] In chapter 6, sec. 2, I raise potential worries about the claim that adopting ends cannot be coerced.

(respect for the moral law), one performs a *virtuous action* (an action having moral worth), even if one is not performing a duty of virtue.

5.6 The Doctrine of Right

Because the doctrine of virtue presupposes some familiarity with the doctrine of right, a few remarks about the latter are in order. The doctrine of right represents Kant's legal and political philosophy and focuses on rights of individuals as citizens and of states that can be legitimately enforced by external coercion. Its primary focus is on "external freedom"—freedom of action unhindered by others. Part I, Private Right, addresses the rights of individuals associated with property, contract, and "rights to persons akin to rights to things," the latter including for example the rights of parents over their children. Part II, Public Right, concerns a *"system of laws for a people, that is, a multitude of human beings, or for a multitude of peoples, which, because they affect one another, need a rightful condition under a will uniting them, a constitution (constitutio), so that they may enjoy what is laid down as right"* (DR 6:311). Here, Kant distinguishes the right of states over its citizens, the right of nations (i.e. states in relation to each other), and cosmopolitan right, which concerns a possible peaceful union of all nations. These two parts are preceded by a dedicated introduction which, among other things, explains the concept of a right, the universal principle of right, and the ultimate basis of acquired right in one's innate right as a person. Let's take these in order.

First, the moral concept of a right in the context of a doctrine of right, has primarily to do with external relations among persons insofar as the actions of persons (as deeds) can affect other persons, where no account is taken of one's motives. All that matters is how one's actions affect the freedom of others to set and pursue their own ends. *Second*, the universal principle governing right is:

> UPR: "Any action is *right* if it can coexist with everyone's freedom in accordance with a universal law, or if on its maxim the freedom of choice of each can coexist with everyone's freedom in accordance with universal law" (DR 6:230).

Someone thus wrongs me if what they do hinders me in my activities where such hindrance cannot "coexist with freedom in accordance with a universal law" (ibid.) Furthermore, this conception of right is analytically associated with an authorization to use coercion in cases where coercion is a "hindrance to a hindrance" thus protecting a potential victim's freedom of action. The basis of UPR and the authorization to use coercion is Kant's claim that all persons have an innate right of freedom in the sense of an *entitlement* to be allowed to do or omit actions without interference from others, subject to the condition that acting on this entitlement is compatible with a like entitlement of all. This is the only innate right; all others are acquired. What acquired rights there are and how they can be acquired is treated in DR's doctrine of elements.

Relating these ideas to the two types of lawgiving explained in the previous section, one fundamental contrast between DR and DV is that the former is only concerned with external actions and coercion from others (including the state)—external coercion—as a legitimate motivating reason (incentive). By contrast, virtue has to do with adopting ends, apparently something one cannot be externally coerced into doing and so involves an exercise of what Kant calls one's "inner freedom" through which one is able to exercise self-constraint. While external coercion is the incentive associated with the rule of positive law (laws enacted by a state), only the incentive of respect for the moral law can be associated with the kind of lawgiving proper to a doctrine of virtue. As we shall see in the coming chapters, there are other contrasts Kant draws between the doctrines of right and of virtue; all of them listed in the Appendix.

5.7 Concluding reflections

In this chapter and the previous two, we have covered quite a lot of material mostly from the four sections of the general introduction to MM and also from the introduction to *The Doctrine of Right*, material that will help prepare readers for *The Doctrine of Virtue*. Chapter 3 was devoted to explaining Kant's conception of philosophy in order to explain his idea of and necessity for having a metaphysics of morals.

Chapter 4 was devoted to the elements of Kant's theory of action, including the structure of both nonmoral and moral motivation. In this chapter we considered a battery of concepts fundamental to Kant's doctrine of morals, including the concepts of freedom, practical law, obligation, duty, and others. We then considered Section IV, where Kant distinguishes two types of lawgiving as a basis for dividing the doctrine of morals into a doctrine of right and the doctrine of virtue and lately considered some basic elements of the former doctrine.

Before moving forward to *The Doctrine of Virtue*, let us reflect a bit more on Kant's conception of moral requirements as categorical imperatives with a comment on lawgiving. The concluding reflections in chapter 3 considered the idea of moral requirements as both categorical and authoritative. It is worth recalling what was said, since it is so central in Kant's conception of morality and his moral philosophy built on that conception. To say that an imperative, directed toward oneself, is *categorical* refers to its conditions of application. The contrast here is with hypothetical imperatives, whose conditions of application depend on those ends one happens to desire, which can vary from person to person. The ends in question are usually ultimately adopted on the basis of judgments about which of them will contribute to one's happiness. And Kant refers to them using various labels, including 'discretionary', 'relative', 'optional', and 'contingent.' Thus, hypothetical imperatives only conditionally apply, depending on one's contingent ends.[13] A moral imperative, by contrast, is unconditional; it applies regardless of the contingent ends one happens to have adopted. This is what makes it *categorical* in its application.

However, as we noted in chapter 3, there is more to Kant's conception of a categorical imperative than its application conditions. Such imperatives also have superior normative authority. Thus, a further aspect of categorical moral imperatives, at least those associated with perfect duties, is that they provide reasons for choice and action that

[13] Strictly speaking, if hypothetical imperatives merely express means/ends relationships without regard to the source of the end (whether sensible inclination or the moral law) then there can be both nonmoral and moral hypothetical imperatives. However, given contemporary usage as well as Kant's own, going forward 'hypothetical imperative' will refer exclusively to those means/ends imperatives that refer to ends one might adopt based on one's desires and aversions.

are normatively superior to competing reasons of self-love—reasons ultimately grounded in one's contingent desires and inclinations. Thus, a fundamental idea in Kant's ethics is that moral requirements are *categorically authoritative*.[14] This conception will be refined once we get to the Elements of *The Doctrine of Virtue*, where Kant spells out his system of duties of virtue.

Finally, a brief remark about the concept of lawgiving. To be morally obligated to do or refrain from doing something essentially involves standing in a relation whose relata are (*i*) the one who is put under an obligation and (*ii*) the one who does the obligating. In the case of juridical lawgiving (and assuming the established criminal, civil, and other laws are legitimate), the one doing the obligating is the State. In the case of ethical lawgiving, Kant's view is that one "gives oneself" the moral law; one is both the lawgiver and the one being given the law and thereby put under obligation. This might strike readers as odd, perhaps paradoxical: How can one be categorically bound if one is both the one who is bound and the one who does the binding? However, as we shall see when we come to duties one has to oneself, Kant addresses this apparent "antinomy" as he labels it.

Further Reading

- On the distinction between moral worth and moral merit in Kant's ethics, see Johnson 1996.
- On Kant's division of *The Metaphysics of Morals* see chapter 2 of Gregor 1963.
- On the two types of lawgiving and the division between DR and DV, see Timmons 2002b [2017].
- On the topic of lawgiving and legislating the moral law, see Reath 1994a [2006] and as mentioned above in note 3, Kleingeld and Willaschek 2019.

---

[14] What about the reason-providing force of moral imperatives associated with wide, imperfect duties which allow latitude concerning when to comply with them? Here I want to say that such imperatives provide sufficient, even if not overriding reason to comply with them on occasions where one has the opportunity to do so. (Thanks to Robert Audi for prompting this qualification.) On complying with imperfect duties and the possibility of moral worth, see chap. 9, sec. 1.

PART III

INTRODUCTION TO *THE DOCTRINE OF VIRTUE*

6

The Doctrine of Virtue as a Doctrine of Ends

Preface, Introduction, and Sections I–III

We now turn to Kant's *Doctrine of Virtue*. It begins with a relatively short preface followed by a lengthy introduction. The book is then divided into the Doctrine of Elements of Ethics (Elements, hereafter) and the Doctrine of Methods of Ethics (Methods, hereafter). In the Elements, Kant sets forth his system of duties of virtue, dividing them into duties to oneself and duties to others. The Methods briefly discusses the teaching of ethics and the practice of virtue. The book ends with a Conclusion explaining why a metaphysics of morals does not include reference to religion, understood as a doctrine of duties to God.

The four chapters in this third part of the book cover the preface and the book's eighteen Section introduction. These Sections deal with issues that Kant took to be preparatory for elaborating his doctrine of virtue in the Elements. The present chapter covers the preface and the first three Sections of the introduction whose primary focus is Kant's conception of ethics as both a doctrine of virtue and, relatedly, a doctrine of ends. The next chapter covers Sections IV–VIII where Kant discusses the most fundamental ends of the doctrine of virtue, namely self-perfection and the happiness of others. However, as for the remainder of the introduction to DV, I have found it best not to follow Kant's exact sequencing of Sections, but rather to treat them thematically and so somewhat out of order. Chapter 8 is about Kant's conception of virtue and concentrates on Sections XII, XIV, and XV. Chapter 9 considers the overall project of grounding the system of duties of virtue we find in the Elements—the project of developing a science of ethics that

Kant's Doctrine of Virtue. Mark Timmons, Oxford University Press (2021). © Oxford University Press.
DOI: 10.1093/oso/9780190939229.003.0006

Kant discusses in Sections IX, X, and the final two Sections of the introduction.

⚜⚜

Together, the preface and first three Sections of the introduction address these questions:

- Why must there be metaphysical first principles for a doctrine of virtue?
- Why is ethics as a doctrine of virtue only possible if it is also a doctrine of ends—ends one has a duty to adopt?
- What distinguishes duties of virtue from duties of right?
- Why must there be ends that are duties?

There are other issues brought up in these Sections; however, for the most part, the focus is on Kant's answers to these questions.

A brief remark about terminology before we begin: In the general introduction to MM, Kant consistently refers to moral *laws*. As explained in chapter 5, sec. 1, he defines a broad sense of 'moral law' that applies to both holy, perfectly rational beings (like God) and to nonholy, imperfectly rational beings (including human beings). Moral laws as they apply to beings of the latter sort are properly expressed as categorical imperatives, which can alternatively be expressed as moral ought-statements. In DV, we find talk of moral *principles*, which is equivalent to talk of moral laws as they apply to human beings.

6.1 The necessity for a doctrine of virtue

The seven-paragraph preface discusses two topics. First, in paragraphs 1–4, Kant explains why there is a need for a doctrine of virtue grounded in metaphysical first principles, thus addressing the first of our four questions. Second, in paragraphs 5–7, he argues against the coherence of any attempt to understand a doctrine of virtue as grounded on happiness, which Kant refers to as "eudaimonism" (from the Greek 'eudaimon,' often translated into English as 'happiness'). I will skip over Kant's arguments against eudaimonist ethics, which is less important for our concerns. So, let us focus on the first four paragraphs.

Kant begins the preface telling readers how he conceives of metaphysics, properly understood. In chapter 3 we saw that Kant's conception of metaphysics, as a genuine field of inquiry, refers to those a priori principles of pure reason that govern the proper employment of some mental faculty. Metaphysics, so understood, is a science in which the first, most fundamental principles pertaining to a particular employment of a mental faculty are set forth systematically, and thereby ordered according to a particular scheme, thus constituting a *system*, rather than a mere aggregate. The contents of such a system is referred to as a *doctrine*. Kant's doctrine of virtue, then, is that branch of moral philosophy whose primary aim is to derive a system of principles of duty from the supreme principle of morality, the categorical imperative. Associated with the various derived principles of duty are virtues and vices.

After the reminder about metaphysics, Kant raises the issue of whether a doctrine of virtue, like a doctrine of right, requires metaphysical first principles. After all, virtue is concerned with motivation, and one might wonder how questions about motivation can be addressed by metaphysics, rather than just empirical psychology. And one may also wonder whether metaphysics is of any value in teaching ethics. In response to these worries, Kant repeats a theme we found in Section I of the general introduction to MM, where he argues that a metaphysics of morals is necessary to secure the authority and purity of fundamental moral principles. We find similar remarks here where Kant is claiming that without grounding a doctrine of virtue in metaphysical first principles—principles whose ultimate source is pure reason—one cannot secure the "certainty or purity" (DV 6:376) characteristic of such principles. The principles in question, because they are strictly universal and necessary, are only properly cognized a priori and thereby with complete certainty. The *purity* in question derives from the fact that fundamental metaphysical principles of the doctrine of virtue are grounded in reason alone and so independently of any empirical considerations. However, purity also concerns the type of incentive that must be available if there are to be categorical requirements of morality. As we learned in chapter 4, the pure incentive (or motive) of duty is contrasted with incentives related to one's contingent likes, dislikes, desires, aversions, and inclinations. Only if one can be motivated by the pure incentive of doing one's duty from duty, can one be morally obligated by a moral principle (or law). With respect to teaching ethics, Kant warns teachers against attempting to base morality on feeling, since this undermines the certitude and purity of morals. He urges them to understand for themselves the metaphysical grounding of a doctrine of virtue so that they can properly engage in moral education, including early moral education where the aim is to help cultivate in students (without teaching them metaphysics) a proper sense of duty and virtue.

Having thus explained the need for metaphysical first principles in a doctrine of virtue, in a one-paragraph opening to the introduction to DV Kant notes that although the term 'ethics' had been used in ancient times to refer to the entirety of the doctrine of morals, he is following the current use that reserves it exclusively for the doctrine of virtue. Thus the doctrine of right, concerned with "external law" and coercible duties, is not part of ethics. He then proceeds in Sections I–III to address our second and third questions.

6.2 Discussion of the Concept of a Doctrine of Virtue

Section I, as its title indicates, is about the very concept of a doctrine of virtue. It has seven paragraphs. The first three explain why ethics is properly understood as a doctrine of virtue, paragraphs 4 and 5 argue that ethics is also a doctrine of ends, paragraph 6 briefly contrasts DV with DR, and 7 summarizes the Section. Important for our purposes is why ethics is properly understood as both a doctrine of virtue and a doctrine of ends.

Ethics as a doctrine of virtue

In chapter 5, sec. 5, we learned that the division of MM into a doctrine of right and a doctrine of virtue concerns two types of lawgiving (juridical and ethical), yielding two corresponding kinds of obligation, and that the key difference concerns the type of incentive or motive associated with each. To review: juridical lawgiving, which only pertains to duties that either require or prohibit "external" actions, are properly subject to coercion by others— "external coercion." Thus, they concern the use of one's "external freedom"—freedom of external action from the hindrance of others. The motives associated with juridical duties are sensible, empirical motives—motives that have mainly to do with avoiding consequences that would conflict with one's happiness. Duties of virtue, by contrast, are not subject to coercion from others. Rather, the only motive or incentive possible for ethics is the "pure" (nonempirical) motive of duty, compliance with which requires *self-constraint* ("inner freedom") and excludes external constraint via coercion from others.

In the opening paragraphs of Section I Kant does not mention lawgiving; however, the themes here do relate to the two types of lawgiving. He points out that the concept of duty involves that of constraint ("necessitation") and that there are two types of constraint: external constraint and self-constraint. He then points out that when the subject matter of duty is the "internal determination of the will" (DV 6:380), which is not subject to external constraint, the only incentive possible is one of self-constraint in which one exercises one's "inner" freedom of choice by overcoming contrary-to-duty motives and acting solely out of respect for the moral law (solely from duty). This is the "ethical" conception of duty. The developed capacity based on a "considered resolve" to act solely from duty—"the moral disposition *within us*" (ibid.)—is virtue. In chapter 8 we examine in detail Kant's conception of virtue, but the idea is that to be an overall virtuous person is to have made a firm resolve to comply with all duties solely from the motive of duty, together with the developed strength of will (fortitude) to overcome "impulses of nature" (ibid.) enabling one to follow through on one's resolve. So, ethics (as a system) is properly understood as a doctrine of virtue. Beginning in paragraph 4, Kant next explains why ethics is also properly viewed as a doctrine of ends.

Ethics as a doctrine of ends

One reason why the duties featured in DV are not subject to external constraint (coercion) concerns its primary subject matter—ends that one has an obligation to adopt. Compared, then, to the duties featured in DR, ethics "furnishes a *matter* (an object of the free faculty of choice), an END of pure reason that is represented at the same time as an objectively necessary end, i.e. as a duty for the human being" (DV 6:380). What immediately follows this claim is an argument that there *must* be ends one has a duty to adopt—ends set by pure practical reason. The idea is that there must be such ends, otherwise "lawgiving reason" itself (which does not work through sensuous inclinations) would not be able to "check the influence" of contrary-to-duty inclinations. This argument somewhat anticipates Kant's main argument in Section III for the necessity of ends one has a duty to adopt, and I will return to it then. However, given its placement, the argument here can only be read as arguing for a conditional claim: *if* legislative reason is able to check the influence of inclinations, then it must be a source of ends. The argument is conditional because, in the final paragraph of Section I, Kant explains that so far he has only argued that the very idea of ends that it is a duty to have is conceptually coherent; not (yet) that one is subject to such duties.

If there are (and indeed must be) ends that one has a duty to adopt, then because adopting them is not subject to coercion (as Kant claims) such duties cannot belong to the doctrine of right. The sort of moral constraint possible in relation to the adoption of ends is self-constraint which, as noted, pertains to ethics. This is roughly Kant's reasoning in paragraph 5, which concludes with the first sentence in 6: "For this reason ethics can also be defined as the system of *ends* of pure practical reason" (DV 6:381).

As noted earlier, and to repeat, Kant's section-ending remarks make clear that all he takes himself to have done so far is argue that the very idea of an end that is also a duty is not self-contradictory. What he thinks he must go on to show is *how* such an end is possible—that is, he must argue that there really are such ends; the task of Section III. In Section II, there is further discussion of ends as duties. However, before turning to II, we should ask ourselves whether Kant's claim that one cannot be coerced into adopting an end is true. One might have doubts. Suppose I am a championship athletic trainer, specializing in diving, and that you very much want me to train you for the next Olympics; being in those games is an end you have chosen. I tell you that I'll agree to train you but that you must gain muscle mass by weight training. You dislike the idea of gaining muscle mass. But I insist, and so you rather grudgingly adopt the subsidiary end of gaining muscle mass by weight training. Have I not coerced you into adopting an end that you would not otherwise have? After all, I threaten not to train you if you refuse. Of course, you are the one who decides to adopt the intermediate end and so exert your freedom of will in doing so. But the same is true if, under the threat of imprisonment, you decide to repay a loan—a matter of external coercion that falls within the realm of juridical duty. Of course, in the Olympics example, the subordinate end of gaining muscle mass represents a necessary means to a more basic end of yours. So, Kant's claim might be that one cannot be coerced into adopting *basic* ends—ends that one adopts, but not as a means for realizing some further end.

What about basic ends? Kant claims that all human beings necessarily have as an end their own happiness—not an end one adopts, but an end everyone has "by a *natural necessity*" (G 4:415). For Kant, happiness is a matter of taking satisfaction in one's inclinations being realized. Can one be coerced into adopting basic ends whose realization one believes are constitutive of one's happiness? Such ends seem to be ones that one typically adopts whole-heartedly, based on what one is naturally attracted to, and so perhaps at least with respect to them, coercion by others to adopt them is not possible. Kant makes the very strong claim that the very idea of being coerced by someone to make something one's end involves the contradictory idea of "an act of freedom that at the same time is still not free" (DV 6:381). Of course, whenever someone coerces you by threatening harm unless you, say, keep a promise you've made, then if you do comply, there is a sense in which you do not act freely, a point that applies to cases of being coerced to perform external actions. It seems, then, that all Kant needs, or is entitled, to claim is that adopting an end *wholeheartedly as one's own*, excludes being coerced by someone else.

6.3 Discussion of the Concept of an End that is also a Duty

Section II continues the discussion from I. It, too, has seven paragraphs, the final one labeled "Remark." The section's main task is to explain why ends that are duties are properly called "duties of virtue" (DV 6:383). The Section begins with a methodological contrast between the doctrine of right and doctrine of virtue (paragraphs 1 and 2), and then proceeds to contrast duties of virtue with both ethical duties and with duties of right (4 and 5). Following these contrasts, Kant proceeds to offer a few remarks on human virtue itself (5–7).

Methodology

The key methodological difference between DR and DV concerns the relation between ends and duties. DR is only concerned with constraint on external actions; it says nothing about ends one might adopt. Based on judgments about which ends whose realization will likely contribute to one's overall happiness, one adopts various ends—so-called contingent (discretionary) ends. The doctrine of right is concerned with constraints on action (or, as Kant here puts it, *maxims* of action) in the pursuit of such ends. In pursuit of ends that one happens to choose (out of self-love) one is to act only on maxims of action that are consistent with the freedom of others in accordance with universal law, as set forth in the universal principle of right (UPR). Thus, for duties that comprise a doctrine of right, "we begin with the end to detect the *maxim* of actions that conform with duty" (DV 6:382). By contrast, methodologically, ethics "cannot begin with ends that a human being may set for himself" (ibid.). This is because if, relative to one's contingent ends of self-love, duties featured in the doctrine of virtue were to *require* adopting maxims of action (and not just constrain which ones to adopt, characteristic of duties of right), the required maxims would thereby only be in the service of contingent ends of self-love (empirical incentives). But then the maxims of action would not be unconditional moral requirements—the resulting doctrine would not feature duties—and so it would not be a doctrine of virtue as part of a doctrine of morals. Kant concludes from this line of reasoning that if there is to be a doctrine of virtue featuring genuine duties, then there must be ends that are at the same time duties. "So, in ethics the *concept of duty* will have to lead to ends and ground *maxims* with regard to ends we *ought* to set for ourselves, according to moral principles" (DV 6:382). As Kant makes clear in paragraph 3, having reached this conclusion about ethics, he still must argue that there are such ends and identify them—tasks reserved for Sections III and IV, respectively. The remainder of Section II (beginning with paragraph 4) is to show "that and why a duty of this kind goes by the name of a *duty of virtue*" (DV 6:383).

One might think that it is unnecessary at this point for Kant to defend this claim, since he has already argued that a doctrine of virtue will include, as part of its content, ends one has a duty to adopt, and so it seems to follow that such duties are duties of virtue. However, what we find in paragraphs 4 and 5 are observations that importantly clarify the concept of a duty of virtue by contrasting it with the concepts of duty of right and ethical duty. He also adds a few remarks that help clarify his conception of virtuous disposition. Here, then, are five clarificatory remarks we find in these passages.

Enforceable rights, duties, and the correlativity thesis

For each duty one has, there is what Kant refers to as an "authorization" (a right in the sense of permission) to perform any action that is one's duty. Of course, this holds for duties of right as well as for duties of virtue. However, to have a legal right (a claim backed by state law) against someone or some institution (e.g. that others not trespass on one's property) imposes duties on others not to violate that right. All duties of right of the sort featured in DR are correlated with enforceable rights that individuals and institutions have. Call this the "correlativity thesis." So, one contrast Kant draws between duties of right and duties of virtue is that for the latter there are no correlative enforceable rights. This is because having such rights involves the permissible use of coercion to enforce those rights, and the use of coercion as an incentive for compliance does not apply to duties of virtue. Hence the

correlativity thesis—that for each duty there is a corresponding enforceable right on the part of others—only holds for duties of right.[1]

Duties of virtue distinguished from ethical duties

In paragraph 4, Kant writes, "to every ethical *obligation* there
corresponds the concept of virtue, but not all ethical duties are
therefore duties of virtue" (DV 6:383). What does this mean? To
begin, *all* duties, whether of right or of virtue, are subject to what
Kant calls "ethical obligation." As we learned in chapter 5, sec. 5,
ethical obligation (associated with ethical lawgiving) connects a
duty with the incentive (or motive) for complying with the obligation from the sole motive of duty. Since, as we learned in chapter 5,
sec. 1, a duty is the content of an obligation, corresponding to any
ethical obligation is an *ethical duty*. For example, even if, on some
occasion, one cannot be coerced to comply with a duty of right,
one is still morally obligated to do so; the motive of duty can
then serve as a sufficient motive for compliance. The concept of
an ethical duty, then, invokes the *formal* incentive of complying
with duty from the sole motive of duty which applies to all duties;
ethical duties are not the special province of a doctrine of virtue.
This means that if there is to be a distinctive subject matter for the
doctrine of virtue it will have to be ends one has a duty to adopt,
hence, such duties are properly called 'duties of virtue.' Worthy of
note is the contrast between having an overall virtuous disposition,
whereby one is motivated by the sole motive to duty to comply with
one's duties (ethical duties), and the variety of ends one has a duty
to adopt (duties of virtue). Virtue as an overall character trait, formally characterized, is something singular, while there is a multiplicity of virtues (specific character traits) associated with the
duties of virtue. Collectively, the virtues provide "material" content
to an overall virtuous disposition.

---

[1] However, in DV Kant recognizes rights associated with respect due to others.
Presumably, such rights to respect are not properly subject to legal enforcement.

Coercion and the essential difference between a duty of virtue and a duty of right

In paragraph 5, Kant repeats his claim that duties of right, but not duties of virtue, are properly subject to coercion, that coercion as an incentive is, as he says, "morally possible." As noted in the previous paragraph, for each of the duties in DV that prohibit or require certain types of action, there are virtues (and vices) associated with them. In the Elements, Kant mentions chastity as a virtue corresponding to one's powers of sexuality. Coming to have a particular virtue requires freely adopting an end and being disposed to act in accord with it. And so if one focuses on the particular virtues corresponding to the duties of virtue, Kant's point about the impossibility of being coerced into acquiring a virtue holds.

Virtue as morality in its highest stage

For a *finite* holy being (e.g. as Jesus Christ is sometimes characterized), who can't be tempted to violate duty, there is no doctrine of virtue. Kant marks this by saying that for a holy being whose actions necessarily comply with the moral law, the will of such a being manifests an ideal of the *autonomy* of practical reason. Although human beings, in virtue of having free will, are capable of acting autonomously, their *developed* capacity to overcome contrary-to-duty inclinations and act from the sole motive of duty is *autocracy* of practical reason. The sense of 'autocracy' here is that of self-mastery—ruling over one's inclinations, being able to overcome any that conflict with duty. This sort of developed capacity is virtue (virtuous disposition as an overall character trait). Virtue conceived as an *ideal* is "personified poetically" by the sage (DV 6:383) as someone who is "completely free from the influence of any alien kind of incentive, other than that of duty" (ibid.). However, human beings can approximate this ideal through a process of adopting "deliberate, firm, and ever more purified principles" (ibid.). Kant makes this latter point explicitly in opposition to any view that takes virtue to be a mere, mechanical habit one might acquire. (These remarks about virtue as an ideal and the kind of aptitude it involves will come up in later chapters, particularly in relation to the duty of moral self-perfection.)

Virtue, lack of virtue, vice

In the concluding "Remark," Kant distinguishes three ethically significant states of character: virtue, lack of virtue, and vice. Presumably, this three-fold distinction can refer to one's overall character, or it can refer to particular character traits, some of them virtues, others corresponding vices, and still others in which one manifests mere lack of some particular virtue. Examples of such traits include beneficence (virtue), malice (vice), and mere lack of beneficence. Again, these distinctions will be illustrated in coming chapters that take up the various obe. Finally, Kant goes on to explain that true "strength of soul" refers to being in possession of one's use of one's powers—a state of health in which, through reason, one gains mastery over one's inclinations. Thus, to say that great crimes require more strength of soul than does virtue is to confuse the force of inclinations that weaken one's free use of one's rational capacities with true strength of soul.

6.4 Why there must be ends that are at the same time duties

As earlier noted, here is where Kant attempts to establish the reality of ends one has a duty to adopt—positive duties, the most general of which are self-perfection and the happiness of others. The section has three paragraphs. The first begins with a central thesis of Kant's theory of action, "An END is an object of the free faculty of choice, the representation of which determines it to an action (by which the former is produced). *Every action* thus, has its end . . . " (DV 6:384–385, my emphasis). The passage continues, stating that adopting an end is an exercise of one's freedom of choice, rather than a mere effect in nature. However, the third and final sentence of paragraph 1 is potentially confusing:

> But since this act, which determines an end, is a practical prin-
> ciple that commands the end itself (hence unconditionally), not the
> means (consequently not conditionally), it is a categorical impera-
> tive of pure practical reason, and hence one that connects a *concept of
> duty* with that of an end as such (DV 6:385).

It is potentially confusing because "this act" seems to refer to *any* act of
adopting an end; the immediately preceding sentence, after all, begins
with a claim about "every action." Of course, not every act of freedom
whereby one adopts (determines) an end is something prescribed categorically and thus a duty.[2] Perhaps Kant should have begun the third
sentence with "But *when* this act . . . ," which would more clearly signal
a transition from speaking of every instance of adopting an end to the
topic of obligatory ends. In any case, it is in the second paragraph that
Kant addresses our fourth bulleted question: Why must there be ends
that are duties? Here is what he writes (brackets inserted):

> [1] Now, there must be such an end and a categorical imperative cor-
> responding to it. For [2] since there are free actions [3] there must
> also be ends to which, as an object, these actions are directed. [4] But
> among these ends there must be some that are at the same time (i.e.
> according to their concept) duties.—For [5] were there no such ends,
> then—since [6] there can be no action without an end—[7] all ends
> would hold for practical reason only as a means to other ends and
> [8] a *categorical* imperative would be impossible, [9] eliminating any
> doctrine of morals (DV 6:385).

What follows the first dash is the crucial bit—a *reductio* argument.
Kant takes himself to have established the categorical imperative as
the supreme principle of morality in his foundational works, and thus
that the morality of duty must be represented as a system of categorical imperatives. So, the key claim in this argument is that if there were
no obligatory ends, there would be no categorical imperatives at all.

---

[2] This assumes that Kant is referring to all uses of one's freedom to adopt ends, including those grounded in self-love. Potter 1985 argues that it refers more specifically
only to those free actions motivated by duty.

He thus concludes not just by saying that *sans* obligatory ends there would be no doctrine of virtue, but rather there would be no doctrine of morals *at all*, which includes the doctrine of right.

Let us ask two questions about this argument. First, why think that if there were no ends that one has a moral duty to adopt "all ends would hold for practical reason only as a means to other ends"? I believe Kant meant to say all *adopted* ends would hold for practical reason only as means. Here is why. As noted earlier in section 2, Kant claims that it is part of our nature as human beings that we have an inborn natural inclination to promote our own happiness. To promote one's own happiness requires that one have certain ends. Some of these ends one has by nature as a living being corresponding to basic needs including, for example, the end or goal of being nourished, safe, and so forth. These seem to be ends that hold in virtue of the kinds of beings human beings are; it isn't clear that they hold for pure practical reason as such. Securing these, which is not always under one's control, enables one to set further ends whose realization one believes will constitute happiness. On Kant's view, one does not have an unconditional duty to promote one's own happiness (a claim which we take up in the next chapter). Nevertheless, given that happiness is an end we all have, there are hypothetical imperatives and prudential counsels that make it rational for one to adopt various ends as means to those basic ends (corresponding to needs) whose realization at least partly constitutes one's happiness. Therefore, even if there were no obligatory ends—ends one is morally required to adopt—there could still be ends that it is rational to adopt as means contributing to the end of making oneself happy. So far, so good.

The second question is: why does Kant claim that if all ends (except the final end of happiness) hold only as means to other ends, and ultimately as means to happiness, a categorical imperative would be impossible? One way to conceive an answer to this question is to recall from chapter 4 that one's ends are the basis of reasons for action. For instance, setting the end of becoming a lawyer gives one reasons for doing various things, including setting more specific ends (like applying to law schools). Concerning big life decisions such as setting the end of entering a profession, one's ultimate reason for doing so is likely because one believes this will contribute to a satisfying life—to one's overall happiness. If all reasons for action bottomed out in this way, then all reasons for action would be, in Kant's terminology, conditional. But by their conception, moral reasons for action and corresponding duties are unconditional in application, in the sense that those reasons and corresponding duties hold independently of one's inclinations. Thus, there must be an end (or ends) other than one's own happiness that grounds morality. And, indeed, according to Kant (something he argues for in his foundational works) humanity is an end—an end in itself—that demands respect. And so, one's humanity (in Kant's technical sense) as an end in itself is the basis for unconditional, categorical reasons for action that yield duties. Again, so far, so good; there must be at least one end that "holds for practical reason" unconditionally if there are to be categorical imperatives.

The question is whether this is enough to show that there must be positive ends that one has a duty to adopt. This is a potential sticking point in the argument. Granted, as just noted, it is part of Kant's conception of morality that humanity is an end-in-itself—an element of our rational nature that demands respect. However, why couldn't there simply be categorical imperatives (moral requirements) that forbid one to perform certain actions because the maxim of one's action fails to respect the humanity of oneself or others? Kant's example of a lying promise from the *Groundwork* seems to be a case in point. Because such "promises" treat others merely as a means (which entails acting on a non-universalizable maxim), acting on a lying promise maxim is categorically (unconditionally) forbidden by the CI. Indeed, in the *Groundwork*, when Kant claims that persons *as such* have a certain standing that he calls "dignity," which must "serve as a limiting condition of all merely relative and arbitrary ends" (G 4:436), this latter remark suggests that the fact that persons have such standing serves as a constraint—a *negative end*, so to speak—that imposes particular moral constraints on one's treatment of persons. Again, no need to bring in positive ends that one has an obligation to adopt. A similar problem seems to beset the argument from Section I where Kant claims that there must be ends set by reason (positive ends) in order to combat ends whose source is one's sensible nature.

Perhaps, then, the doctrine of morals (including the doctrine of right) should be understood as a fundamentally negative doctrine where the ethical system that is part of the doctrine largely contains duties of omission. Granted, some of these duties, such as the duty not to break promises, could be expressed as positive duties (e.g. to keep one's promises), but this is just because keeping one's promises is the only way to avoid breaking them. The worry, then, is that morality, so understood, could be represented as a system of negative categorical imperatives that rule things out, and only by logical implication yield positive duties. And note, too, that if there were no duties to adopt positive ends, the doctrine of morals would not be restricted to a doctrine of right. After all, in Kant's system there are duties of omission to oneself and others that are not subject to external coercion. This means that there could be a distinct doctrine of virtue composed of directly ethical duties that are not properly subject to external coercion—duties to avoid the vices of arrogance, backbiting (defamation), and derision (ridicule) are some of Kant's own examples. It looks as if the argument for the claim that there must be duties to adopt positive ends, even granting that the morality of duty is a system of categorical imperatives derivable from the supreme principle (CI), is a non sequitur. If so, this is disappointing. Or is it?

Suppose as a stand-alone argument for positive ends that one has a duty to adopt, it cannot be made to work. I say this pessimistic assessment doesn't matter much for Kant's project of developing and defending ethics as fundamentally a doctrine of positive ends. For one thing, and as we shall see in chapter 13, Kant provides an argument for the duty to adopt the happiness of others, one of the two fundamental positive ends governing duties of love toward others. His argument can be viewed as an extension of the claim that morality is about respecting humanity as an end in itself. A similar point can be made about the duty of self-perfection, although Kant does not explicitly argue for this duty. In any case, we aren't finished with this issue; another argument for there being positive ends that are duties comes later in Section IX of the introduction to DV, which we examine in chapter 9.

What one can say, based on the first two sections of the introduction to DV, is that the doctrine of virtue, as Kant conceives it, is clearly committed to the claim that pure practical reason necessarily sets ends that one has a duty to adopt, and is tantamount to the claim that unless there are ends that one has a duty to adopt, there can be no doctrine of *virtue*.

In Sections IV through VIII, taken up in the next chapter, Kant introduces and then elaborates the most fundamental obligatory ends (self-perfection and the happiness of others) that serve to structure his system of ethical duties that we find in the Elements.

6.5 Concluding summary

Before going forward, let us review. We began this chapter with four questions to help guide us through these opening sections. Here they are again now with Kant's answers in brief.

- Why must there be metaphysical first principles for a doctrine of virtue? Because metaphysical principles are needed to ground the certainty and purity of fundamental moral principles pertaining to ethics as a science.
- Why is ethics as a doctrine of virtue only possible if it is also a doctrine of ends—ends that one has a duty to adopt? Because virtue is a matter of character and, in particular, how one organizes one's life around ends that constitutes the core of specific virtues.
- Which features distinguish duties of virtue from duties of right? Duties of right are essentially correlated with enforceable rights of others; duties of virtue are not. The former are subject to external coercion, the latter are not. Duties of virtue concern duties to adopt maxims; duties of right only concern external actions.
- Why must there be ends that are duties? Kant's answer is that without such ends, there can't be categorical imperatives at all and thus no doctrine of morals, including both the doctrine of right and of virtue.

Further reading

- For attempts to shore up the argument for there being ends one has a duty to adopt see Potter 1985, Allison 1993, and Potter's 1993 reply to Allison.

7

General Ends that Are Also Duties

Introduction, Sections IV–VIII

Having argued that a doctrine of virtue is fundamentally a doctrine of ends, Sections IV to VIII discuss the two most general ends that are also duties. Here, the guiding questions addressed are:

- At the most general level, which ends are also duties?
- What distinguishes them from duties of right?
- What is the specific nature of these duties?

7.1 What are the ends that are at the same time duties?

Kant's answer is: *one's own perfection* and the *happiness of others*. In Section IV, after giving this answer, he proceeds to explain why one does not have a duty to promote one's own happiness or a duty of perfection toward others. *First*, one does not have a duty to set as an end one's own happiness because "[w]hat everyone unavoidably already wants by himself, does not belong under the concept of *duty*; for that is *necessitation* to an end adopted reluctantly" (DV 6:386). The concept of duty, as we've seen, is the concept of a particular kind of constraint; one that would be out of place given that one naturally pursues one's own happiness.[1]

Second, one doesn't have a duty to perfect others because their *self*-perfection requires that they do something no one else can do,

---

[1] Could there be persons who do not *naturally* pursue their own happiness? If so, do they have a duty to promote their own happiness? As we have noted, Kant claims that necessarily all human beings naturally have their own happiness as an end. And, we shall see, Kant does allow that there can be a duty to promote one's happiness in cases where doing so is necessary to avoid immoral behavior. On this point, see section 7.2 later.

Kant's Doctrine of Virtue. Mark Timmons, Oxford University Press (2021). © Oxford University Press.
DOI: 10.1093/oso/9780190939229.003.0007

namely, adopt for themselves a final end of perfecting themselves. After all, it is "self-contradictory to require (make it my duty) that I ought to do something that no other than he himself can do" (DV 6:386). And surely it is true that I cannot adopt *for you* the end of your self-perfection; only you can set your own final ends. Of course, I can set for myself the goal or end of doing what I can to encourage you to adopt your own self-perfection as one of your final ends and I can help you achieve that goal. As we shall see when we consider Kant's views on moral education (chapter 16), one job of a moral educator is to do what she can to lead a student to adopt ends that are also duties.

Section V clarifies the *concepts* of self-perfection and promoting the happiness of others. Section VIII explains the *duties* associated with these concepts, while Sections VI and VII are transition sections that identify certain distinctive characteristics of duties of virtue that then figure in the Section VIII exposition of the two ends that are also duties. Let us proceed to take up these sections in their order.

7.2 Clarification of these two concepts

One's own perfection

Kant begins this section explaining that the concept of perfection is ambiguous. It can refer to the totality of individual elements that constitute a single thing. This is the quantitative perfection of a thing. However, it is qualitative perfection we are concerned with here, a concept "belonging to *teleology*" (DV 6:386). The qualitative perfection of a thing is where there is a harmony between its characteristics and its end or purpose. An artifact (e.g. a watch) displays qualitative perfection when its parts collectively work together to realize its purpose (giving correct time). In the *Critique of the Power of Judgment,* Kant argues that we can only understand living things such as plants and animals by assuming they are designed. From a teleological perspective relevant to ethics, Kant conceives of human beings as rational and morally accountable beings, as having capacities whose realization constitutes the qualitative perfection of such beings. The two most fundamental such capacities are (*i*) one's "natural" mental and physical capacities, and (*ii*) one's will.

Regarding (*i*), Kant claims that one has a duty to develop those natural faculties (here he only mentions understanding) that enables one to raise oneself up from "the crudity of his nature, from animality . . . more and more toward humanity, by which alone he is capable of setting ends for himself" (DV 6:387). Kant's remark here is rather opaque. Can't one set ends even if one's understanding is not cultivated? Perhaps he means that the *range* of ends it is possible to set requires cultivation of these faculties. In any case, Kant's later discussion of this duty is clearer where he says that the cultivation of our natural faculties serves as means to all sort of possible ends. (We will revisit this in chapter 12.) Of course, one has reasons of self-love to develop one's capacities, but Kant's point here is that one has a moral obligation to develop them so that one may "be worthy of the humanity that dwells within him" (ibid.) Regarding one's will—in particular, one's capacity for free choice—one's duty is to cultivate "the purest disposition of virtue" by striving not only to comply with one's duties, but to do so solely out of respect for the moral law.

Teleology, then, plays a role in Kant's ethics. As rational beings, members of an intelligible realm of freedom, one has the end or purpose of striving to achieve a state of natural and moral perfection. To achieve such a state of self-mastery is to maximize one's inner freedom—freedom from undue influence of mere inclination and correspondingly the freedom to set ends grounded solely in reason. This is one element of Kant's *moral* teleology; the other being the end of happiness.[2] Recall from chapter 2, the highest, most complete good, according to Kant, is happiness in proportion to virtue.

---

[2] Kant's moral teleology is to be distinguished from *natural teleology* according to which organisms as parts of the natural world have ends or purposes that are intrinsic to them. The difference between these types of teleology is important and we will return to it in chapter 10.

The happiness of others

This duty is to promote the happiness of others by making others' (morally permitted) ends one's own. Of course, it is up to others to choose and pursue those ends that they believe will contribute to their happiness. And, unless I'm otherwise morally obligated, I am permitted to refuse to help others achieve those ends that I do not think will contribute to their happiness.

Kant adds a qualification about one's own happiness. As he explains, one does or can have an "indirect duty" to promote one's own happiness. The idea is that one has a direct duty to preserve one's own moral integrity (adherence to moral principles) which itself grounds a duty to take preventive measures that safeguard one's own happiness by, for example, "fending off poverty" (DV 6:388). Arguably, this does not undermine Kant's claim that one has no duty to adopt one's own happiness as an end (which one naturally has anyway), because the indirect duty in question concerns guarding against adversity and pain that can tempt one to violate one's duties—its explanation as an indirect *duty* refers to morality, not happiness.

7.3 How duties of virtue are distinguished from duties of right

After clarifying the concepts of self-perfection and the happiness of others as they figure in his system of ethics, Kant follows with two sections, each of which compares duties of virtue with those of right along two related dimensions. *First*, only the principles (laws) of duties of right set forth requirements for *actions*, while the principles of duties of virtue set forth laws only for *maxims* of actions. *Second*, and supposedly following from this first contrast, ethical duties featured in DV "are of *wide* obligation, whereas duties of right are of *narrow* obligation" (DV 6:390). What do these claims mean, and what is their significance? At noted earlier, the placement of these sections is between the immediately preceding Section on clarification of the concepts in question and discussion of the duties corresponding to these concepts in Section VIII. Presumably, this is to be able to explain more precisely the nature and ground of these duties. For instance, in VIII Kant mentions that these two general ends that are also duties are of "wide" as opposed to "narrow" obligation, a distinction he introduces in VII. Both VI and VII are difficult and raise a number of questions about interpretation that require some attention.

Ethics does not give laws for actions (Ius does that), but only gives laws for maxims of action

Before commenting on the contents of this section, its title requires comment. All intentional actions, according to Kant, are actions on a maxim, and so it might initially seem peculiar that Kant would say that the doctrine of right (*Ius*) sets forth laws for actions, while ethics only gives laws for maxims of action. Don't all moral laws that are part of the doctrine of morals as set forth in MM, whether of right (i.e. justice) or of ethics have to do with maxims? As we learned from chapter 4, strictly speaking the answer is yes. Indeed, maxims are mentioned in Kant's formulation of the fundamental principle of the doctrine of right: "An action is *right* if it can coexist with everyone's freedom in accordance with a universal law, or if on its *maxim* [emphasis added, M.T.] the freedom of choice of each can coexist with everyone's freedom in accordance with a universal *law*" (DR 6:230). So, what is the contrast between laws for actions and laws for maxims of actions Kant is here concerned with?

I believe the answer is that by referring to maxims of action in this context Kant has in mind the duty not just to do or refrain from doing particular actions, but the duty of shaping one's character to conform to virtues corresponding to the various duties of virtue. This can only be done, according to Kant, by coming to have character traits, that is, dispositions to comply with the various duties from the motive of duty. In forming such dispositions, one may be described as adopting maxims—general policies—pertaining to actions prescribed by positive duties of virtue and those that are proscribed by negative duties of virtue. Thus, strictly speaking, ethics as a branch of moral philosophy does not give laws for actions, it gives laws (sets forth principles) for adopting and complying with general policies (maxims of action) and doing so from the sole motive of duty. Chapter 4 introduced the distinction between a maxim of action and a maxim of ends. One might have thought the contrast Kant is drawing at this point between DR and DV should be expressed in terms of these two types of maxim. Indeed, he formulates the fundamental principle of DV using such terminology: "act according to a maxim of *ends* that it can be a universal law for everyone to have" (DV 6:395). In any case, going forward, let us stick to 'maxim of action' as Kant is using it in these passages, that is, as referring to general policies of action.

Turning now to the content of V, if what is distinctive of ethics in contrast to duties of right (featured in DR) is that there must be laws for maxims of action, *how* this can be—is the question Kant now addresses in this Section. Already in III he has argued that there must *be* ends that one has a duty to adopt. What he seems to be doing here is connecting his thesis about obligatory ends with the kinds of law featured in DV—laws for maxims of action. Only if there are such ends providing a foundation can there be maxims of action that one is obligated to adopt—maxims concerned with general policies of action. Kant's reasoning seems to be along these lines. Suppose one has the end of benefitting others. So long as one's maxims of action adopted as means to that end are consistent with the universal law formula, "so act that the maxim of your action could become universal law" (DV 6:389), acting on such helping maxims is permitted, not required. The only way in which ethics makes maxims of action required is by there being ends one has an obligation to adopt. So, if ethics as a doctrine of virtue is possible, there must be such ends—a much weaker claim than what Kant argued for in III.

Ethical duties are of wide obligation, duties of right are of narrow obligation

Kant begins this five-paragraph section with the assertion that what is stated in its title is a consequence of the claim expressed in VI's title, namely, that DV only gives laws for maxims of action, while DR only gives laws for actions. To see how the one is supposed to be a consequence of the other, we first need to understand Kant's distinction between wide and narrow obligation.[3]

What Kant is getting at with the narrow/wide distinction is intuitive. For example, consider the duty to promote the happiness of others. The duty, thus stated, is unspecific and so allows some leeway for complying with it. As Kant points out, "in what way and to what extent" (DV 6:390) to promote the happiness of others is left up to one's discretion. For instance, I might donate money to some charitable organization or instead donate my time. In one of these *ways* or another, I can act to comply with the duty. *How much* money or time I donate is a further consideration. Moreover, the question of *when* and *for whom* one is to promote the happiness of others is generally left open. The duty to promote the happiness of others, construed as a duty of charity, then, is wide along four dimensions of compliance. Contrast this wide duty with the narrow duty pertaining to legal contracts. Suppose I contract with you to build a fence around your property within a specific time period. This duty, so characterized, is specific regarding *what* I am obligated to do, *who* it is owed to, and *when* the job is to be done. Thus, duties of right and duties of virtue differ in *degree* of compliance concerning how much latitude one has in deciding what one is to do, how much one is to do, how often one is to do it, and for whom. Notice that a duty can be narrow in some respects and wide in others. For example, parents have a duty to raise their children to be good persons. The duty is narrow regarding to whom the parents owe this duty, yet there are many ways and opportunities for compliance and so it is otherwise wide.

Kant makes an important observation about wide duties.[4] A wide duty is not to be "taken as a permission to make exceptions" to the unspecific maxim of promoting the happiness of others, "but only as [permissions,

---

[3] One might suppose the reference in the title to ethical duties is only to duties of virtue and, if so, the more accurate title would refer to *directly* ethical duties, because duties of right are indirectly ethical. However, the title is arguably not imprecise since a duty of right *as an ethical duty* is only of wide obligation; one need not comply with it from the sole motive of duty, nor is it part of a duty of right as such that one must strive to comply from the sole motive of duty.

[4] I will come back to Kant's remarks (in the second paragraph of Section VI) about merit, the fulfillment of duties of virtue, failure to fulfill them, and principled opposition to them (vice) in the next chapter.

M.T.] to limit one obligatory maxim by another (e.g. general love of one's neighbor by love of one's parents), by which the field for the practice of virtue is indeed expanded..." (DV 6:390). What counts as making an exception to the maxim in question? Since, generally speaking, complying with an end that is a duty leaves one much freedom in deciding when and how to do so, clearly I am not necessarily violating this duty when I decide on some occasion to forgo an opportunity to do volunteer work (that would promote others' happiness) in order to play soccer. Kant may make it sound as if in order to be justified in not complying with a wide duty on some occasion there must be some other duty (supported by stronger grounds of obligation) that takes precedence over it. But this would be overly demanding of a moral theory, not allowing one sufficient freedom to pursue one's own interests. However, Kant's idea here, suggested by his example, is that in adopting a maxim of ends to promote others' happiness, I am permitted to qualify the content of the duty by, for example, giving priority to loved ones over that of strangers. As we shall see when we get to the treatment of this duty in the Elements, Kant's remarks about permissible variation in *degrees* of beneficence toward different people fits nicely with the idea of priority.

Closely related to the narrow/wide distinction is the perfect/imperfect distinction. One might wonder whether they mark any genuine difference concerning a particular duty, since Kant never explicitly gives an example of a narrow and imperfect duty nor of a wide perfect one.[5] Yet, in the first paragraph of this section, Kant strongly suggests there is some difference between them when he writes, "[t]he wider the duty—the more imperfect therefore a human being's obligation to do the action..." (DV 6:390). And he consistently describes some duties as narrow *and* perfect, others as wide *and* imperfect, again, indicating a difference of some sort.[6] One might suppose, then, that *duties* are

---

[5] I will qualify this claim in chapter 12 in relation to the duty of moral self-perfection.

[6] Interestingly, in a draft of MM, Kant writes: "An obligation... presupposes a law. If this law determinately and immediately concerns the action so that the kind—how to act?—and the extent—how much to do?—is determined in the law, then the obligation is perfect (*obligatio perfecta*) and the law is *stricte obligans* (narrowly obligatory); no choice remains to us either for exceptions if the law is valid in its universality or for the measure of compliance with it" (DrMM 23:394). The passage continues: "However, if the law does not directly command the action but only the maxim of the action, it leaves open to the subject's judgment the kind of act—how—and the measure—to what extent—the thing

properly narrow or wide and *obligations* are properly perfect or imperfect. (Recall from chapter 5, sec. 1, a duty is the content of an obligation whereby one is necessitated to do or refrain from doing something.) But Kant does not restrict his application of these distinctions in this way. For instance, in the Section's title, wide obligations are contrasted with narrow ones, the second paragraph of this section begins with a remark about "imperfect duties," and in the Elements a major division is between perfect and imperfect duties.

For the sake of clarity, I propose the following regimentation: let us use the narrow/wide distinction to refer respectively to the difference between those obligations requiring specific actions (or omissions) and those only requiring maxims of action (general policies). This distinction concerns what Kant in some places refers to as the *quality* of the obligation. Let us then use the perfect/imperfect distinction to refer to the degree of latitude one has in complying with the obligation—its *degree*. Narrow obligations, in requiring or prohibiting specific actions rather than policies of action, lay down conditions that do not allow the kind of latitude in compliance that one enjoys with imperfect obligations, they require "perfect" compliance. They are perfect regarding *when* one is required to comply, which is the dimension of compliance Kant seems most concerned with in the Elements. Wide obligations (wide in quality by only requiring the adoption of general policies—maxims of action) are of imperfect obligation (imperfect in the degree of compliance demanded). This sort of regimentation helps highlight that fact that there are two related dimensions of obligations (and duties)—their quality and degree—that can be marked using the 'narrow/wide, perfect/imperfect' language Kant uses.[7]

---

commanded should be realized, provided only that it would be necessary for us to do as much as possible under given conditions, then the obligation is imperfect and the law is not narrow but a broad obligation *late obligans* (widely obligatory)" (ibid.). Although the contrast is between law and obligation rather than duty and obligation, I don't believe this is of any import. In any case, my proposed terminological regimentation attempts to capture the contrast in the passage between what the law lays down as a duty, either an action (narrow) or a maxim of action (wide), and the corresponding conditions of compliance (perfect or imperfect). Note, too, that these remarks directly connect the claims in the titles of Sections VI (about laws) and VII (about obligation).

[7] Whatever difference Kant had in mind, the difference between narrow and perfect and between wide and imperfect seems to be merely one of focus: one can focus on the

The remaining four paragraphs of VII relate wide duties of imperfect obligation to the concept of merit. Kant begins paragraph 2 claiming that wide, imperfect duties alone are duties of virtue. To comply with a wide imperfect duty is to do something morally meritorious because one has done more than the moral law strictly requires. Kant gives the example of complying with a duty of right solely out of respect for the rights of others, which goes beyond what is strictly demanded and is thus meritorious. Such an action also (given its motivation) has moral worth. He also gives the example of "the universal ethical command" to comply with duty from the sole motive of duty. This turns out to be an imperfect duty and thus meritorious (for reasons explained in chapter 12, sec. 2). These examples may suggest that an action is meritorious when and only when done from duty, and thus that meritoriousness and moral worth apply to the very same set of actions. In chapter 5, sec. 4, I argued against this. You may recall that merit is a matter of degree. The greater the sacrifice (and hence the greater the opposition from inclination) and less demanding the moral obligation (as when one has leeway to help others and is not otherwise bound by a duty of right to help someone in particular), the greater the merit. Moral worth results from doing one's duty solely from duty. So 'merit' and 'moral worth' refer to different properties of action. It might still be that all meritorious actions have moral worth and the other way around. Certainly, all cases of acting solely from duty are meritorious; the duty to strive to make the moral law one's sole motive is a wide imperfect duty (as we will see in the next section). However, sometimes saving a stranger's life at some risk to oneself (Kant's example from MM 6:228) is surely going beyond what is strictly owed to others even if one was not motivated from the sole motive of duty but rather out of fellow-feeling for the person in peril. Complying (in the sense of conforming to) a wide imperfect duty is typically

---

content of a duty and its relative specificity or focus on how much leeway one has in complying with the duty. A mere difference of focus may explain why (i) Kant does not clearly distinguish narrow from perfect or wide from imperfect, (ii) why members of both pairs are applied indifferently to duties and to obligations, and (iii) why a duty/obligation is either both narrow and perfect or wide and imperfect.

meritorious—deserving of praise from others.[8] Yet it need not have moral worth—one may not have complied with the imperfect duty of moral self-perfection (the "universal ethical command").[9]

In paragraphs 2 and 4, Kant mentions bringing duties of wide obligation "closer in compliance" to duties of narrow obligation, presumably by (*i*) becoming disposed to take obligations of, say, promoting the happiness of others, as approaching duties of narrow obligation in strength and thereby (*ii*) coming to act on the corresponding maxim of action more frequently. He also mentions a "subjective principle of ethical *reward*" (DV 6:391) one may experience in doing so—a kind of moral pleasure that goes beyond the kind of contentment that comes from complying with duties of narrow obligation. Although in so acting it isn't the expectation of pleasure that motivates the action, but the "reward" of experiencing such pleasure, is how in a sense "virtue is its own reward" (DV 6:391). (In this Section, Kant also mentions the distinctions among virtue, lack of virtue, and vice, which we touched on in the previous chapter and will come up again when we get to the Elements.)

Finally, let's return to the first sentence of Section VII, namely, the fact that ethical duties are of wide obligation and duties of right are of narrow obligation follows from the claim made in the title of VI. If, as the title of VI claims, ethics (the doctrine of virtue) *only* gives laws for maxims of action—understood as broad policies for guiding action— then indeed ethical duties are all of wide obligation, or, more precisely, they are comparatively wide in quality and correspondingly imperfect in degree. Hence, were the claim expressed in the title of the previous section true, then what is stated in the title of this section would also be true.

An apparent problem is that in the Elements there are duties of omission that concern actions one must avoid and that Kant classifies

---

[8] Only typically meritorious because arguably being able to easily save a child (not one's own) from drowning is an act of beneficence that it would be wrong not to do. There are also cases, as Adam Cureton reminded me, where one's motivation would seem to undermine any merit for saving a life, as when it is done just for the sake of feeling good about oneself, or simply to make the other person indebted to you.

[9] For a scholarly defense of the claim that for Kant moral merit and moral worth are distinct properties, see Johnson 1996.

as perfect duties, which are narrow in specifying to whom the duty is owed (oneself), the action one is to avoid (e.g. lying), and on which occasions one is obligated to comply (always). One way to reconcile these two claims about ethics is to say that the title of Section VI is referring only to the positive duties, including, of course, self-perfection and the happiness of others. This would mean he is saying that only ethics gives such laws, which does not rule out its giving laws for actions.

7.4 Exposition of duties of virtue as wide duties

Now that Kant has explained that ethics is primarily concerned with maxims of action (general policies of action) and that its duties are characteristically wide, he proceeds to further elaborate the duties of self-perfection and the happiness of others. He does this by specifying in more detail their content and by explaining why they are duties. He refers to this task as one of *exposition*.[10] Because Kant also treats these same duties in the Elements, I will here be brief and save elaborating this material until later chapters.

One's own perfection as an end that is also a duty

Earlier in V, Kant called attention to two types of perfection: perfection of one's "natural predispositions" and perfection of one's will. Here, Kant refers to the former as "physical perfection"—the "*cultivation* of all *capacities* in general, for the advancement of ends presented by reason" (DV 6:391). He proceeds to give an argument for this duty that will be taken up later in chapter 12. Here, Kant makes the point that this duty is ethical—and thus of wide obligation. The command corresponding to the duty of *moral* self-perfection is the duty to strive to have an overall virtuous disposition. Here, the maxim expressing this duty is: "Cultivate your powers of body and mind to make them fit

---

[10] An exposition, for Kant, is an explanation of something that falls short of a definition, only found in mathematics. On this point, see CpuR, A 727–731/B 755–759.

for any ends you might encounter" (DV 6:392). Concerning the perfection of one's will—"the greatest moral perfection of human being" (ibid.)—the duty is to strive to comply with one's duties from the sole motive of duty. Kant remarks that at first sight it seems to be a narrow obligation, yet in fact it is a wide obligation—a thesis we consider in some detail in chapter 12.

The happiness of others as an end that is also a duty

Kant distinguishes benevolence (*Wohlwollen*—literally well-wishing) from beneficence (*Wohltun*—well-doing). The duty is not one of mere benevolence, but of beneficence—*doing* something to promote the happiness of others. He also distinguishes a person's "natural welfare" from one's "moral well-being." One has a duty toward both. Regarding the first, the duty is to adopt a maxim of beneficence. As lately noted, this wide, imperfect duty permits latitude in complying with it. One should be willing to endure some sacrifice of, say, time or money, to help others satisfy their (morally permissible) ends, particularly their basic needs. But, as we've seen, who to help, when to help, how to help—these are aspects of complying with the duty that are typically up to those individuals who have the resources and opportunities to help others.

In these passages, Kant appeals to the universal law formula to argue for the claim that promoting the welfare of others is a duty. He also explains one of the duty's limits, namely, that it is impermissible to promote the welfare of others if doing so would put one in a position of needing help from others to satisfy one's basic needs. Here, again, because the argument for the duty comes up later in the Elements, I put off discussion of it and the argument limiting self-sacrifice until chapter 13.

Concerning the moral well-being of others, Kant claims we have a negative duty of refraining from doing anything that would tempt someone to act immorally which would then likely cause that person to suffer the pangs of conscience in the form of guilt, shame, or both. Such suffering contributes to their unhappiness.

7.5 Brief review

We are now poised to examine Kant's conception of virtue—the topic of the next chapter. Before that, let us briefly review some key ideas from Sections I–VIII of the introduction to DV.

- Ethics refers to that branch of moral philosophy concerned with virtue.
- Virtue as an ideal is "autocracy"; the developed capacity to successfully overcome contrary-to-duty inclinations and comply with one's various duties from the sole motive of duty, i.e. respect for the authority of categorical moral requirements.
- In the pursuit of autocracy, there are ends that one has an obligation to adopt, the most general of which are self-perfection and the happiness of others.
- Because ethics is primarily concerned with ends, its requirements concern the adoption of maxims expressing general policies of action.
- Kant distinguishes the *quality* and *degree* of duties. He also distinguishes narrow from wide duties and perfect from imperfect duties. To relate these distinctions, I've proposed that quality refers to the narrow/wide distinction and concerns whether the duty is a narrowly specified action or the adoption of a maxim of action. Degree, then, refers to the latitude one has in complying with the duty.

Further reading

- On the general topic of obligatory ends, see Herman 2007.
- As noted in the previous chapter's Further Reading, the articles by Potter 1985, 1993, and Allison 1993 [1996] are also recommended for discussion of Kant's attempt to argue that there must be ends that one has a duty to adopt.

8

Radical Evil and the Nature of Virtue

Sections XII–XV & IX

Kant's conception of virtue, as mentioned already, is a matter of resolving to comply with one's duties solely out of respect for the moral law together with acquiring the strength of will to comply with that resolve. This, however, is only a threadbare description of what is a rich conception of virtue, whose full appreciation requires understanding the rudiments of Kant's theory of human nature as they bear on his ethics. As Kant explains in his 1793 *Religion within the Boundaries of Mere Reason*, while it is part of human nature that we have an "original predisposition" toward the good, to become virtuous one must overcome the innate "radical evil" characteristic of human beings. This chapter, then, explores Kant's conception of virtue, against the background of his theory of human nature as it relates to good and evil. The first three sections address the following questions relating themes from the *Religion* to *The Doctrine of Virtue*:

- What are the rudiments of Kant's theory of human nature as they bear on his ethical theory?
- What place, if any, does feeling have in this theory?
- What is the thesis of radical evil?

After addressing these questions, section 4 returns to DV's introduction to flesh out the just-cited threadbare description of virtue. Then, with Kant's conception of virtue fully in view, two questions remain, the first of which returns us to the *Religion*:

- How is radical evil manifested in human psychology?
- What must one do to overcome manifestations of evil in striving toward virtue?

Kant's Doctrine of Virtue. Mark Timmons, Oxford University Press (2021). © Oxford University Press.
DOI: 10.1093/oso/9780190939229.003.0008

8.1 The original predisposition to good

The *Religion* is divided into four parts. Part I is entitled "Concerning the Indwelling of the Evil Principle alongside the Good or Of the Radical Evil in Human Nature." In the first section, "Concerning the Original Predisposition to Good in Human Nature," Kant distinguishes three "elements" of this original predisposition: the predispositions to animality, humanity, and personality.

The predisposition to *animality* concerns our innate drive of self-love, which "may be brought under the general title of physical or merely *mechanical* self-love, i.e. a love for which reason is not required" (R 6:26). This element includes the drive for self-preservation, the sexual drive that serves the propagation of the species, and the social drive to be in community with other humans. Kant remarks that various "bestial vices" of gluttony, lust, and wild lawlessness (in relation to others) can be "grafted" upon these drives by failing to properly control them. Animality—one's animal nature—is the basis for one kind of duty to oneself, the topic of chapter 10.

The predisposition to *humanity* pertains to the human being "as a living and at the same time *rational* being" (R 6:26). This is also a predisposition of self-love, but one that leads to self-other comparisons, and so requires the use of reason. By comparing one's condition to that of others, one judges whether one is happy or unhappy. This way of seeking happiness initially inclines one "*to gain worth in the opinion of others*" (R 6:27), initially as having equal worth. However, this sort of interpersonal comparison, if not properly tempered by the moral law, can lead to the vices of envy, ingratitude, and malice—vices of hatred taken up in chapter 14.

Finally, the predisposition to (moral) *personality*[1] is "the susceptibility to respect for the moral law *as of itself a sufficient incentive to the power of choice*" (R 6:27). This susceptibility is manifested in "simple respect for the moral law within us" (ibid.) which, in this passage, Kant identifies with moral feeling—feeling in the *capacity* sense to be further

---

[1] You may recall from chapter 5, sec. 2 that Kant distinguishes moral personality from psychological personality. The latter refers to the capacity to be conscious of one's identity over time.

explained in the next section. This predisposition, of course, includes the predisposition to humanity, but goes beyond it because "[t]he most rational being of this world might still need certain incentives, coming to him from the objects of inclination, to determine his power of choice" (R 6:26n). Strictly speaking, it is the predisposition to personality in virtue of which human beings are not only rational beings qua members of the sensible world, but morally accountable as members also of the intelligible world. One can think of this predisposition as a central element in one's freedom of the will, necessary for being subject to the moral law. Moreover, it is one's moral personality that grounds the kind of standing Kant refers to as dignity. It is notable that Kant refers to moral personality here as "the idea of humanity considered wholly intellectually" (R 6:28).

Here, it is worth recalling what was said in 5.2 about Kant's use of 'humanity' and (moral) 'personality.' There we noted that Kant often contrasts humanity with animality, where the former includes moral personality—the source of one's dignity that finds expression in the formula of humanity as the command to always treat humanity in oneself and others never merely as a means, but always at the same time as an end in itself. In the passages under consideration from the *Religion*, he explicitly refers to humanity in a narrower sense, contrasting it with moral personality. To anticipate: in the Elements, where Kant employs the formula of humanity to ground various midlevel duties, he uses 'humanity' and 'personality' indifferently, thus using the former term in its inclusive sense.

8.2 Aesthetic preliminaries of the mind's receptivity to concepts of duty as such

Returning to DV's introduction, Section XII concerns those moral endowments—referred to as "natural predispositions"—"such that if one lacks them there can be no duty to put oneself in possession of them . . . because they lie at the foundation of morality not as objective conditions, but as *subjective* conditions of receptivity to the concept of duty" (DV 6:399). They are "*moral feeling, conscience, love* of one's neighbor, and *respect* for oneself (*self-esteem*)" (ibid.) One's consciousness of them is "not empirical in origin" (ibid.), rather, one becomes aware of them as *effects* of the moral upon the mind. Given Kant's rationalism, at first it might seem jarring that feeling is now entering the picture. However, as the quote indicates, these predispositions are not part of the objective conditions of morality; feelings don't represent anything as objective—they "yield no cognition" (DV 6:400) as Kant says. Rather, they have to do with how the law (the objective standard of morality) is experienced in beings who are members of both the intelligible and sensible realms and in whom feeling is involved in producing action. Let us briefly consider each of them.

Moral feeling

Kant writes that "Any determination of the faculty of choice proceeds *from* the representation of the possible action *through* the feeling of pleasure or displeasure, taking an interest in it or in its effect, *to* the deed . . ." (DV 6: 399). (This remark was quoted in chapter 4 in explaining the rudiments of Kant's theories of moral and nonmoral motivation.) Regarding feelings and the moral law, those feelings that do not result from a representation of the moral law are "pathological"; their source is one's sensible nature. Feelings that do result from such consciousness of the moral law are moral feelings. Here, it is helpful to distinguish moral feeling as a *capacity*, or "*receptivity*" to use Kant's language, from *episodes* of feeling that result from the activation of this capacity. It is the former that is in focus here. The general capacity in human beings "of the free faculty of choice to being moved by pure practical reason (and its law)" (DV 6:400) is what Kant means here by moral feeling.[2] In the *Religion*, the predisposition to personality is described as a susceptibility to "simple respect for the moral law within

---

[2] Kant here claims that *consciousness* of obligation presupposes moral feeling—an epistemic condition. In the opening paragraph of XII, he makes the stronger, seemingly metaphysical claim that it is "by force of them [the natural predispositions, M.T.] that he can be bound by duty" (DV 6: 399). This latter claim, focused specifically on moral feeling, fits with the kind of ethical internalism I've been attributing to Kant. See chapter 5, sec. 5.

us" (R 6:27). Moral feeling (as a capacity), then, is another label for this susceptibility or "receptivity." It is an aspect of human nature[3] through which consciousness of the moral law is able to have an effect on one's temporal choices—the "affection of the inner sense" (DV 6:399). Thus, one does not have a duty to acquire moral feeling, rather, having it is presupposed in the ability to be bound by, as well as to become aware of, the law and the duties it imposes. One does, however, have an indirect duty to cultivate and thereby strengthen it by dwelling on its "inscrutable source" (ibid.); inscrutable because (as I will put it on Kant's behalf) unlike the source of nonmoral reasons for action grounded in self-love, its source is inscrutable because it is an aspect of one's autonomy whose nature, as supersensible, is inscrutable to us.

Conscience

Related to moral feeling is conscience. This is the inborn capacity of reason to hold oneself accountable to the moral law. The operation of conscience involves judging whether a deed one has performed (or is considering performing) complies with the moral law; it is not itself a feeling. And so it cannot be a duty to act in accord with conscience because that would require "yet a second conscience in order for one to become aware of the act of the first" (DV 6:401). The operation of conscience, then, presupposes the moral law; it is *not* some faculty or sense that detects or otherwise determines what is right or wrong, virtuous or vicious. The verdicts or *acts* of one's conscience either acquit one of wrongdoing or condemn one's action. They also warn us of such possible judgments when we are deciding to act. And although conscience itself is not a feeling, its role in the psychological economy of an agent is "to affect moral feeling by its act" (DV 6:400). Kant makes additional

---

[3] Does it belong to one's intelligible nature (human being as *homo noumenon*) or to one's sensible nature (*homo phenomenon*), or partly to both? Clearly, Kant here is referring to certain phenomena manifested in one's sensible nature (they are *natural* predispositions of the mind) that result from consciousness of the moral law (or perhaps the determination of the power of choice by such consciousness). Thus, as described here, they belong to one's sensible nature. How *exactly* these empirical manifestations are related to one's noumenal self and the predisposition to moral personality is a matter for scholarly debate.

remarks about conscience concerning the possibility of an erring con-science, the relation between acting on one's conscience and being blameworthy, and the duty of conscience as indirect. However, because the duty of conscience receives further treatment in the Elements as one of the duties to oneself, let us defer elaboration of these additional points and others until chapter 12.

Love of humanity

Love as a kind of emotion (or "sensation" as Kant writes) is not within one's direct voluntary control, and so there can't be a duty to somehow produce it at will. This is "pathological love." Disinterested beneficence *is* within one's voluntary control and so something one can be obligated to act on; it is the primary duty of love toward others featured in the Elements. This is "practical love"—doing good for someone in order to benefit them. Insofar as "love of humanity" is a natural predisposition of one's sensible nature, it is "an aptitude of the inclination to beneficence generally" (DV 6:402). The idea is that regardless of whether one finds oneself loving others (in the emotion sense) and regardless of whether one finds others lovable (worthy of the emotion), one has an aptitude (receptivity) for loving them, and practicing the duty of beneficence (promoting the happiness of others) can enliven this aptitude, which in turn is manifested in an inclination to beneficence.

Admittedly, the four paragraphs discussing love of humanity are far from crystal clear. And if the reading I've just proposed is correct, then it raises a question about virtuous action. As we've learned, vir-tuous action is action done solely from the motive of duty, which gives it moral worth. At least this is how Kant typically describes it. Yet here Kant seems to be recommending that one develop one's aptitude for an inclination to feel a certain way toward others. The seeming problem is that 'inclination' refers to habitual (sensuous) desire, and no action done even partly from desire has moral worth. Given that the doctrine of virtue is concerned with moral motivation, the remarks about love of humanity seem strikingly out of synch with Kant's views. I suggest the following for dealing with this issue.

In the general introduction at 6:213, Kant introduces the label "sense-free inclination" which, he notes, can be used to refer to the sensuous effect—an "intellectual pleasure"—resulting "from a pure interest of reason" (in the moral law). In light of this: if (*i*) one takes an interest of reason (as explained in 4.4) in disinterested beneficence, and (*ii*) if this interest alone is what motivates one to benefit others for their sakes, and finally (*iii*) if, as a result, one's "aptitude of the inclination to beneficence" (as an aspect of one's sensuous nature) is enlivened, then one may describe the resulting inclination as having a sense-free origin, which fits with Kant's claim that these natural predispositions are not of empirical origin. Acting from this "inclination," then, presumably has moral worth that is transmitted, as it were, from the original source of motivation to the deed, i.e. action on this inclination. In any case, this predisposition is an aspect of one's duties of love toward other human beings that includes beneficence, gratitude, and sympathy which we examine in chapter 13.

Respect for oneself (self-esteem)

Kant's title for this subsection is simply "On respect." Yet in his remarks introducing these four characteristics he mentions respect for oneself (self-esteem), hence my title. He is here referring to a particular feeling—respect—directed toward oneself, or self-esteem. As with the other three characteristics, Kant denies that one has a duty of self-esteem. In the *Groundwork*, Kant characterizes the concept of duty as "*the necessity of an action from respect for the law*" (G 4:400). The concept of duty already includes the concept of action from respect for the moral law. Thus, a duty of self-respect would have to be the necessity of bringing about the feeling of respect for the law (the necessary "action") from the feeling of respect for the law. Kant explains that this amounts to the nonsensical idea of being "bound by duty to duty (DV 6:402). Kant also says that the feeling of respect for oneself "is a ground of certain duties, i.e. of certain actions that can be consistent with his duty to himself" (DV 6:403). He doesn't elaborate this remark, but to anticipate, this feeling predisposes one to comply with the various duties to oneself, taken up in chapters 10, 11, and 12. Since duties of respect toward others are grounded in the duty of preserving others' self-esteem, this predisposition is also implicated in those duties that we come to in chapter 14.

Notably, Kant is identifying self-esteem with self-respect. Yet, as we shall see, there are places where the two are not identified. Egotistical ("*self-gratifying*") self-esteem (mentioned at 6:441) is not a kind of self-respect. It is also important to note that what Kant here denies is a duty to have a *feeling* of respect (or moral self-esteem), since the feeling of respect—as a capacity—is a presupposition of being subject to the moral law and as an episodic feeling is something involuntarily experienced from recognition of being subject to the moral law. Later, in his treatment of the vice of servility, he says we do have a duty of moral self-esteem, where what he seems to be referring to is the *manner* in which one should seek to perfect oneself—with "consciousness of the sublimity of his moral predisposition" (DV 6:435). Of course, we will re-visit the issue of a duty of self-esteem in chapter 11, and I will have more to say about Kant's concepts of respect, esteem, self-respect, and self-esteem in chapter 14.

Before moving forward, two comments about Section XII are in order. *First*, Kant doesn't explain why he includes discussion of these predispositions at this place in the introduction. As "preliminary concepts" of receptivity to the various duties, perhaps he viewed it as a suitable transition from a general discussion of the concepts figuring in a doctrine of virtue (ending in XI with a summary chart outlining his scheme of duties) to the succeeding sections that discuss virtue and its acquisition. Moral feeling and conscience are the two most general preconditions of being bound to, and aware of, the moral law, while self-respect and love of human beings are more specific manifestations of moral feeling that relate respectively to the duties to oneself and to others explained in the Elements.

Second, given the predispositions to good (moral personality in particular) and the natural presuppositions on the part of sensibility as both essential elements of human nature, why must human beings *strive* to become virtuous? After all, the constitution of such beings would seem to lead them without struggle to have a virtuous disposition. An indication of Kant's answer is: "If it is said, The human being is created good, this can mean nothing more than: He has been created for the *good*, and the original *predisposition* in him is good; the human being is not thereby good as such . . ." (R 6:44). To explain this remark brings us to Kant's doctrine of radical evil.

8.3 Radical evil

Section III of *Religion* I is entitled "The Human Being is By Nature Evil." Kant claims that although all human beings have a predisposition to (moral) personality whose full realization would result in having a virtuous disposition, nevertheless all human beings are evil in that each "is conscious of the moral law and yet has incorporated into his maxim the (occasional) deviation from it." The quote continues:

> "He is evil *by nature*" simply means that being evil applies to him considered in his species; not that this quality may be inferred from the concept of his species [which would make the thesis analytically true, M.T.] . . . , but rather that, according to the cognition we have of the human being through experience, he cannot be judged otherwise, in other words, we may presuppose evil as subjectively necessary in every human being, even the best (R 6:32).

So according to the radical evil thesis, necessarily all human beings are evil, and since it is not analytically true, the thesis is a necessary synthetic claim, thus only cognizable a priori. Oddly, Kant does not seem to offer an a priori justification ("deduction") of this thesis.[4] Rather, he points to "a multitude of woeful examples that the experience of human *deeds* parades before us" (R 6:33) indicative of the evil that is woven into the human species as such. In explaining the nature of radical evil, Kant refers to one's "fundamental maxim" which expresses one's freely chosen orientation of the power of choice with respect to the moral law. That is, all humans are responsible for allowing themselves at least occasional deviations from the moral law. In so far as

---

[4] For an illuminating discussion of this apparently missing deduction, see Laura Papich 2018, ch. 5 and Pablo Muchnik 2010, who each attempt to provide the missing deduction.

this maxim is a *principle* governing one's orientation of the exercise of choice as both an intelligible and sensible being, it is a source of one's intentional deviations from the moral law. The "choice" of this fundamental maxim is itself a timeless noumenal act that cannot be explained, yet it is something for which each is responsible. (I won't dwell on the paradoxical idea of choosing—on what basis?—one's basic orientation of the will; something Kant admits is paradoxical.)

While this "natural propensity to evil" (R 6:32) as an aspect of human nature is inextirpable, its influence can be overcome by becoming virtuous. But the struggle to become virtuous requires overcoming those propensities that lead one to violate the moral law, which will be explained in section 5 after examining more closely the nature of virtue. The thesis of radical evil then provides the anthropological backdrop to the task of becoming virtuous.

8.4 Virtuous disposition

In Sections IX and XIII, Kant explains his "formal" conception of virtue—the characteristic of having an overall virtuous disposition. The many individual virtues comprise its "material" or matter. The virtues correspond to the duties of virtue, and so while there are many virtues, "there is only one virtuous disposition" (DV 6:410). In places, we have noted that a virtuous disposition includes two elements: a commitment to morality that is constitutive of a good will and the acquired strength to follow through. Kant provides a concise description of virtuous disposition in the first paragraph of Section IX. With brackets inserted, the paragraph begins:

> [1] *Virtue* is the strength of the maxim of a human being in following his duty.—Any kind of strength can be recognized only by hindrances it can overcome, and [2] in the case of virtue these hindrances are natural inclinations, [3] which can come into conflict with his moral intent. (6:394).

The first bracketed remark is an extremely compressed definition of virtuous disposition, followed by an unpacking of it (suggested by the dash). Regarding the reference to human beings in 1, in a later passage (at 6:405), Kant notes that the concept of virtue only applies to nonholy rational beings (including human beings). As we have learned, a holy being is one whose nature is such that it always and necessarily conforms to the moral law; a being whose will is not susceptible to the kinds of hindrances mentioned in 2, or any other hindrances. Remark 2, then, draws out something implicit in 1, against the background of Kant's conception of human agency and his motivational dualism. The reference in 3 to one's moral "intent" refers to one's commitment to act on maxims of duty. So, Kant is thinking of agents who intend to do what they take to be their duty (they have adopted a maxim of duty) but, in addition, the intent or "resolve" of such agents to act accordingly (the strength of their commitment to their maxims in fulfilling duty) is strong enough to overcome contrary-to-duty inclinations. Furthermore, the sort of resolve in question is a *moral* resolve involving a kind of self-constraint, and so

> ... [4] virtue is not merely a self-constraint (for then one natural in-clination could strive to overcome another), but [5] also a constraint according to a principle of inner freedom, and hence [6] through the mere representation of one's duty, according to its formal law (DV 6:394).

Comment 4 rules out as a matter of virtue cases in which an agent has sensuous inclinations that favor doing incompatible things on some occasion (play versus study) and where one of them proves motiva-tionally strongest. But more generally, this comment rules out pruden-tial self-constraint as equivalent to virtue.[5] The constraint essential to virtue is *moral* self-constraint of the sort indicated in 5 and 6.

Inner freedom as the *capacity* for moral self-constraint is (or is part of) autonomy of the will (6:396); fully realized, it is what Kant refers to as "autocracy" of the will (DV 6:383). The "principle of inner freedom" Kant is referring to in 5 is indicated in 6: the principle of

---

[5] Nor is virtue a matter of having a firm resolution to comply with duty out of self-interest. In the *Religion*, Kant refers to this as virtue "in a legal sense," which he explicitly distinguishes from genuine moral virtue. See R 6:47.

observing one's duties from the sole incentive (motive) of duty or, as Kant says, "through the mere representation of one's duty." This is "moral strength." Successfully striving to become virtuous involves strengthening one's respect for the law, thus strengthening one's moral resolve.

Moral resolve, good will, and virtuous disposition

To fully appreciate Kant's conception of virtue, it is worth saying more about the sort of moral resolve constitutive of a good will. Here, I will elaborate (on Kant's behalf) a conception of the good will and virtuous disposition that represents an ideal toward which human beings can strive.[6]

Moral resolve is a matter of having a proper normative orientation of one's will by subordinating nonmoral incentives to moral incentives. This subordination has both cognitive and volitional components. The cognitive component involves use of one's faculty of understanding; "the faculty of concepts, and hence also of those that aim at duty" (DV 6:387). Moral understanding fundamentally involves a basic grasp of the concept of duty together with some grasp of both the content and structure of the normative realm—the realm of both moral and nonmoral reasons for choice and action. The *content* of this realm includes the basic duties set forth in the Elements together with the various associated virtues to be acquired and vices to be avoided. Part of having proper moral understanding, then, is to understand the virtues and vices, and their significance in striving to acquire a virtuous disposition.

To grasp the *structure* of the normative realm involves taking moral reasons that impose strict requirements on one's behavior to be normatively superior to reasons of self-love. Doing so is what I will call "normative subordination" of the nonmoral to the moral. However, moral understanding also involves recognizing that some moral reasons for

---

[6] Kant's theory of virtue includes two ideals—the one that I am about to explain and an ideal of complete holiness that cannot be fully achieved by beings with a sensible nature. On this ideal of holiness, see CprR 5:84.

action, associated with wide, imperfect duties such as beneficence, favor without requiring specific actions, and provide one with sufficient reason to do so, but only in cases where such action would not violate a narrow, perfect moral obligation or involve excessive self-sacrifice.[7] Kant claims that narrow, imperfect duties always take precedence over complying with wide, imperfect duties. This is another species of normative subordination, one within the moral realm (See Vig 27:537).

Of course, mere understanding of the basic content and structure of this complex normative realm is not sufficient for having a good will. In addition, one must also have a commitment to comply with one's moral understanding—a "moral cast of mind." This is the volitional component of a good will; the *resolve* to comply with duty from the sole motive of duty (respect for the moral law). This component, then, calls for motivational subordination of the nonmoral to the moral. Thus, when fully mature, the cast of mind in question includes the following complex resolution constitutive of a good will:

> Moral resolve. (*i*) One resolves (i.e. firmly intends) to comply with one's perfect duties and do so by acting solely out of respect for the moral law. (*ii*) Regarding general ends that one has a moral obligation to adopt (the obligatory ends of self-perfection and happiness of others) one's resolve includes adopting such ends and doing so solely out of respect for the moral law, and then acting to promote those ends on appropriate occasions. (*iii*) Finally, one resolves to cultivate those particular qualities of character (the virtues) that dispose one to exercise good judgment in complying with one's general obligations, while avoiding particular vices and again cultivate them solely out of respect for the moral law.

Because mere compliance with duty does not require acting from the sole motive of duty, each of these three provisions of moral resolve includes two elements: comply with duty and comply by acting

---

[7] Given that one has sufficient moral reason to be beneficent (assuming I'm right about this), excessive self-sacrifice must defeat one's reason because of how it will likely affect one's duties to oneself. Thanks to Adam Cureton for prompting this remark.

from the sole motive of duty—respect for the moral law. These two elements are reflected respectively in the commands: Be ye perfect! Be ye holy! that Kant mentions in his discussion of moral self-perfection in the Elements (DV 6:446). With this conception of a mature good will in view (composed of proper moral understanding and associated resolve), we can now characterize more fully Kant's conception of someone with a virtuous character as one who fully realizes their predisposition to moral personality.

Virtue, then, in its highest degree achievable for human beings, includes having moral resolve (as just elaborated) together with the acquired strength to comply with one's resolve. In succeeding at this, one thereby *fully* exercises one's inner freedom by realizing one's predisposition to personality. However, because, according to the thesis of radical evil, as human beings we each have "chosen" to have a power of choice that may allow principled opposition to the moral law, we must strive to overcome this inextirpable property of our power of choice. At the level of empirical human psychology, what stands in the way of such overcoming? The answer is that corresponding to the elements constitutive of virtue, there are propensities to evil leading to vice. Here we return briefly to the *Religion* I, Section II, "Concerning the Propensity to Evil in Human Nature."

8.5 Propensities to evil

A propensity, for Kant, is the psychological basis ("subjective ground") for acquiring an inclination upon experiencing the object of that inclination. Propensities are thus properties of the capacity for choice. They can be good or evil, morally speaking. Although they can be innate and thus characteristic of the human species, they *may* be represented as not being such, that is, "they can be thought of (if it is good) as *acquired*, or (if evil) as *brought* by the human being *upon* himself" (R 6:29). A propensity to evil, then, is a "subjective ground of the possibility of the deviation of maxims from the moral law" (R 6:29). There are three such propensities to evil—weakness, impurity, depravity—which represent distinct ways of failing to be virtuous.

First, there is the propensity to frailty in which one experiences weakness of will and fails to do one's duty because the strength to comply is weaker than competing inclinations. (This is a failure of motivational subordination.) Weakness of will is compatible with moral resolve; with having a good will. The result of such weakness is lack of virtue to some degree.

Second, impurity is where one does comply with the moral law, but only because, in addition to whatever motivating force respect for the moral law has, one (luckily) has cooperating inclinations that favor doing one's duty and complies with duty on the basis of those motivations. So, in such cases, one has not complied with duty from the *sole* motive of duty. What goes distinctively wrong[8] in cases of impurity is that one has failed to resolve to comply with duty solely from the motive of duty. So described, impurity results from a lack of good will that does not thereby constitute an evil will, i.e., depravity.

Finally, depravity is the "propensity of the power of choice to maxims that subordinate the incentives of the moral law to others (not moral ones)" (R 6:30). It is this normative subordination that represents a principled opposition to the moral law and constitutes "true *vice*" (DV 6:408). While impurity results from *not resolving* to comply with duty from the pure motive of duty (a lack of good will), depravity is the *resolving not* to comply with duty from the sole motive of duty.[9] To have adopted this as a general policy is to be a morally vicious person. To allow select principled opposition to the moral law is to suffer from particular vices.[10] Here we have an evil will, directly opposed to a good

---

[8] The propensity to impurity has been a subject of some dispute in the secondary literature. For defense of this understanding of impurity, see Timmons 2017b.

[9] As Kant remarks in Book II of *Religion*, "genuine evil consists in our *will* not to resist inclinations when they invite transgression, and this disposition is the really true enemy" (R 6:58n, bold added).

[10] In *Religion* I, 6:22–25, Kant defends what is referred to as "character rigorism," according to which one either has a good will or an evil will; there is no in-between—no mere lack of good will, or mixture of partly good and partly bad. In Timmons 2017b, I explain that the rigorism thesis should be thought of as holding only regarding Kant's transcendental psychology and not his empirical psychology. Making this move enables Kant to respond to the objection (most thoroughly developed by Claudia Card 2010, 2016) that his theory of moral evil fails to accommodate common character flaws, including lack of character.

will, thus one's predisposition to evil is manifested in one's behavior as an embodied rational being.

So, in order, the three propensities to evil represent ways of falling short of virtuous disposition: lack of virtue, lack of good will, and evil will.

8.6 The task of acquiring virtue

But then how does one go about the task of virtue acquisition? Kant's short answer is "by means of elevating the moral incentive (the representation of the law) by contemplating (*contemplatio*) the dignity of the pure law of reason in us, and at the same time by practice (*exercitio*)" (DV 6:397). It is the longer answer that will occupy us in this section, where I will briefly outline Kant's conception of virtue acquisition in which contemplation and practice play a role. (Part of Kant's developed answer is provided in the Doctrine of Methods, taken up in chapter 16.)

Kant writes that the decision to adopt this maxim of virtue (moral resolve) must be done all at once. That is, it requires a "*revolution* in the disposition of the human being" (R 6:47, see also Anth 7:294), since committing oneself to break away from vice gradually, "could in itself be impure and even vicious, and hence produce no virtue (which rests on a single principle)" (DV 6:477). Kant admits that we lack insight into how this revolution is possible (R 6:50). But something in one's moral education or perhaps just one's reflection must trigger it. Presumably, contemplation of the dignity of the moral law—of its authoritativeness—plays a role in coming to embrace this normative orientation of the will. In various places Kant describes the phenomenology of such contemplation as something more than merely apprehending that in fact moral reasons have the kind of authority just mentioned. Fully appreciating the law's authority includes experiences of the law "checking self-love" and "striking down self-conceit"— experiences that have both a negative effect on feeling, but also "awakens *respect* . . . insofar as it is positive and a determining ground" (CprR 5:74). Such experiences are presumably part of what leads one toward having a proper normative orientation.

However, as explained earlier, having moral resolve is compatible with being subject to bouts of weakness of will where one knowingly fails to comply with one's duty, and it is only strength of moral resolve that is properly considered virtue. And so the task is to strengthen one's respect for the authority of the law so that considerations of strict moral obligation become motivationally dominant in a way that overcomes weakness and also excludes cooperating incentives of self-love. Doing so, as noted earlier, is a matter of realizing one's inner freedom which involves both a negative and a positive task. The negative task is two-fold:

> being one's own *master* in a given case . . . and being *lord* over oneself . . . i.e. *taming* one's affects and *ruling* over one's passions.—The *frame of mind* in these two states is noble (*erecta*), while in the opposite case it is ignoble (*indoles abiecta, serva*) (DV 6:407)

Affects (*Affekten*) and passions (*Leidenschaften*), Kant tells us in Section XVI, are "essentially different from each other" (DV 6:407), and are treated in some detail in Kant's *Anthropology*, Book III, where he discusses the faculties of feeling and of desire. There, he claims that both sorts of motivational state "shut out the sovereignty of reason" (Anth 7:251).[11] Affects such as anger (including indignation, fear, and exuberant joy) are sensible, occurrent feeling states that (typically) arise spontaneously, thus making rational reflection on choice and action difficult.[12] Failing to "tame" such affects as they arise in a given case is a kind of weakness which, when they interfere with one's doing one's duty, manifest a *lack of virtue*. For instance, being overcome by momentary fear (an affect) of speaking up for one's moral convictions and thereby failing to do so manifests a lack of moral courage on that occasion. To tame one's affects is not always to eliminate such feelings. Rather, it involves reflection on them, recognizing that they can and often do usurp rational choice, and then getting oneself into a condition in which one is able to check their motivational influence on

---

[11] See also CJ 5:272–273.

[12] "Affect is surprise through sensation, by means of which the mind's composure . . . is suspended" (Anth 7:252).

one's action. In the highest stage of human virtue, one reaches a state of "moral apathy" involving a kind of strength in which affects "lose their influence on moral feeling only through respect for the law becoming more powerful than they are, one and all" because respect for the law is more powerful than all such feelings together (DV 6:408). Such apathy is *self-mastery* in the sense relevant to virtue.

A passion is a "sensuous desire that has become a lasting inclination (e.g. *hatred* as opposed to anger)" (DV 6:408) and is thus a dispositional state. Kant proposes a two-fold classification of the passions (Anth 7:267–268): those grounded in the "innate" natural inclinations to freedom and to sex, and those grounded in "acquired" inclinations having to do with influencing others—inclinations to honor, authority, and possession. These inclinations ground maxims to pursue these ends. But when a person is not properly constrained in the use of means for achieving these ends, they become passions. Specific manifestations of them shut out the sovereignty of reason because, for example, when in the grip of a passion "the enchanted human being sees very well indeed the reasons against his favorite inclination, but he feels powerless to give them active emphasis" (EMH 2:261). If, for example, the inclination to be honored by others is not properly governed, it becomes a "mania" (as Kant says) for being honored by others—an unjustified demand that others view one as worthy of greater esteem than is owed to those others. One who succumbs to this passion is not merely lacking in virtue; the individual is guilty of *vice*; specifically, the vice of arrogance. Kant's conception of a vice as a character trait is that of an "intentional transgression" of the moral law that has become a deep-seated principle of action.

Taming affects and ruling over passions, then, helps to strengthen one's moral resolve by removing hindrances to the incentive of respect. This is the chief negative requirement of the practice of virtue emphasized by Kant (see, for example, CprR 5:75–76). However,

> Virtue, in so far as it is founded on internal freedom, thus contains a positive command for human beings, namely to bring all his capacities and inclinations under his (reason's) control, and hence a command of ruling himself, which is added to the prohibition,

namely not to let himself be ruled by his feelings and inclinations (the duty of *apathy*). (DV 6:408)

This "positive command" involves the cultivation and thus strengthening of one's respect for the law—the positive component of the practice of virtue, achieved through contemplation and practice. In the Methods, Kant emphasizes the importance of recognizing both the dignity of virtue as well as one's capacity for it as "exalted." Contemplation of this dignity (mentioned earlier in connection with having a proper normative orientation) and awareness of one's power "must bring about an elevation of the soul that only animates it to hold its duty the more sacred the more it is challenged (DV 6:483). Further, the practice of virtue at a more concrete level involves the cultivation of the virtues, which not only requires avoiding vice, but also engaging in activities that positively contribute to the cultivation of such virtues as sympathetic feeling (presumably a way in which the natural predisposition of love of human beings is realized). The hoped-for effect of such contemplation and practice is a strengthening of one's moral resolve, inspiring a positive interest in morality. Additionally, the practice of virtue aims for a frame of mind, that of a "*mind at rest*," ruling over one's affects and passions "with a deliberate and firm resolution to put its law into practice" (DV 6:409). Finally, the feeling of elevation that accompanies such self-mastery naturally leads to a frame of mind both "*robust* and *cheerful* . . . in observing its duties" (DV 6:484).

To sum up: for Kant, virtue involves a two-part resolution plus moral strength. The resolution is to (*i*) comply with one's moral obligations, based on one's moral understanding of the content and structure of the normative realm, and to do so (*ii*) from the sole motive of duty—out of respect for the moral law. Having this resolve is to have a good will. Virtue, then, is having a good will and (*iii*) the strength of will to overcome temptation in complying with one's resolution. Strengthening one's commitment to morality requires a kind of self-mastery whereby one can avoid vices, which are grounded in passions, as well as being able to tame affects that may interfere with being a morally virtuous person. This is the negative dimension of virtue. The positive dimension concerns cultivating and strengthening one's moral resolve. How is one to go about this? A significant part of Kant's answer to this question involves cultivating those virtues that help inoculate one against the vices—against the propensity to depravity. Kant has more to say about virtue acquisition in the Methods where he takes up the "practice of virtue," a topic we revisit in chapter 16.

8.7 Concluding reflection

Kant's conception of virtue is often compared unfavorably to Aristotle's. In his *Nicomachean Ethics*, Aristotle distinguishes a person of mere continence from a person of true virtue. Persons of the former sort must sometimes overcome sensible inclinations that oppose doing one's duty, while persons of true virtue have reached a state of character where inclination is in "harmony" with the requirements of duty. Surely, the Aristotelian picture of virtue is of a higher caliber than the Kantian continence picture.

In the secondary literature, there are attempts by sympathetic scholars arguing that Kant's conception is closer to Aristotle's than critics have supposed, and so the apparently stark contrast between Kantian continence and Aristotelian harmony is not that great. One route to pursue in defending this claim is to first note that for Kant virtue as strength is something one must acquire, thus allowing for gradations in degree of virtue. One might then argue that at the highest degree of humanly possible virtue (which necessarily falls short of the ideal of complete holiness), the Kantian view recognizes something at least close to the Aristotelian picture. A more fully virtuous person is one who has been able to strengthen her moral resolve and thus her respect for the law by acquiring a range of particular virtues that help inoculate her against succumbing to and even being seriously tempted by any contrary-to-duty inclinations she may have. Yet, the "propensity to evil," i.e. the susceptibility to the influence of contrary-to-duty inclinations, is something that is inextirpable (R 6:43). Thus, it is not possible for human beings to reach a state in which the susceptibility (however remote for a fully virtuous human being) is completely eliminated. Rather, as Kant puts it, "Virtue is always *progressing* . . . it is an ideal that is unobtainable" (DV 6:409, see also CprR 5:32–33, 83–84). Presumably, the particular ideal in question is holiness which, strictly speaking, transcends virtue as strength in combatting a propensity to evil, since a holy will lacks this propensity. However, insofar as a nonholy human being can acquire the virtues through self-mastery over affects and self-governance over one's passions, one can at least approach a humanly possible ideal of virtue.

Note, however, that there arguably remains a difference between the moral psychologies of Kant and Aristotle that separates their views. To put it in Kantian terms, Aristotle's moral psychology allows one's emotions and inclinations to be "shaped" by moral principles so that they are restructured to be in harmony with morality. To take an example much discussed in the literature—the feeling of sympathy. Sympathy unconstrained by moral principles can lead one to wrong action, as when, in Barbara Herman's (1981) example, out of sympathy for someone needing help one helps them to carry out a theft. According to Aristotle's moral psychology, moral principles can affect the structure of this feeling so that in cases like the burglary, one is not at all motivated to help. However, whether Kant's moral psychology allows for such shaping of feelings, emotions, and inclinations is questionable, for reasons we cannot pursue here. If not, then Kant's account of virtue, even when developed as far as humanly possible, cannot embrace the Aristotelian view. Yet, it can still recognize grades or degrees of humanly possible virtue.

Further reading

- For a book-length study of Kant's theory of virtue, see Baxley 2010. See also the essays in Beltzer 2008 and in Jost and Wuerth 2011.
- For an illuminating discussion of Kant's theory of Section XII on the aesthetic predispositions, see Guyer 2010 [2016].
- For discussion of Kant's moral psychology as it bears on his conception of virtue and how his moral psychology differs from Aristotle's, see Thomason 2017. See also Grenberg 2010.
- Engstrom 2002 explores Kant's conception of inner freedom as it relates to virtue.
- On Kant's conception of moral evil, see Timmons 2017b, Papish 2018, and the collection of papers edited by Anderson-Gold and Muchnik 2010.

9

The Science of Ethics

Sections XIII, IX–XI, XVII, & XVIII

As we learned in chapter 3, for Kant, the metaphysics of morals is the science that comprises a system of a priori principles and propositions (including especially synthetic a priori principles) that pertain to the use of one's freedom of choice. The main project of *The Doctrine of Virtue*, then, is to set forth a system of midlevel ethical duties by deriving them from the supreme principle of morality, the categorical imperative. This is Kant's 'grounding project.' But there is more to the science of ethics; it also involves a scheme of internal organization whereby duties are categorized according to principles of division. Kant explains this scheme in some of the latter sections of the introduction to DV. In earlier sections, he formulates the supreme principle of the doctrine of virtue, comments on its status, and provides a justification ('deduction') for it. Regarding the internal scheme of organization, the guiding questions are:

- What are the governing principles of a scientific ethics?
- How is the science of ethics organized?

And regarding the supreme principle:

- What is the fundamental principle distinctive of the doctrine of virtue?
- How is the fundamental principle (a version of the universal law formula of the CI) related to the humanity formulation, which plays a prominent role in many of the derivations featured in the Elements?
- What is the principle's status compared to the supreme principle of the doctrine of right?
- How is it justified?

Kant's Doctrine of Virtue. Mark Timmons, Oxford University Press (2021). © Oxford University Press.
DOI: 10.1093/oso/9780190939229.003.0009

The concluding section raises a worry about Kant's grounding project.

9.1 The science of ethics

As noted at the outset, for Kant, a science in the strict sense features synthetic a priori metaphysical principles at its foundation. A science also requires that the principles be organized according to a rational scheme that befits the realm of inquiry. Regarding the scheme of organization for the doctrine of virtue, we find: (*i*) governing principles for a doctrine of virtue, (*ii*) a "schema" that organizes the duties of virtue, and (*iii*) principles of division for the Elements. Let us take these in order.

Governing principles

In the first part of Section XIII (up to the heading, "On virtue in general"), Kant distinguishes his conception of a doctrine of virtue from his understanding of certain ancient doctrines. His objections to these doctrines allow him to articulate "three maxims of scientific treatment of a doctrine of virtue" (DV 6:405).

The first maxim is that there is a multiplicity of virtues and vices, opposed to the view, sometimes associated with Socrates, that there is only one virtue and one vice. Rather, according to Kant, while there is a single virtuous disposition, there are many individual virtues. The first paragraph argues that two alleged proofs of the same duty are either not genuine proofs, or they prove distinct duties. Kant's example is that the harm a lie does to another is not the basis of a proof of the duty of *truthfulness*—a duty to oneself (treated in chapter 11)—rather it is the basis of a proof of a duty of benevolence. The duty of truthfulness is grounded in the fact that the liar violates a duty to herself. The relation between this observation and the first governing principle is that because there are distinct grounds of obligation and thus a multiplicity of distinct types of duty, correspondingly, there is a multiplicity of virtues and vices.

The second maxim says that virtues are distinguished from vices by the *quality* of maxims, not by the *degree* to which one acts on them. Here, the quality of a maxim depends on its relation to the moral law; whether it is required or prohibited. Degree, in this context, refers to one's level of engaging in some activity that the maxim (characteristic of the virtue) concerns. On Kant's understanding of the Aristotelian doctrine of the mean (and employing the concept of a maxim of action) the essential difference between a virtuous maxim of thriftiness and the twin vices of miserliness and prodigality is that misers take thrift too far in skimping on necessities and enjoyments, while prodigals fail to take thrift far enough by excessive spending.[1] Kant's complaint, then, is that the Aristotelian view misses the true nature of the virtues of vices. Vices are a matter of adopting bad maxims. The vice of prodigality results from a maxim that elevates immediate enjoyments over long-term welfare. Insofar as this maxim violates duty and not just prudence, it is at least partly because not guarding one's welfare can lead one to other vices and thus away from a virtuous disposition. This reflects Kant's claim at 6:388 that one has an "indirect duty" to promote one's happiness as a safeguard against vice. But also, because prodigals slavishly subject themselves to the pursuit of immediate enjoyments, they lack the kind of self-mastery that is constitutive of a virtuous disposition; they lack, indeed oppose, some degree of inner freedom. The virtue of thrift, then, rests on adopting a maxim of economizing (unlike the prodigal) at least partly for the further end of enjoyment of life's pleasures (unlike the miser), where one's reason for doing so is that the moral law requires it as an element of self-mastery.

Finally, according to the third maxim, we *learn* which (direct) ethical duties there are and thus what one ought to do and how one ought to be based on a priori "rational knowledge" (DV 6:404). This maxim is opposed to any empirically grounded view where one only learns which duties and corresponding virtues there are by empirical means,

---

[1] Kant supposes that this view of the nature of virtue and vice has implications about *coming to have* a virtue, namely by either spending less if one inclines toward prodigality or spending more if one inclines in the other direction. The footnote makes clear that the real nature of Kant's concern is with what distinguishes virtue from vice and thus with the nature of these traits. Whether Kant is working with the most plausible version of the doctrine of the mean can be left open.

as one learns what does and does not contribute to one's happiness. Were it possible to learn them in this way it would entail that there are no a priori moral *laws*, and thus no metaphysical first principles of ethics.

Schema for duties of virtue

Section XI features a diagram that organizes the basic categories of duties of virtue according to distinctions Kant has drawn thus far: material/formal; internal/external; one's own end/the ends of others; and morality/legality. Quoting from the text, the categories are:

1. My *own end* that is also my duty
   (My own *perfection*)
2. *The end of another*, the promotion of which is also my duty
   (The happiness of others)
3. The *law* which is also the incentive
   On which the *morality* of every free determination of the will is based.
4. The *end* which is also the incentive
   On which the *legality* of every free determination of the will is based.

1 and 2 concern what is material in duties of virtue, while 3 and 4 concern what is formal.

1 and 3 concern internal duties of virtue; 2 and 4 external duties of virtue.

Worth noting here is the distinction between the *morality* in observing a duty of virtue and the *legality* of doing so. In acting on the end of promoting the happiness of others one complies with the moral law (whether one's motive is respect for the law or simply fellow feeling for others). When the law is also the incentive or motive for acting on a maxim of promoting the happiness of others, then one's action has moral worth. This is to emphasize and reinforce a theme from chapter 5, namely that complying with duties of virtue is possible without doing so from the sole motive of respect for the moral law. However, this is not to deny that the issue of motivation is paramount in Kant's doctrine of virtue.

Here it is worth remarking on a seeming puzzle about how one can be beneficent on some occasion from the motive of duty if the beneficent act in question is not one's duty. In general, how is it possible to comply with an imperfect duty from the motive of duty if particular actions in accord with them are not themselves duties? That I could donate money to a particular charitable organization on some occasion is not something I have a duty to do and I know that. So, how can such actions have moral worth? I believe the answer is that although I'm not required to donate to any particular charity nor do I have a duty to donate at any particular time, when I consider donating at this time to a particular charity, I conceive the action as a way of partially complying with imperfect duty and this is what motivates me to donate. This strikes me as a way of acting from duty and so I don't think there is a puzzle with these kinds of cases.

Division of the doctrine of virtue

We skip ahead in the text to the last two sections of the introduction. The first is entitled, "Preliminaries for the Division of the Doctrine of Virtue," while the second, a continuation of the first, has no title. These sections: (*i*) bring together and summarize the key elements that distinguish DV from DR, (*ii*) including an explanation of why the former, but not the latter includes a doctrine of methods, and in the final section, (*iii*) Kant explains the various ways in which ethics, as a science, is organized.

In XVII concerning concepts "preliminary to the division," Kant considers how the two parts of MM differ both formally and materially with respect to the types of obligation that differentiate the duties featured in the two parts. Kant also comments on the distinction between an *obligation of virtue* and a *duty of virtue*, familiar from Section IV of the general introduction to MM and discussed in chapter 5, sec. 5.

Abstracting, then, from material differences in contents of the two parts of MM, their formal differences concern: types of lawgiving and corresponding species of obligation, the proper "objects" of the two species, and the resulting type of duty. Taking these up in order:

- For duties of virtue no external lawgiving is possible; all lawgiving in ethics is *internal*. Juridical obligation corresponds to external lawgiving, ethical obligation corresponds to internal lawgiving.
- These two species of obligation differ in the type of response they require. While the doctrine of right obligates one to perform actions, the doctrine of virtue obligates one to adopt maxims (policies of action).
- Ethical duties[2] are of wide obligation unlike the narrow duties of DR.

Note the progression here. The most fundamental distinction between the two parts of MM, as Kant conceives them, is in terms of lawgiving. Because no external lawgiving is possible for duties of ethics, it must be that maxims (which do not allow of being coerced) are the objects of ethical obligation. And because maxims are the objects of ethical obligation, one's ethical duties must include those of wide obligation.

Turning from formal (structural) to material (content) differences between DR and DV, the field of ethics, unlike the field of juridical right, is primarily concerned with *ends*, the "matter" of choice. As we learned at the outset of DV's introduction, ethics is aptly characterized as a doctrine of ends. This explains why Kant identifies the "supreme principle" of the doctrine of virtue in terms of ends: "act according to a maxim of *ends* that it can be a universal law for everyone to have" (DV 6:395).

Concerning how the two parts of MM are related, Kant again stresses that it is important to distinguish the "*one* obligation of virtue" (DV 6:410) from the many duties of virtue. The former refers

---

[2] Here and in a few other places, 'ethical duty' seems to refer to duties of virtue. (See MM 6:234, DV 6:390, and 6:468). However, Kant's official characterization of ethical duties refers to the fact that all actions in conformity with duty must also be done *from duty*. This singular "obligation of virtue" (DV 6:410) pertains to both duties of right as well as duties of virtue.

to one's moral mission in life to comply with all duties—juridical and ethical—from the sole motive of duty, or respect for the moral law. This obligation, then, refers to Kant's conception of a virtuous disposition which, as explained earlier, is something singular. In this way, all juridical duties are "indirectly ethical" (MM 6:221). But while the concept of virtue (in the sense of being a virtuous person) is singular, there is a multiplicity of duties of virtue, namely, those featured in DV.

In addition to these formal and material ways of distinguishing DV from DR, the penultimate section also includes a "Remark" in which Kant explains why DR, but not DV, includes a doctrine of methods, which we will consider later in chapter 16.

With preliminaries out of the way, in the final section of the introduction, Kant explains two complementary ways in which a system of ethics as science is to be organized. According to the very concept of such a system, the main division is between an Ethical Doctrine of Elements and an Ethical Doctrine of Method. In the former, the task is to set forth and defend a system of ethics which includes the most fundamental ethical duties (its so-called Dogmatic part). Appended to many of these duties are various questions and remarks, mainly about hard cases that Kant leaves for the reader to ponder. This part is Casuistry. The casuistical remarks are not part of the science of ethics, rather, they raise issues about the interpretation and application of the system of duties when it comes to judging concrete cases. Method concerns matters of moral education and virtue acquisition— Catechizing and Ascetics, respectively. Because this manner of classification into Elements and Method has to do with the concept of a science, Kant refers to it as a "formal" organization.

The second principle of division concerns the subjects of ethical duties—human beings—and the "relation between the being bound by duty and the being that imposes duty" (DV 6:412). This manner of division takes into consideration the subjects of duty and thereby structures Dogmatics. Here, the main division is between duties that human beings have to human beings and duties they may or may not have to nonhuman beings. Regarding the former, Kant holds that there are duties to oneself and duties to other human beings. Regarding the latter, which concerns one's moral relations (whatever they might be)

to "subhuman" and "superhuman" beings—animals and God—Kant
argues later that humans have no duties to such beings.

In contrast to the division of MM according to the very form of
a moral science (its formal division), this second sort of division
concerns the "matter" of ethics—what, in general terms, the science
is about: human beings. Because it is about *human* (rational) beings,
ethics requires that considerations of human nature figure importantly
in deriving a system of ethical duties, as we shall see in the coming
chapters.

Let us now backtrack to Sections IX and X which I saved until now
because here Kant articulates and justifies the supreme principle of DV,
which provides the normative foundation of the system of duties of
virtue.

9.2 The supreme principle of the doctrine
of virtue

In Section IX, the supreme principle of DV is formulated thus: "Act according to a maxim of *ends* that it can be a universal law for everyone
to have." This principle is a version of the universal law formula tailored to a doctrine of ends. However, in commenting on this formula,
Kant relates it directly to the formula of humanity: "According to this
principle a human being is an end for himself as well as for others, and
it is not enough that he is not warranted to use either himself or others
merely as means (when he can still be indifferent to them), but it is
in itself a human being's duty to make the human being as such his
end" (DV 6:395). This comes close to how the formula of humanity is
expressed in the *Groundwork*: "*So act that you use humanity, in your
own person as well as in the person of any other, always at the same time
as an end, never merely as a means*" (G 4:429). How is the formula of
humanity related to the supreme principle of DV? For something to
be an end that it can be a universal law for everyone to have it must
be an end that is commanded by reason alone. Only such an end can
ground a categorical imperative and thus "be a universal law for everyone to have." Any other end would be a contingent, discretionary

end grounded in inclination that can vary from person to person and thus could only ground hypothetical imperatives. In the *Groundwork*, Kant argues that the only end that can ground categorical imperatives is humanity in the person—moral personality—which has the status of being an end-in-itself. It is humanity, understood as one's rational nature including one's moral predisposition to personality, that finds expression in the formula of humanity. More on this formula in the following chapter. In the meantime, let us consider the status and derivation of the supreme principle of DV.

Status

In Section X, Kant contrasts the status of the supreme principle of DV with the supreme principle of *The* Doctrine of Right. Both are a priori principles of practical reason. Kant has argued that the latter is an analytic truth—true in virtue of the concepts contained in the principle. The supreme principle of DV is said to be synthetic and a deduction for it is required. Without going into any detail, the reason why the former principle is analytic is that the concept of coercion, included in the principle, is implicitly contained in the concept of freedom. By contrast, the reason Kant gives for why the latter principle is synthetic is that the concept of an end which is also a duty is not contained in the very concept of freedom.

Deduction

Kant claims that the supreme principle of DV can't be proved, presumably because that would require deriving it from some more fundamental moral principle. But then it wouldn't be supreme. However, Kant offers the following "deduction" in the sense of a justification for accepting it (brackets inserted).

[1] What *can* be an end in the relation of human beings, to oneself and others, *is* an end for pure practical reason; for [2] it [pure

practical reason, M.T.] is a faculty of ends in general, and [3] for it to be indifferent with regard to them, i.e. to take no interest in them, is therefore a contradiction, [4] since then it would not determine the maxims for actions ([5] which always contain an end) either, and hence [6] it would not be practical reason. [7] But pure reason can command no ends a priori without at the same time announcing them as one's duty; and [8] this duty is then called a duty of virtue (DV 6:395).

The passage is complicated to say the least, involving multiple arguments. Claim 1 seems to be the main conclusion of the passage. However, it isn't clear how it is supported by other claims in the passage. Nor is it clear what it means.[3] Put it aside and consider claim 2 including the argument for it, which occupies center stage in the passage. Presumably, what it means to say pure practical reason is a faculty of ends is that it is a source of ends that does not rely on inclination—a pure source—and so a source of ends that can be universally commanded a priori; ends that are duties. If 2 can be established, then there is a reasonably clear path to the supreme principle of DV as follows.

1. There must be ends prescribed a priori by pure practical reason. [2]
2. Pure practical reason can prescribe no ends a priori without setting them forth as duties—duties of virtue. [7, 8]

Therefore,

3. There must be ends that are also duties; ends that one is obligated to adopt and act on (from 1 and 2).

---

[3] Much depends on what is meant by 'can.' Perhaps it has the sense of 'what is universally legislatable.' It would thus read: What, in the relation of a human being to himself and others, is universally legislatable as an end, is an end for pure practical reason. If this is a correct rendering, then I would read it as saying what it *is* to be an end for PPR is for it to be universally legislatable. It would thus entail step 5 of the argument in the subsequent text.

Therefore,

4. One is obligated to adopt and act on ends prescribed by pure practical reason (from 1–3).
5. If an end is prescribed by pure practical reason, then it must be an end for which there is a universal law commanding everyone to adopt it.

Therefore,

6. One is obligated to adopt and act on those ends it can be a universal law for everyone to have (supreme principle of DV).

If this reconstruction adequately captures Kant's thought, then the question is why there must be ends prescribed by *pure* practical reason; why accept 2? Presumably, the ends in question are, or at least include, the positive ends of self-perfection and the happiness of others. The argument for 2, expressed in 3–6, is a reductio ad absurdum to the effect that if pure practical reason is incapable of setting ends, then it could not determine maxims of action either. If it can't do that, then it isn't "practical reason." (Note that 'pure' in 6 is dropped. Was this intentional? Does it matter?) The gist of the reductio seems to be that unless pure practical reason is a source of positive ends, there really isn't such a thing as pure practical reason. But why not? Let's grant that humanity is an end of pure practical reason and can thus be a source of reasons to refrain from various actions. We now seem to encounter the same gap we discovered in the argument for obligatory ends featured in Section III. It could be that humanity as an end of pure practical reason only requires that we not treat ourselves and others merely as means. Granted, Kant claims that this negative constraint is "not enough" and that the supreme principle of DV requires that we "make the human being as such an end" (DV 6:395), presumably by adopting and acting on positive ends. But the argument under consideration was supposed to establish this claim, not presuppose it. Perhaps there is a rendering of the arguments in the quoted passage that saves Kant from this objection. If so, I'm not sure how it goes.

9.3 Concluding reflection

I conclude with some observations about Kant's grounding project. For this project to succeed, it is not enough to simply derive duties from some principle; the principle should also serve to help *explain why* certain actions are duties (or contrary to duty). A principle that serves merely as a test for whether an action is or is not contrary to duty need not also serve as an explanation of why the action has the deontic status it does. And this is how I view the formula of universal law. Intuitively, the fact that some maxim cannot be universalized might reliably indicate that acting on that maxim is contrary to one's duty, but to be a reliable test of permissibility it need not also serve to explain why an action on some maxim is wrong. The formula of humanity, it would seem, fills the role in Kant's ethics of an explanatory principle.[4] And indeed, as we are about to see in coming chapters, Kant mainly relies (sometimes implicitly) on the humanity formulation of the CI in deriving a system of duties.

I will leave readers with a looming worry about Kant's project, particularly as it related to grounding duties to oneself. There is a difference between deriving duties from a principle, on one hand, and the duties merely serving as an interpretation of that principle, on the other. A commonly raised misgiving about FH is that it is vague; that it does not itself possess enough content to serve as a basis for deriving conclusions about duties. To convey the worry, consider what James Griffin says about the concept of equal respect as it figures in moral theorizing:

> Every moral theory has the notion of equal respect at its heart: regarding each person as, in some sense on an equal footing with every other one. Different moral theories parlay this vague notion into different conceptions. Ideas such as the Ideal Observer, or the Ideal Contractor specify the notion a little further, but then they too are very vague and allow quite different moral theories to be got out of them. And the moral theories are not simply derivations from these

---

[4] I defend this at length in Timmons 2017a, chaps. 2–4.

vague notions, because the notions are too vague to allow anything as tight as derivation. (Griffin 1986, 208).

Arguably, the command to treat oneself and others never merely as a means but always as an end captures an idea of equal respect. So, considering Griffin's remarks about the concept of equal respect, one might worry that Kant's formula of humanity is too vague to be the basis of genuine derivations. That is, one might suspect that what is really going on in the Elements is that Kant's system of duties constitutes one possible *interpretation* of treating humanity always as an end, never merely as a means, but that there are other ways of interpreting the formula of humanity appealing to a somewhat different set of duties. This result would mean that Kant is not offering genuine derivations. I believe he is and the only way to address the worry is to examine the various derivations in the Elements to which we now turn.

Further reading

- On Kant's grounding project, see Smit and Timmons 2013 [2017a].
- On Kant's doctrine of virtue as normative ethical theory, see Hill 2006, 2010.

PART IV

THE DOCTRINE
OF ELEMENTS

10

Perfect Duties to Oneself as an Animal Being

Part I, Book I, Chapter I

The Doctrine of Elements represents Kant's normative ethical theory, comprising a system of midlevel duties to oneself (Part I) and to others (Part II) that can be derived from the categorical imperative. Part I is divided into: Book I, "Perfect duties to oneself" and Book 2, "On a human being's imperfect duties to oneself (with regard to his end)." Book I has two chapters, "The duty of the human being to himself, as an animal being," and "The duty of the human being to himself, merely as a moral being." Book II concerns imperfect duties to oneself. The Elements begins with an introduction followed by the treatment of various duties to oneself, spanning 22 subsections, each marked with '§' (a section symbol). This chapter will cover the introduction and perfect duties to oneself as an animal being. Chapters 11 and 12 are devoted respectively to perfect duties to oneself as a moral being only and imperfect duties to oneself.

The guiding questions addressed in this chapter are:

- Why must there be duties to oneself and how are they possible?
- Which principles organize duties to oneself?
- What are the duties to oneself as an animal being and how are they justified?
- What role does teleology play in justifying the duties to oneself?

After explaining Kant's answers to the first two questions, and before getting to the duties themselves, I have devoted a brief section (10.3) to explaining some of the themes in Kant's arguments that we encounter in his treatment of duties of virtue.

Kant's Doctrine of Virtue. Mark Timmons, Oxford University Press (2021). © Oxford University Press.
DOI: 10.1093/oso/9780190939229.003.0010

10.1 Duties to oneself *as such*

Kant begins (§1) with an apparent antinomy featuring, on one hand, an argument that the concept of a duty to oneself is incoherent that is opposed by, on the other hand, an argument that there must be such duties. A duty to oneself involves being both the one imposing the obligation and (at the same time) the one who is obligated. How can this be? After all, in cases of interpersonal obligation, one can be released, for instance, from an obligation to repay a loan by the other party simply forgiving the debt. It would then seem possible that for any alleged duty to oneself, one could (as the one imposing obligation) always release oneself from the obligation. However, duties in which one can release oneself *at will* violates the conceptual claim that duties involve an inescapable constraint. Thus, the very concept of a duty to oneself seems to be conceptually incoherent. And, of course, if this very concept is incoherent, there cannot be duties to oneself. Opposing this conclusion is the claim (§2) that if there are no duties to oneself there are no duties, period. Thus, if we assume there are duties (which is here not in doubt), then there must be duties to oneself. But why and how?

In answer to the 'why' question Kant writes: "For I can cognize myself as obligated to others only in so far as I at the same time obligate myself, since the law by force of which I regard myself obligated springs in all cases from my own practical reason, by which I am necessitated in that I am at the same time the one who necessitates with regard to myself" (DV 6:417–418). Kant adds a footnote pointing out that talk of "I owe it to myself" in the case of some duties is commonplace. Of course, he is correct about what is commonplace; nevertheless it is hard to follow Kant's reasoning here. Despite the wording, the point does not seem to be about a condition of *cognizing* that one is under an obligation,[1] rather the point is about a condition on there *being* duties to others, namely, that there must be duties to oneself.

---

[1] On this point, see Timmermann 2013.

One thought, suggested by the quote, is that having obligations (for Kant) requires autonomy and thus the ability to act based on the moral law whose source is practical reason (the legislative component of autonomy). The idea is that being obligated at all requires that one can constrain oneself to comply with the moral law. As we have seen, in the introduction to DV Kant does highlight the significance of self-constraint in connection with duties of virtue. Additionally, self-constraint is significant for all duties because even in cases in which one cannot be compelled by others to comply with a duty of right, one can still comply *from duty*; an act of self-constraint.

However, if this is the extent of Kant's reasoning, it is inadequate. From the claim that obligation requires being able to constrain oneself, it simply does not follow that one has any duties to oneself. Self-constraint is a necessary, but not sufficient, condition for having duties to oneself. Perhaps, then, something can be made of the idea that moral self-constraint sufficient to comply with any duty for the sake of duty requires cultivation of the sort of willpower needed to overcome contrary-to-duty inclinations. And perhaps based on the idea that one has such a duty to oneself—a duty of moral self-perfection—one can go on to defend more specific duties to oneself.[2] In any case, dialectically Kant does not need to argue for the strong claim that there can't be duties to others unless there are duties to oneself. Rather, all that is needed is an explanation of how duties to oneself are conceptually possible, followed by arguments for specific duties to oneself, bolstered by the commonplace thought that there are things I (morally) owe to myself. What, then, about the conceptual possibility of duties to oneself— the 'how possible' question?

In section 3, "Unlocking this apparent antinomy," and having sided with the claim that there are duties to oneself, Kant proceeds to explain how one can make sense of such duties by invoking his distinction between human beings as members of a sensible realm of nature (as *homo phenomena*) and as members of the intelligible realm of things in themselves (as *homo noumena*). Kant's claim is

[2] See Potter 2002 for defense of this strategy.

that as a member of the noumenal realm one has the power to impose obligations on oneself as a member of the phenomenal realm. That is, the obligating intelligible self is distinct from one's obligated phenomenal self; the former holding the latter to account. Now, this may be a way to make sense of such duties, but the invocation of the phenomenal/noumenal distinction seems unnecessary. After all, the law of autonomy—the moral law—determines the content of one's moral obligations. Moreover, the obligations imposed by the moral law are categorical and thus not hostage to one's inclinations, including any inclination to be free from such constraints. One simply does not have the power to unbind oneself from an obligation at will. Given this, there doesn't seem to be any conceptual difficulty in making sense of duties to oneself.[3]

10.2 On the division of duties to oneself

Section 4 of the introduction is entitled "On the principle of the division of duties to oneself." Here, Kant explains the basis for the various divisions within the Elements. Having a principled basis for division is important if a doctrine is to be a science because a science (as explained in chapter 3) must be an organized collection of principles and claims, not just some random aggregate. Accordingly, Kant explains two principles of organization regarding duties to oneself. The "objective division" focuses on the objects of obligation—the duties themselves. Some duties to oneself are negative duties of omission that have to do with *preserving* one's nature. Positive duties to oneself, by contrast, concern actively *perfecting* oneself. The "subjective division" concerns the self as the subject of such duties and concerns two perspectives one can take on human nature—as an animal being and as a moral being only. Because the substance of these divisions is developed in the Elements, efficiency favors moving ahead.

[3] See Timmermann 2006b for a more sympathetic reading of Kant's use of the *homo phenomena/homo noumena* distinction in this context.

10.3 Themes in Kant's treatment of duties
to oneself

As we shall see, Kant's handling of the various duties in the Elements is both complex and often confusing. Therefore, it will be helpful to sort out various themes and strands of thought in Kant's treatment of duties to oneself before turning to the text. These include: (*i*) the general idea of arguments for the inherent wrongness of certain types of action, (*ii*) the role of moral teleology in Kant's scheme of duties, to be distinguished from (*iii*) references to natural teleology, and finally, (*iv*) some fundamental theses concerning the concept of obligation that figure in Kant's arguments. Each requires brief comment.

Inherent wrongness

In his treatment of perfect duties to oneself, Kant appeals to the humanity formulation of the CI which, tailored to the type of duty in question, commands one to refrain from treating oneself merely as a means. Such treatment makes one unworthy of the "humanity in one's person." Kant argues that engaging in suicide and the other vices associated with negative duties to oneself expresses an attitude that is "degrading" or "debasing" of one's humanity, or in some cases a "defiling" of one's humanity, and in general "surrendering one's personality"—all for the sake of satisfying inclinations of self-love. Such degradation is inherently wrong because one inverts the proper order among reasons for action; subordinating reasons of morality—going forward call them "humanity-based" reasons—to reasons of self-love. In so acting, one manifests a kind of irrationality making one unworthy of one's humanity. This is the dominant mode of argument we find in the treatment of negative duties to oneself. With respect to the positive duties to oneself such as the duty of self-scrutiny (treated in chapter 12), failing to fulfill them is to fail to "harmonize" positively with one's humanity, thus failing to fully "live up to" one's humanity.

Such argumentation is based on the claim that moral (i.e. humanity-based) reasons are superior in their normative force compared to reasons of self-love. This reflects the now familiar categorical authority of morality. However, the fact that certain considerations such as the need for self-preservation constitute a humanity-based reason to avoid suicide, and not just a prudential reason grounded only in self-love, needs explanation. This brings Kant's moral teleology into focus, which was briefly mentioned in 7.2 in connection with the duty of self-perfection

Moral teleology

'Teleology' derives from the ancient Greek term 'τέλος' (or 'télos') that is translated as 'end' or 'purpose'. Intelligent agents including, of course, human beings, adopt ends or purposes that serve as part of a so-called rationalizing explanation of a series of actions performed *for the sake of* one or another end. One makes sense of various doings and activities by reference to ends they are supposed to serve. There are ends or purposes one in fact adopts and there are those that one ought to adopt, and among the latter are ends that are duties. As we have learned, the two most fundamental such ends are those of self-perfection and the happiness of others.

Focusing now on duties to oneself, there is a way of viewing Kant's arguments that relates them to the end of moral self-perfection. This end is fundamental from a teleological perspective in that it explains why certain reasons for action (or omission) are humanity-based reasons and thus serves to unify the other duties to oneself. As lately noted, Kant's mode of argument for the various duties to oneself is that certain actions and attitudes are inherently wrong because one subordinates moral, humanity-based reasons to reasons of self-love. However, one may ask what explains why the considerations that ground duties (e.g. that some action is or would be suicide) are *morally* relevant in the first place and not just a matter of self-love. I believe the answer comes from Kant's moral teleology. In brief, the idea is that the negative duties to oneself concern preserving one's animal and moral natures whose destruction or hindrance interferes with striving toward the end of moral self-perfection. The positive duties to oneself concern activities that are partly constitutive of moral self-perfection. What I'm saying is not explicit in Kant's text; however, recognizing this element helps make sense of an obvious teleological dimension in Kant's ethics. Moral teleology should be distinguished from natural teleology, which also plays a role in Kant's theory.

Natural teleology

This refers to the supposition that nonintelligent, naturally occurring things and, in particular, organic things (e.g. plants and animals) have purposes—purposes *intrinsic* to them. To get a handle on this, consider artifacts like cars. In their initial phase of production, cars are the result of a designer or team of them coming up with an engineering plan for a model—the design guiding the building of a particular car. According to the design, the various parts of the car including wheels, engine, engine parts, and so forth, are designed with the whole car in mind and are meant to work together to make the vehicle operational. To understand the parts of a car is to understand their function in relation to the whole car itself whose main purpose is transportation. In the case of such artifacts, the design and what it is designed for are *external* to the car itself, as plans in the minds of engineers. Partly for reasons of comparison and contrast, consider now organic things, such as an apple tree. To view the tree from the perspective of natural teleology is to view it and its parts as having purposes *internal* to the tree and its parts, that is, as part of its intrinsic nature, rather than being the product of an intelligent designer. The end or purpose of the tree itself is to become and then flourish as the kind of thing it is—an organic being with the powers to grow, reproduce, and in our example to produce a particular fruit. Viewed teleologically, its constituent parts (roots, trunk, and leaves) each have a particular purpose in contributing to the tree's life. The roots, for example, have the purpose of absorbing water and inorganic nutrients that help maintain the existence of the tree including its other parts. Viewed this way a tree is a self-organizing thing—organized according to purposes that serve the whole. Appealing to ends or purposes in explanation is to appeal to so-called *final causes* of things.

Natural teleology, associated with Aristotle, conflicts with the sort of mechanistic view associated with Newton according to which one explains natural phenomena solely in terms of efficient causality—what we ordinarily think of as cause and effect relations, as when one object hits another and causes the latter to move in a certain direction. Kant was a Newtonian who thus held that scientific explanations of natural phenomena can be given solely in terms of efficient causality. Yet he also thought that there is a place for teleological thinking and reasoning about the natural world. And although he denied that one is justified in attributing intrinsic purposes to organisms (or any naturally occurring phenomena as elements in the sensible realm), he thought that it is useful for scientific inquiry to view organisms *as if* they had intrinsic purposes in order to guide the search for mechanic explanations of them. (We need not get into further detail about this heuristic value of teleological thinking, which would take us to Kant's extensive treatment of teleology comprising Part II of the *Critique of the Power of Judgment*.)

Appeals to natural teleology play a role in Kant's ethics. In the introduction to duties to oneself (§4), Kant identifies basic "impulses" of the animal nature of human beings, which may be viewed teleologically as naturally directed toward the ends of: (1) self-preservation, (2) preservation of the species, and (3) preservation of one's capacity to enjoy life. The animal powers corresponding respectively to these natural ends are: the power of life itself, which in one place (DV 6:424) Kant refers to as "love for life," one's sexual power, and one's power of nourishment. Appealing to these natural ends, Kant argues that it is wrong to employ one's animal powers in ways that "go against" their natural ends. Appeal to natural teleology is most prominent in Kant's handling of the duty to oneself involving the use of one's sexual powers and in his treatment of lying (which goes against the natural end of communication). Exactly what role it plays will be explained when we take up specific duties.

Theses

Although Kant's conception of the categorical authority of morality has been covered in previous chapters, it will be convenient for what follows to remind ourselves of the key ideas.

Inescapability thesis: humanity-based reasons are always in principle applicable to one's choices, actions, and attitudes. There is no "moral free zone," so to speak, within which actions are immune from moral evaluation (although many of our morally indifferent actions, like which shoes to wear, will not involve such reasons.)

Supremacy thesis: humanity-based reasons that either require or at least favor certain responses in choice, action, and attitude enjoy normative supremacy over reasons based in self-love.

These two together reflect the categorical authority of morality.

Finally, as we learned from the general introduction to *The Metaphysics of Morals*, in cases where there are humanity-based (and thus moral) reasons for incompatible courses of action, Kant claims that "practical philosophy says, not that the stronger obligation takes precedence . . . , but that the stronger *ground of obligation* prevails" (MM 6:224). Here I understand talk of "grounds" of obligation as equivalent to humanity-based reasons. This idea of competing grounds is registered in the following:

Authorization requirement: A type of action that normally violates one or more duties can be morally justified (authorized), but only if there are humanity-based reasons favoring the action that are at least as strong (normatively) as whichever humanity-based reasons disfavor the action. Questions of authorization come up in Kant's handling of questions of casuistry.

Considering these themes and theses, let us turn to the duties to oneself as an animal being and Kant's arguments for them. For each of the duties, I have added a footnote that cross-references discussions of the duty in the Collins and Vigilantius lecture notes, where often one finds a more extensive treatment of them.

10.4 Perfect duties to oneself as an animal being

Kant begins with the remark that the first, "though not the foremost, duty of a human being to himself in his quality as an animal being" (DV

6:421), is to preserve oneself in one's animal nature. The overarching first duty is to refrain from willful "physical death," to be understood broadly to include all the vices covered in §§5–8. Total physical death results from suicide (self-disembodiment).[4] Partial physical death results from physical self-mutilation and from depriving oneself either totally or temporarily of the proper use of one's basic animal powers. Suicide, physical self-mutilation, sexual self-abuse, and drunkenness and gluttony are the chief vices in this category that violate one's dignity. We thus have negative duties of omission to refrain from such actions as well as to avoid falling prey to those vicious character traits associated with them. Kant provides a brief discussion of each duty (an "article") followed by "casuistical questions"—questions about hard cases and other matters of fine detail.

Article I: Of Self-Disembodiment

Kant makes clear that he is considering the question whether, apart from violation of any duties to others, intentionally killing oneself is wrong.[5] In the third paragraph, he mentions the "Stoic thought" that killing oneself is one's own prerogative; a position he opposes because of the Inescapability thesis. His anti-suicide argument comes in paragraph four and appeals to the humanity formulation of the CI. The paragraph begins with a sentence denying the Stoic view, and then continues:

> To annihilate the subject of morality in his own person is tantamount to erasing from the world, as far as is within his power, morality itself, in its existence, which is yet an end in itself; hence, disposing of oneself as a mere means to a discretionary end one has is degrading humanity in one's person (*homo noumenon*), whereas the human being (*homo phenomenon*) was nevertheless entrusted to it for preservation (DV 6:422–3).

---

[4] Presumably, this is the *foremost* duty to oneself as an animal being.
[5] See also Collins lecture notes 27:369–378 and Vigilantius 27:603–604, 92–3, and 627–630.

Kant refers to morality as an end in itself; something that one can "erase" in some limited way. The idea is that in committing suicide one is eliminating oneself (as an embodied person) and thus "rooting out" of earthly existence something which is capable of morality. As Kant remarks in the *Groundwork*, that alone which has dignity is "morality [i.e. virtue, M. T.] and humanity in so far as it is capable of morality [i.e. moral personality, M. T.]" (G 4:435). Thus, the moral relevance of suicide, viewed from the perspective of moral teleology, is that it destroys the capacity for being or becoming a virtuous person. Given that considerations of preserving one's own life are *morally* relevant, the wrongness of suicide consists in the subordination of humanity-based (moral) reasons for preserving life to whatever inclination would motivate suicide.

Here, then, are three observations about this argument. *First*, Kant argues that suicide *for discretionary ends* is wrong, not that suicide is necessarily always wrong. You may recall from chapter 6, contingent, discretionary ends are rationally optional and are contrasted with obligatory ends—ends that are also duties. Here, the Supremacy thesis is being brought to bear: humanity-based reasons, including the fact that self-preservation is necessary for striving for virtue, defeat (if not silence) reasons of self-love that may favor suicide.

Second, at the very end of the quote and earlier in paragraph 2, Kant refers to one's humanity being "entrusted" to oneself. This suggests a theological element to the argument: that God has entrusted preservation of one's life to human beings, and commands that we comply. However, Kant's moral theory is incompatible with divine command theory, and anyway in the lecture notes he is reported as emphatically denying that suicide is wrong because it violates a divine command.[6] In Collins we find this telling remark: "So the reason for regarding suicide and other transgressions of duty as abominable must be derived, not from the divine will, but from their inherently abominable nature" (27:343). Rather than appealing to a divine command, Kant invokes the

---

[6] Collins 27:375 and Vigilantius 27:603.

homo phenomenon/homo noumenon distinction, remarking that
the former is entrusted, or, in other words, required by the latter to
preserve one's life.[7]

Finally, one might wonder how it is that one treats oneself
merely as a means in committing suicide. It cannot be that one
does not have one's own consent in doing so; nonconsent would
seem to be a way of treating someone else merely as a means to
one's own ends. Rather, Kant appeals to considerations of honor,
specifically, that there are ways of behaving where in effect one
treats oneself in a way that "debases" one's humanity (more precisely, one's moral personality). And, as explained earlier, this
occurs whenever one intentionally subordinates moral reasons to
reasons of self-love; such intentional (and principled) subordination is Kant's conception of vice. Let us then understand the idea
of treating *oneself* merely as a means to the satisfaction of one or
another discretionary end as just this kind of subordination; this
being a wrong-making feature of an action. In so subordinating,
one violates the Supremacy thesis and is thus dishonoring one's
status as a being with dignity.

Kant concludes the article condemning self-mutilation for
purposes of, say, financial gain.[8] He calls such actions "partial
murder" of oneself. Of course, having a leg amputated to save one's
life is permissible since then one is acting to preserve one's existence
and thus one's humanity. Kant's point is that regardless of whether
one's reason for the amputation is one of self-love, one has a moral
reason—preserving one's humanity—that morally justifies this
choice. By the Authorization thesis, one is morally permitted, if not
required, to undergo a life-saving amputation. This same argument
does not apply to other cases; Kant mentions undergoing castration
to make a living as a singer.

---

[7] Kant does hold that moral laws can (and should be) conceived as commands of God,
but denies that the source and authority of moral laws is that they are commanded by
God. This particular theme comes up in the conclusion to DV and is further elaborated
in the *Religion*. See later, chap. 16, sec. 6.

[8] Kant would presumably be against selling bodily organs, as Robert Audi pointed
out to me.

Casuistical questions

That moral humanity-based reasons might justify sacrificing one's life, or taking one's life (suicide), or taking risks with one's life, is the topic of the various questions of casuistry appended to the main article. Here, again, the Authorization requirement is especially relevant.

Kant poses four examples of individuals who commit suicide or intend to if certain circumstances arise. First is the mythical case of Marcus Curtius, who sacrificed his life "to save [his] native country (DV 6:423);" an apparent act of heroism. Kant asks whether, despite the heroism, his act should be considered self-murder (suicide). If so, it raises questions about competing grounds of moral obligation. On one hand, the fact that an action is a case of suicide is a moral reason against it. On the other, that it is done for the good of one's country is a moral reason that perhaps justifies Curtius's action.[9] The other cases are similar in character. The philosopher Seneca chose to commit suicide rather than be unjustly executed by Nero. In the *Anthropology* (Anth 7:259), Kant explains that execution under the law is disgraceful to the one executed and that killing oneself in cases like Seneca's is choosing a death with honor over one that is both unjust and disgraceful. Arguably, the fact that killing oneself in such circumstances expresses honor for one's humanity justified Seneca's suicide.

Again, the case of the man who (having been bitten by a mad dog and feels the onset of his own madness) kills himself to prevent any harm to others involves two conflicting grounds of obligation. One ground is the duty of self-preservation, another is the duty to avoid injury to innocent others. Kant asks whether he did wrong. Notice that the cases cited here differ from the one about the ruler who carries with him a fast-acting poison in case he is captured by enemies. Here, there is the conditional intention to commit suicide, but also the ruler has an obligation to the people of his nation to do what he can to safeguard their lives. The final example concerns risk-taking. Given that there is a small chance that one might die from vaccination, is it permissible to

---

[9] Kant also mentions "intentional martyrdom" for the salvation of the human race—an apparent reference to Jesus Christ—and whether this case should be considered, along with the case of Curtius, "an act of heroism" (DV 6:423).

submit to it? All of these are hard cases because the characters are not acting for some discretionary reason of self-love, and so their actions are not obviously ruled out by Kant's anti-suicide argument.

Kant does not answer his questions about these hard cases. According to the Vigilantius lecture notes, Kant held that "imperfect duties always succumb to perfect ones, just as several imperfect duties outweigh a single one" (Vig 27:537). This doesn't tell us what happens when two grounds of perfect obligation conflict: the duty of self-preservation and the duty to refrain from bringing harm to innocent others (as in the case of the bitten man).[10] What makes sense to say about these and other hard cases is that the details of the particular circumstances matter and that one will have to rely on moral judgment in determining the right course of action where there are competing grounds of obligation.

The possibility that in some cases self-sacrifice and perhaps suicide can be morally authorized brings into relief the importance of distinguishing questions about moral relevance from questions about wrongness. Appealing to considerations of moral teleology, the fact that killing oneself would destroy the possibility of striving toward the fundamental end of moral self-perfection explains why it is morally relevant. Yet, if there can be authorized cases of suicide, then there must be something further that explains the wrongness in cases where suicide is wrong. That one subordinates morality to self-love and expresses this in an act of suicide is what makes that act inherently wrong and captures nicely the rationalist idea that wrong action is fundamentally irrational.

Article II: On defiling oneself by lust

Our animal impulse to preserve the species through sexual reproduction is the basis for Kant's views on sexual behavior.[11] In *The Doctrine*

[10] A duty to avoid harming innocent others is a duty of right that belongs to *The Doctrine of Right* and thus a perfect duty. In the Vigilantius notes, Kant is reported as claiming that in the case of the bitten man, suicide is wrong because one option is to have oneself tied up (or otherwise confined) to prevent harm to others. There is also mention that a remedy for such bites had been recently developed.

[11] See also Collins 27:384–392 and Vigilantius 27:637–642.

of Right, Kant considers the rights of spouses within a marriage. It is there that he discusses sexual intercourse. He argues that using another person's body for sexual gratification is, as such, to treat that person as "if it were a thing." "In this act, a human being makes himself into a thing, which conflicts with the right of humanity in his own person" (DR 6:278). Thus, each partner both treats the other as if she or he were a thing and allows the other to do the same. Kant goes on to argue (for reasons we won't get into) that only within a legal marriage between members of the opposite sex do the partners avoid treating each other *merely* as means while also allowing themselves to be so treated as a means of sexual gratification.

The article on defiling oneself by lust is, of course, about masturbation. Because using one's sexual organs in this way is inherently non-procreative, Kant classifies it as an "unnatural" use—a use not in accord with nature's supposed end. Here, then, is where the appeal to natural teleology is evident. However, Kant does not propose to rest his case on a claim about what is unnatural. After claiming that it is immediately obvious to everyone that this act is a violation of duty to oneself, Kant admits that "it is not so easy to conduct a rational proof of the inadmissibility of that unnatural, and even of merely unpurposive, use of one's sexual attributes. . . ." He continues: "the *ground of proof* lies in the fact that a human being gives up (throws away) his personality by using himself merely as a means to the satisfaction of animalist drives." (DV 6:425). If we again understand the idea of treating oneself merely as a means in terms of subordinating moral reasons to reasons of self-love, then the argument is that masturbation involves such subordination because in effect one "throws away" one's moral personality (one's predisposition to become virtuous).

But why suppose there is morally significant subordination here? After all, what is wrong with such "complete abandonment" on some occasion? One may completely abandon oneself to sensual pleasure in getting a massage but doing so is not throwing away one's personality. Here, it is worth noting that in the context of discussing the education of adolescents in his *Pedagogy*, Kant condemns masturbation as harmful to the exercise of one's body and mind, a belief typical of that time. More significantly, he remarks that the moral consequences are even worse in that "inclination rages *without arrest* because no real satisfaction takes place" (Ped 9:498, my emphasis). This remark suggests that from the perspective of moral teleology, masturbation is a morally relevant consideration, given that virtue requires the kind of self-mastery over one's inclinations that is incompatible with them "raging without arrest." Even if one finds Kant's argument against individual actions of masturbation quaint, he is on stronger ground if one considers self-abuse as habitual, a kind of sex addiction.

Finally, it is interesting that Kant compares masturbation with suicide and says that at least suicide takes courage and so the disposition to commit suicide allows "a place for respect for the humanity in one's own person" (DV 6:425). By contrast, masturbation as complete abandonment to animal impulse does not.

Casuistical questions

Kant begins by claiming that because the preservation of the species is an "end of Nature" in cohabitation, acting directly contrary to that end is morally impermissible. This presumably rules out certain "artificial" means of birth control. What is open to consideration is whether intercourse is permitted without regard for this natural end. So, for instance, is sex within marriage wrong in cases where partners know that pregnancy cannot result? What about instances where one of them (Kant says "she") has no desire for sexual intercourse? Should either of these be considered instances of acting from "unnatural lust"?[12]

Kant responds to these questions by asking whether, on the supposition that intercourse without taking procreation into account provides grounds (reasons) for concluding that it is impermissible, nevertheless nonprocreative sex is at least sometimes permissible. Here he mentions a "collision of . . . determining grounds" but does not explain what he has in mind. Perhaps the idea is that while there are grounds, even within marriage, to have sexual intercourse only when pregnancy is at least possible, there are even stronger grounds for permitting

---

[12] These questions are not about masturbation, although allowing oneself to be used by another person for sexual gratification is pertinent to duties to oneself (see the duty to avoid servility taken up in the following chapter).

nonprocreative sex in order to help prevent a greater violation such as adultery. The danger in such a moral permission is that it risks allowing "animal inclinations" to gain the upper hand over virtue and thus lead one down a path to the vice which Kant refers to as 'unchastity.' In putting this forth for readers to ponder, Kant asks whether it is not overly puritanical to limit sexual intercourse for this kind of moral reason.

In the final paragraph on casuistry, Kant distinguishes sexual inclination that is sometimes called 'love' from aesthetic pleasure, the love of delight in the perfection of another person, and the moral love of benevolence. He notes that sexual pleasure is of a unique sort which, when limited by moral concerns, can "enter into close union" with the moral love of beneficence between marriage partners. Perhaps the thought here is that within a marriage relationship mutual beneficence is or can be enhanced by sexual intercourse, thereby strengthening the bond of marriage.

Let us return to Kant's argument in the article and his remark that masturbation is a kind of "unnatural use" of one's sex organs. Could this be read as proposing an argument based on unnaturalness? There are good interpretive reasons for not attributing to Kant this kind of teleological argument, besides the fact that he says it is hard to "conduct a rational proof" that unnatural sex is wrong (which wouldn't be hard if one were to suppose that wrongness of the use of some organ followed immediately from its being unnatural). In any case, any such "unnaturalness" argument faces a dilemma. Either the unnatural use of this or that organ means, in effect, 'morally wrongful use of,' or it doesn't. If so, the argument is question-begging, if not, there is a gap in the argument. That is, from the fact that some natural organ evolved to serve the promotion of some end, it doesn't follow that using it for some other purpose is morally wrong. Natural teleology does not (and should not) play a crucial role in Kant's case against masturbation.[13]

---

[13] See Gregor 1963: chap. IX for a defense of this claim. She argues that Kant's appeal to teleology in his discussion of sexual self-abuse, and later, in his discussion of lying, serves merely as helpful exposition of the duty rather than as the basis for a derivation. See also Denis 1999 for a similar view about the role of teleology in Kant's argument here.

Article III: On stupefying oneself by excessive use of food or drink

The vices are gluttony and drunkenness.[14] The general virtue one displays in avoiding drunkenness and gluttony is *temperance*, the corresponding vice is *intemperance*. Kant condemns both as habitual vices (gluttony and alcoholism) but also as individual actions as this passage makes clear:

> In the state of drunkenness a human being is to be treated only like an animal, not as a human being; by overindulging in dishes and in such a condition he is, for a certain time, paralyzed for actions that require him to use his powers with agility and deliberation.—It is obvious that putting oneself in such a state is violating a duty to oneself (DV 6:427).

Kant also refers to these vices as "debasements" of one's humanity. Thus, even apart from any permanent harm to the ability to use one's powers "with agility and deliberation," drunkenness and gluttony express a certain attitude toward one's humanity by elevating one's animal drives for enjoyment over maintenance of one's capacities that contribute essentially to one's end-setting capacity. Again, any harm to one's well-being (or to others) that results does not explain the wrongness of these acts of intemperance or the wrongness of the associated vices. Rather, the wrongness consists in subordinating humanity-based reasons that favor preserving one's natural end-setting capacities to reasons of immediate enjoyment and thus to reasons of self-love. As with masturbation, what makes such vices (individual actions and associated character traits) morally relevant is how they are opposed to the kind of self-mastery partly constitutive of the end of virtue. In drinking or eating to excess, there are at least three ways to be intemperate. *First* are cases in which one resolves out of respect for the moral law to refrain from getting drunk and thus, so far as the virtue of temperance is concerned, one

---

[14] See also Collins 27:380–381 and Vigilantius 27:632–634.

has the right commitment. Nevertheless, under pressure from one's job, say, one suffers a lapse and drinks to excess. This is frailty—one of the propensities to evil discussed in chapter 8. *Second* are cases in which one has not resolved to refrain—not made it is policy grounded in morality—and so may or may not refrain, depending on how one feels on the occasion. This is different from a *third* case in which one recognizes the wrongness of one's action and not caring or even acting in defiance of morality. Speaking for Kant, this third case is fittingly characterized as a vicious action; one resolves not to comply with morality and thus manifests depravity in action. In the immediately preceding case, one only manifests a lack of resolve. This sort of person, even when they do refrain, does so likely for prudential reasons and thus their compliance manifests impurity. Finally, note that here again we find Kant commenting on the comparative wrongness of these vices.

> Gluttony is even lower than that animalistic entertainment of the senses [by alcohol or drugs], in that it merely engages sense as a passive property . . . and hence it approaches even more closely the brutish enjoyment of cattle. (DV 6:427)

Casuistical questions

Kant questions whether allowing "wine a use bordering on intoxication" is morally questionable since its moderate intake can stimulate social interaction. He thinks the use of opium and spirits merely for enjoyment "comes closer to baseness" (DV 6:428) than intoxication given their effects on users who become reticent and silent. Using them for medical purposes however is authorized, whose permissibility can be understood in terms of conflicting grounds of obligation: as medicines they can promote health which is a ground for using them, while the fact that they induce some form of incapacitation is a ground for refusing them. Kant also questions whether it is permissible to accept invitations to banquets, given that on one hand they promote the moral end of sociability, but on the other they are temptations to intemperance.

10.5 Concluding reflection

In contemporary normative moral theory, consequentialism is a type of theory according to which moral permissibility and impermissibility of actions can be fully explained by appeal to the level of intrinsic value (or disvalue) of the consequences associated with the action.[15] The theory of intrinsic value is thus explanatorily prior to the theory of right conduct. Kant defends a nonconsequentialist theory—often referred to as a kind of deontology. Put most generally, the idea is that the deontic status of actions (their legality in Kant's technical sense) depends on how they bear on respecting persons in the sense of complying with the moral law. Of course, their moral worth (morality) depends on whether one's compliance is motivated solely by respect for the moral law. And although in various places I have stressed the legality/morality distinction as applying to the duties of virtue, DV is fundamentally about moral character. As Kant remarks in the third *Critique*, "even if the deed is objectively lawful . . . it is not enough to do what is right, but it is also to be performed solely on the ground that it is right (CJ 5:327).

How then, if at all, do consequences figure in Kant's ethics? In at least three ways. *First*, maxims suitable for moral evaluation often include act descriptions that refer to consequences. Just as voluntarily moving my finger in flipping a light switch can be described as turning on the light (a consequence of my finger movement), an act of pulling a trigger on a rifle can be described as shooting someone. *Second*, in the case of some duties to oneself, Kant appeals to the consequences of, for example, gluttony and drunkenness as these states affect one's capacities as a functioning rational being. Still, it isn't the consequences that explain why such actions are wrong. In the Collins notes we find this remark about duties to oneself, "It is not, indeed, the consequences that are the *principium* of these duties, but rather their inner vileness; yet the consequences help, nonetheless, to provide a better insight into the *principium*" (Col 27:347).

---

[15] This formulation, referring to intrinsic value/disvalue of consequences "associated" with actions, is deliberately vague so that it covers both "direct" (act consequentialism) and "indirect" (rule, motive consequentialism) forms of this type of theory.

A *third* way in which consequences (results) are addressed by Kant concerns responsibility for them. Toward the end of Section III of the general introduction to MM, Kant briefly discusses questions of imputation. He writes: "The good results of a meritorious action, like the bad results of a wrongful action, can be imputed to the subject" (MM 6:228) as results for which one can be praised or blamed and perhaps punished. How exactly to determine which consequences are imputable is an issue we cannot pursue here.

Further reading

- On duties to oneself, see Timmermann 2006b and 2013.
- On Kant's duties to oneself as an animal being, see Timmons, 2013 [2017a].
- For discussion of responsibility for consequences in Kant, see Reath 1994b [2006].

11

Perfect Duties to Oneself Merely as a Moral Being

Part I, Book I, Chapter II

The duties in question—duties of omission—include duties to omit lying, miserliness, and false humility (servility). Earlier, in §4, Kant distinguished the negative duties to oneself from the positive ones according to differences in the object of these duties—the "objective division." Negative duties forbid one to act contrary to "the END of his nature" (DV 6:419), while the positive ones command pursuit of self-perfection. Here, reference to one's nature includes both animal nature and nature as a morally accountable being, that is, as a moral being only. The "subjective division," by contrast, concerns the subject of duty—the human being. Kant remarks that duties to oneself merely as a moral being "consists in what is *formal* in the agreement of the maxims of his will with the *dignity* of humanity in his person" (DV 6:420). He continues explaining that such duties involve "a prohibition against depriving oneself of the *prerogative* of a moral being, namely that of acting according to principles, i.e. of internal freedom, and against thereby making himself a plaything of mere inclinations, and thus a thing" (ibid.). Insofar as this remark distinguishes duties merely as a moral being from duties focused on one's animal nature, it may seem to fail. After all, violation of the duties qua animal being conflicts with one's inner freedom—being free from the force of inclinations. Indeed, as Kant comments in connection with unnatural lust, giving into it is tantamount to handing oneself over to animal inclination (DV 6:425).

Perhaps, then, in the cases of unnatural lust, suicide, drunkenness and gluttony, one abandons oneself to *animal* inclination, as opposed to other sorts of inclination, for instance, the drive of ambition or a sense of self-esteem, either of which might, for example, lead to one or

Kant's Doctrine of Virtue. Mark Timmons, Oxford University Press (2021). © Oxford University Press.
DOI: 10.1093/oso/9780190939229.003.0011

another of the vices under consideration. In any case, Kant concludes Section 4 remarking that "the virtue that is opposed to all of these vices [including the ones concerning animality, M. T.] could be called *love of honor*" (DV 6:420). We gain a better understanding of these remarks about the nature of this category of duty by examining the vices in question. As already noted, lying, miserliness, and servility comprise fundamental duties to oneself as a moral being, however, Kant's inclusion of them raises the following questions:

- Why is lying a violation of a duty *to oneself*?
- Why is there a *duty* to avoid miserliness, rather than its being merely imprudent?
- If false humility is a duty violation, what is the nature of true humility?

Note that Kant drops the use of "Article" he used previously in the headings for the duties to oneself as an animal being and uses roman numerals in the headings of this battery of duties.

11.1 Duties to oneself merely as a moral being

I. On lying

Lying is an "intentional untruth" where the speaker attempts to communicate to the listener what she believes to be false with the intention of getting the listener to believe what is being said.[1] Recall from chapter 5, sec. 5, that a single type of action can violate more than one kind of duty. Suppose someone lies about owning property which he then sells to an unwitting buyer who in turn ends up financially ruined when truth about the property's ownership eventually comes to light. The seller's lie is a violation of a duty of right, subject to state coercion. Because this kind of harmful lie is punishable by the state, it is referred

---

[1] Unfortunately, there is not much in Collins or Vigilantius about lying as a violation of duty to oneself. In Collins 27:444–450 there is an extended discussion of duties of truthfulness to others. See also Vigilantius 27:700–703.

to as lying "in the legal sense," and its wrongness concerns the setback to another's freedom rather than its just being a lie. By contrast, Kant is here concerned with lying "in the ethical sense of the term," which constitutes a violation of a human being's perfect duty to herself. That a lie harms others, whether intended or not, does not explain this violation. Nor is it explained by the fact that the liar does or may bring harm to himself by lying. Nor, finally, is lying justified (authorized) when it is told for some good purpose. Actual or intended consequences are irrelevant. Rather, lying as such is "violating the dignity of humanity in his own person" (DV 6:429) in virtue of the "mere form" of the maxim the liar acts upon. Because lying cannot be justified, one has an exceptionless perfect duty not to lie. It is furthermore the "greatest violation of a human being's duty to himself, considered merely as a moral being" (ibid.).

Kant distinguishes external lies told to others from internal lies involving self-deception. To explain the wrongness of both kinds, he offers the following argument:[2]

[1] Lying is throwing away and as it were annihilating one's dignity as a human being. [2] A human being who does not himself believe what he tells another (even if it were a merely idealized person) has even lower worth than if he were merely a thing; for another human being can still make use of a thing's property of being useful, because it is something actual and given. [3] But communication of one's thoughts to someone through words that yet (intentionally) contain that opposite of what the speaker thinks about the matter is an end directly opposed to the natural purposiveness of his capacity to communicate his thoughts, and [4] hence a renunciation of his personality. . . ." (DV 6:429)

Obviously, the weight of this argument is expressed in step 3 and relies on the assumption that communication through speech has a

---

[2] The argument might appear to only cover external lies. However, reference to a "merely idealized person," which alludes to the "inner judge" of one's conscience (to be treated more fully in the next chapter), suggests that Kant meant the argument to apply to both external and internal lies.

natural purpose—to accurately express one's thoughts on a topic—violation of which constitutes a "renunciation" of the speaker's personality (dignity of the humanity in one's person). However, as noted in connection with masturbation, arguments of this sort relying on *natural* teleology face a dilemma. Either the notion of natural purposiveness is morally loaded or not. If it is, talk of something's natural purposiveness is talk of an end or purpose for which that thing *ought* only to be used. Understood this way, the key premise in the argument simply assumes that lying is wrong and the argument is question-begging. If one does not assume that 'natural purposiveness' is morally loaded, so that it just refers to how things naturally evolve, then there is a gap in the argument: from the fact that some organ or capacity naturally evolved to serve some function, it doesn't follow that using that organ or capacity for some other purpose is wrong. Besides, why suppose that communication through speech only "naturally" serves one purpose? Survival is also served by sometimes communicating what one believes to be false.

By far the most significant aspect of Kant's discussion in this part of the text pertains to inner lies. In the third paragraph Kant first raises the worry that the very concept is contradictory, since lying requires both a liar and someone else who is lied to, a feature apparently lacking in so-called cases of lying to oneself. More generally, internal ("inner") lies raise the thorny issue of self-deception and how such a phenomenon is even conceivable. Kant then goes on in the fourth paragraph to invoke the *homo noumenon/homo phenomenon* distinction which, presumably, is meant to address the apparent contradictory nature of self-deception. His idea seems to be that inner lies involve (in effect) two persons: one's noumenal self which holds one's natural, phenomenal self to the moral obligation of truthfulness, grounded in "the inner end (of communication of thoughts)" (DV 6:430), and one's phenomenal self that attempts to hide something from the former.[3] Whether this only adds to the puzzlement over self-deception, we can leave to

---

[3] Mention of the "inner end" of communication apparently refers to the natural purpose of communication featured in Kant's argument lately quoted, so appeal here to the noumenal/phenomenal distinction does not add anything new to Kant's case against lying.

the side. More important for present concerns are Kant's examples of inner lies.

The first of them alludes to Pascal's wager—betting (when one lacks evidence for or against God's existence) that one does not lose much in proclaiming (to oneself) belief in God, and much to gain (eternal reward) if God exists, but much to lose (eternal damnation) if God exists and one does not believe in him. Kant takes believing (or professing belief) in God out of calculated self-interest to be a kind of inner lie. The person who makes this wager does not *actually* believe in God yet either succeeds in fooling himself that he really does, or says to himself that he does believe without taking care to really consider the matter of God's existence.[4] Kant is also critical of those who believe in God and flatter themselves that their reverence for his laws as such motivates them to comply when the only incentive they are aware of in themselves is fear of punishment. These examples are revealing because, even though not made explicit in Kant's discussion, they relate inner lies to the end of moral self-perfection by way of the duties of conscience and self-scrutiny. In so doing, these positive duties can be leveraged for the purpose of explaining why lying, as it affects oneself, is not just a matter of being imprudent, but morally wrong and deserves to be called the greatest violation to oneself. Let us see how.

As explained in chapter 7, the duty of self-perfection is to strive toward the ideal of maximizing one's inner freedom by gaining mastery over affects, inclinations, and especially passions. The positive duties of conscience and self-scrutiny, as I will argue in the next chapter, should be viewed as constitutive components of the duty of moral self-perfection. That is, because striving for virtue is always in progress, cultivating one's conscience as well as the ability to *honestly* scrutinize one's character are essential ingredients in one's ongoing strivings. To be ignorant of one's motives in complying with duty or, worse, to fool

---

[4] In his 1791 essay, "On the Miscarriage of All Philosophical Trials," Kant's concluding remarks about the moral significance of sincerity points to this second kind of insincerity in proclaiming belief in God. "[I]f someone says to himself . . . that *he believes*, without perhaps casting even a single glance into himself—whether he is in fact conscious of thus holding a truth or at least of holding it to some degree—then such a person *lies*" (MPT 8:268–269). Similarly, if someone says, or thinks to himself, that he believes in his moral uprightness without carefully considering the matter, then he is guilty of an inner lie.

oneself into thinking that one is complying from the motive of duty when one is really motivated by fear, undermines one's chances of becoming virtuous. Viewing the wrongness of inner lies in this way is another example of how the general end of moral self-perfection helps explain why lying is morally relevant and helps unify the more particular duties to oneself.

Finally, in his treatment of lying and truthfulness, Kant remarks that being truthful in one's declarations to others and oneself, in the sense of declaring only what one non-self-deceptively believes to be true (even if in fact one's belief is mistaken) is *honesty*. Truthfulness in promising is *probity*. Both are forms of *sincerity* which demands "*everything said be said with truthfulness*" (R 6:190n2). One might then suppose that insincerity is the vice corresponding to the virtue of sincerity. But Kant denies this. Rather, insincerity is (or need only be) "mere lack of *conscientiousness*—i.e. of *purity* in one's confessions before one's *inner* judge, who is thought of as another person . . ." (DV 6:430). In this same sentence, Kant mentions that this sort of flaw "is given the name of a weakness" (ibid.). So, both lack of purity and weakness are mentioned in connection with this form of self-regarding insincerity, which allude to two of the three propensities to evil considered in chapter 8, namely frailty and impurity. Regarding the case of impurity, someone who simply lacks a firm commitment to compare her conduct and character against the moral law, perhaps conforms her conduct to the demands of the moral law but is not particular about her motivation in so acting (a case of impurity). Indeed, we may suppose that her self-love strongly inclines her to want to feel good about her moral character and she lacks a commitment to moral self-scrutiny of the sort that might reveal lack of pure moral motivation. She is like the lover (of the sort Kant mentions) who only wishes to find good qualities in her lover which then renders his "obvious faults invisible" to her (DV 6:430).

Another possible manifestation of self-regarding insincerity results from the propensity to frailty. This person, unlike the one suffering from the propensity to impurity, has vowed to sincerely measure his conduct and character against the moral law, but (let us suppose) because of the threat of the psychic pain, simply fails to be scrupulous in his moral self-estimation. Perhaps he fits Kant's example of someone who, out of self-love, takes well-wishing for well-doing. This person is too weak to make himself do something good for someone and so at least temporarily fools himself into thinking that mere wishing for the good of others (a good heart) is all the moral law requires.

Kant does not identify by name a vice corresponding to the virtue of sincerity. However, although insincerity as mere lack of conscientiousness does not necessarily rise to the level of the vice, Kant warns that it "deserves the strongest censure" because "from such a rotten spot (falseness, which seems to be rooted in human nature)" DV 6:430–431) being untruthful with oneself spreads to one's relations with others in the telling of external lies. One might add that self-regarding insincerity also deserves the strongest censure because what starts out as mere lack of conscientiousness is likely to become a deeply embedded character trait thus manifesting a form of moral depravity by one becoming *in principle* opposed to always being sincere, in which case it has become a true vice directly opposed to sincerity.

Before turning to issues of casuistry, Kant adds a brief one-paragraph "Remark," as a kind of confirmation of his contention that lying is the greatest violation of one's duty to oneself merely as a moral being. He notes that the Bible cites lying as the "first crime, through which evil entered the world" (DV 6:431).

Casuistical questions

Kant considers cases in which one does not speak her mind out of politeness. I ask you how you like the cover of this book, and supposing that I chose it, you politely, but untruthfully, say, "It's nice." More serious are cases of being responsible for unforeseen consequences that are brought about by, or contribute to, someone committing a crime. Kant's example is the servant who, if asked, is instructed to deny that his employer is at home, and then lies to a guard sent to arrest the employer. This lie allows the employer to slip out and commit a serious crime. Is the servant partly morally accountable for the consequences of his lie? Kant here takes a stand, remarking that the servant shares blame for the consequences of his lie, which his conscience imputes to him.

II. On miserliness

This duty to oneself concerns the vice of restricting one's own use and enjoyment of the means to a good life so much that one's "true needs" go unsatisfied.[5] Kant calls it "scanty miserliness" that he contrasts with "avaricious miserliness" or prodigality where one squanders the means for good living. He notes that this latter type of miserliness, when it is a violation of the duty of beneficence, is not of concern here. Perhaps the thought is that an avaricious person not only lacks resources to help others but is likely to be a burden on others. In any case, the distinguishing feature of scanty miserliness is that the miser's end is only *possession* of the means for all sort of ends without "being willing to use any of them for oneself and thus depriving oneself" (DV 6:432) of life's enjoyments. Like the vices of intemperance, miserliness pertains to the end of enjoying life, though presumably, unlike drunkenness and gluttony, this vice is not conceptualized as a violation of one's brute animal nature. Rather, the miser is guilty of "slavish subjecting" (DV 6:434) himself to acquisition (typically of money) and so "looks upon the means given for the purpose [of enjoyment] as though *he* were himself a means in that regard" (Vig 27:659–660, my emphasis).

Besides condemning miserliness, Kant revisits the Aristotelian doctrine of mean, mostly repeating what he said in Section XIII of the introduction to DV, explaining why he rejects the view. On Kant's own view, virtues are fundamentally a matter of firm maxims and vices are psychologically embedded maxims that directly oppose duty. The virtue related to this duty of omission involves the maxim of good economy (management) of one's resources. Vices, as noted in chapter 8, are matters of principle. A miser acts on a maxim of acquiring the means to good living *"with no intention of enjoyment"* (DV 6:432). Failure to follow through on a maxim of good economy is mere lack of virtue.

---

[5] See Collins 27:399–405, "Of the mind's attachment to wealth, or avarice," and Vigilantius 27:659–662.

Casuistical questions

One might wonder whether prodigality and scanty miserliness are simply matters of imprudence, in which case, miserliness might be considered mistaken thrift rather than a vice. (This was the second question posed at the outset of this chapter.) However, as noted earlier, Kant insists that scanty miserliness "is not just thrift misunderstood, but rather slavishly subjecting oneself to the goods of fortune, not being their master, which is a violation of one's duty to oneself; it is opposed to *liberality* (*liberalitas moralis*) of one's way of thinking" (DV 6:434). The root moral objection, then, involves a principled opposition to self-mastery of the sort that is partly constitutive of virtue.

Miserliness as well as greed and stinginess are manifestations of the more general vice of *selfishness*. Good economy and generosity to others are instances of the more general virtue of *liberality* of mind, which, in this context apparently refers to reaching a state of inner freedom regarding possessions. Finally, Kant raises these (unanswered) questions: if the moral law of good economy is given to oneself by oneself, how can one not know how to apply it? For instance, "[o]ught I to cut back on my bread and butter or only on non-essential expenditure? In old age, or already in youth? Or: is thrift a virtue at all?" (DV 6:434). The worry here seems to be that not knowing how to apply a law because it does not give one precise directions perhaps suggests that thrift (good economy is not a virtue after all. This would call into question the soundness of Kant's derivation of the duty and associated virtue of good economy. But the worry is specious. Applying these midlevel duties (virtue rules) to cases is sometimes hostage to one's lack of empirical knowledge and thus questions of the sort just raised remain problematic. However, this fact about normal life does not disrupt Kant's a priori derivations of the various midlevel duties.

III. On servility

Kant begins by once again appealing to the *homo phenomenon/homo noumenon* distinction, this time relating it to the distinction between what has relative, extrinsic value and what has an absolute value or worth.[6] A thing's extrinsic value depends on how it can be used. It can thus be given an exchange price. Things that have a price are therefore fungible. As mere *homo phenomenon*—that is, as a being with certain natural capacities—a human being, too, is something fungible that can be given a price. However, as *homo noumenon*—as a *person*—a human being has dignity in virtue of their moral predisposition to good (moral personality/humanity). Dignity (an "absolute inner worth") demands respect that prohibits being treated merely as means to some end. Because every human being has this predisposition as part of her rational noumenal nature, and equally so, each person is deserving of a level of basic (recognition) respect or esteem.

The duty to oneself, then, is to cultivate and maintain a proper sense of moral self-esteem. This involves both proper recognition of one's standing as a person and a proper comparison of oneself with the moral law. Regarding the first, one's self-awareness as a being who is capable of the sort of internal legislation constitutive of autonomy naturally "compels" a sense of elevation "and the highest self-esteem, as a feeling of his inner worth" (DV 6:436) or dignity, which does or should instill in him self-respect. In the Collins notes, Kant refers to this kind of self-regard as "true noble pride," which puts everyone on an equal footing, thus grounding the requirement of mutual recognition respect. To genuinely regard oneself as not equal to others, and to regard oneself as lower than others, in this way is the vice of servility. Of course, one might feign inferiority by, for instance, "disparaging one's own moral worth (hypocrisy and flattery) merely as a means to acquiring the favor of another . . ."—a case of false humility "(obtained by lying), and as a degradation of one's personality is contrary to one's duty to oneself" (DV 6:435–436).

The other face of proper self-esteem involves comparison of oneself (deeds and character) against the standards set by the moral law. This can only result from a sincere and impartial comparison of oneself with the requirements of the moral law—this sort of comparison constituting the duty of self-scrutiny is addressed in the following chapter. Because any such comparison reveals how far one is from fully

---

[6] See Collins 27:348–351, "Of proper self-esteem," and Vigilantius 27:664–667.

meeting these requirements, one's response should be one of *true humility* vis-à-vis the moral law. *False moral pride* (a kind of arrogance or moral self-conceit) results from an overinflated sense of how one fares in complying with all of one's duties and doing so from the pure motive of duty (respect for the law). True noble pride together with true humility, then, compose the virtue of proper self-esteem.[7] Servility and false moral pride are the corresponding vices.

Before moving ahead, it is worth noting that in the final paragraph of this Section, Kant repeats a claim from his discussion of respect for oneself (self-esteem) in Section XII in the introduction to DV. There, he argues that there is *no* duty of self-esteem because having a predisposition to have this feeling is a presupposition of duty. Here, he writes (as already noted) that one is compelled to experience a sense of "*elevation* and the highest self-esteem, as a feeling of his inner moral worth" (DV 6:436) from the fact that one is capable of internal legislation. How, then, can there be a duty of self-esteem? Well, the duty is not to have or acquire the presupposition in question nor is it to have the feeling on some occasion for reasons explained in XII. Rather, the duty is to act only in those ways that avoid the vice of servility, which is what §11 is mainly about. What are some of these ways?

In §12, Kant answers this question. For instance, allowing others to "tread with impunity" on one's rights, accepting unnecessary favors, complaining and whining, prostrating oneself on the ground even to show one's veneration of "heavenly objects"—all such actions are "unworthy" of a being with dignity; they are ways of dishonoring oneself. As a negative duty, then, the duty of self-esteem is the duty to avoid such ways of behaving.

Casuistical questions

In his discussion of true humility, Kant denies that one has a duty to compare oneself to others and that striving to equal or best others as a means of somehow gaining an "inner greater worth is *arrogance*" (DV

---

[7] That proper self-esteem has this dual nature is especially clear in the Collins passages mentioned in the previous footnote.

6:435), contrary to one's duty of modesty (treated in chapter 14). As we have learned, true humility results from an honest moral self-appraisal against the demands of the moral law, rather than basing it on a comparison of oneself to others. Here, Kant worries whether the kind of moral self-esteem—one's *"elevation of mind"* (DV 6:437) productive of true noble pride that results from one's recognition of one's own dignity—might be "too closely akin to *self-conceit (arrogantia)*" (ibid.); an attitude opposed to true humility. In other words, the worry is about simultaneously maintaining both true noble pride and true humility. Perhaps, then, the remedy after all is to cultivate or perhaps safeguard one's humility by engaging in self-other comparisons. How would this work? Kant does not say, but the idea seems to be that by outwardly humbling oneself in the presence of others one will reinforce one's sense of the true humility, warding off the kind of self-conceit damaging to true humility. The obvious rebuttal to this ploy, according to Kant, is that the kind of "self-abnegation" expressed in overt acts of humility in the company of others would likely result in their disdain, thus harming one's self-esteem. In other words, this ploy is likely to backfire.

Kant concludes his discussion of casuistry by wondering whether the kind of preferential tributes of respect toward others (who have no civil authority), beyond mere courtesy, is not a sign that there is a widespread tendency toward servility.

11.2 Concluding reflection

Kant's ethics is sometimes accused of "rigorism": the idea that certain duties Kant identifies—the perfect duties of omission—allow for no exceptions. This interpretation is encouraged by an essay, "On a Supposed Right to Lie for Benevolent Purposes," where he argues that one never has a right to lie, even if one's aim is to save an innocent person from likely being murdered. This essay was a response to French politician Benjamin Constant's 1797 essay, "On Political Reactions," in which Constant argues that one's duty to be truthful in one's declarations to others only applies where one's audience has a right to the truth. Murderers asking the whereabouts of an intended victim do not have a right to be told the truth, thus lying is not always wrong, contrary to Kant. In Kant's reply to Constant he explains that he is only considering whether one ever has a *juridical right* to lie, adding a footnote saying that he is not officially claiming that untruthfulness is a violation of a duty to oneself. Nevertheless, it is hard to deny from what we read in DV and elsewhere that Kant thought lying is always a violation of duty to oneself and thus morally wrong.

Some sympathetic scholars argue that Kant fails to demonstrate that lying must always be wrong based on the CI. Furthermore, we have already seen that when it comes to suicide Kant does not argue that killing oneself is always wrong, no matter what. Rather, he argues that suicide for reasons of self-love is always wrong. As his examples in the section on casuistry make clear, he officially leaves open whether killing oneself for moral reasons is permissible. In the case of lying to a murderer, the reason for telling a lie is to save an innocent life. And so, one might plausibly argue that if moral reasons can justify suicide, they can justify some lies. I am sympathetic to this line of thought but will not defend it here.

Further reading

- See Bacin 2013 for an overview and interpretation of Kant's duties to oneself as a moral being only.
- Denis 2010b is an illuminating overview of the somewhat distinct accounts of duties to oneself to be found in the Collins and Vigilantius lecture notes and DV revealing a unique relationship with freedom.
- Kant's perfect duty that prohibits lying to others is treated in some detail in Mahon 2006.
- On servility from a Kantian perspective, see Hill 1973 [1991].
- On Kant's rigorism with focus on the case of lying, see Hill 1992 [2000], Korsgaard 1986 [1996].

12

Imperfect Duties to Oneself

Book I, Chapter II continued, and Book II

After addressing the vices of lying, avarice, and servility, Chapter II on perfect duties to oneself merely as a moral being continues with discussion of the related duties of conscience and moral self-scrutiny, followed by an "episodic section" that discusses the range of beings to whom one can be morally obligated. Finally, Part II, which completes the coverage of duties to oneself, addresses imperfect duties to oneself—the positive duties of natural and moral self-perfection. The duties of conscience and self-scrutiny are included in Part I on the perfect duties to oneself. However, they are naturally discussed along with the imperfect duties of self-perfection because, besides being positive, together they provide the "cognitive basis" for achieving (or at least approximating) the end of moral self-perfection.[1]

12.1 The duties of conscience and self-scrutiny

Section I: On the Human Being's Duty to Himself as His Own Innate Judge

As we learned in chapter 8, sec. 2, in the introduction to DV Kant introduces several natural predispositions pertaining to one's sensible nature without which one would not be conscious of duty.[2] One of

---

[1] Somewhat oddly, the text identifies "The Human Being's Duty to Himself Merely as a Moral Being," §§9–12, which we just covered in chapter 10 as "Chapter II." But "Chapter II" also appears at the start of the discussion of the duties of conscience and self-scrutiny. It would have been less odd for the second use to have been, "Chapter II continued."

[2] In Collins, see 27:351–376 and in Vigilantius 27:575–576, 613–620. See also *Religion* 6:185–190, where Kant stresses the importance of exercising due care in appraising one's deeds in the "internal court" of conscience. Due care, then, is a second-order duty—a

---

Kant's Doctrine of Virtue. Mark Timmons, Oxford University Press (2021). © Oxford University Press.
DOI: 10.1093/oso/9780190939229.003.0012

these is conscience. Therefore, one has no obligation to acquire one, only to cultivate it. In §13, Kant describes conscience in some detail and together with remarks from the introduction and help from the lecture notes, we can address these questions, which we proceed to take up in order:

- What is conscience—its nature and roles in moral life?
- How is conscience experienced?
- Can it be mistaken?
- What are the duties of conscience and how are they justified?
- What is the connection between conscience and blameworthiness?

Regarding its *nature* and *roles*, in the introduction to DV, Kant describes conscience as "practical reason as it confronts the human being in every case of a law with his duty for acquittal or condemnation" (DV 6:400). As we learned in chapter 8, the role of conscience is not to provide a standard that determines which duties there are— that's the job of the moral law. Conscience, rather, acts as an internal judge—judging whether a deed of one's own, as one conceives it, complies with the moral law. It is through conscience that one holds oneself morally accountable. An act of conscience is meant to "affect moral feeling by its act" (DV 6:400) prompting behavior that contributes to one's moral self-improvement. Conscience may judge a prospective action one is contemplating ("warning conscience"), though perhaps more commonly it judges past actions ("retrospective conscience"). The engagement of conscience can be deliberate, as when one consciously deliberates about the morality of something one has done or is considering doing. However, one can be "hit" with spontaneous pangs of conscience over some past deed by, say, being confronted with damning evidence of a past wrongful deed.[3] From Kant's description of conscience, he is mainly focused on the

duty to ensure that one carefully consider the morality of one's deeds. On this point, see Hill 1998 [2002] and Herman 2019.

[3] As in the case of Tony Webster from Julian Barnes' novel *The Sense of an Ending*, who, being confronted with incontrovertible evidence of a grievous long-past wrongdoing of his, is immediately gripped by unrelenting remorse.

deliberate engagement of conscience focused on past actions whose act of judgment either acquits or condemns. Let us stick to this sort of case.

One's *experience* of conscience (our second question) is as of "an *internal court* in the human being ('before which his thoughts the meanwhile accuse or excuse one another')" (DV 6:438). This court, played out in one's head, includes oneself as a defendant as well as an accuser, a defender, and a judge. Of course, all these characters are aspects of the same human being—aspect of one's psyche. The way to make sense of this, according to Kant, is to conceive of there being two persons—the one being accused and the other being the judge. This may be done by conceiving the latter as an idealized person (God) or as an actual person. Conceived in the former way, Kant explains, does not entitle one to assume that this idealized person exists. Rather, one thinks of being accountable to a "scrutinizer of hearts," who is "distinct from ourselves and yet intimately present for us" (DV 6:440). As Kant puts this:

> [One thinks] of a "twofold personality" . . . a double self, that on the one hand must stand trembling at the bar of a court that is yet entrusted to him, but on the other holds in its hands the office of the judge by innate authority. (DV 6:439n)

To make sense of a doubled self, Kant once again invokes the distinction between oneself as a member of the intelligible realm (and thus as *homo noumenon*) in the role of prosecutor and judge as distinct from oneself as a member of the sensible realm (and thus as *homo phenomenon*) in the role of the accused.

Our third question is about conscience and error, which takes us back to remarks from the introduction. Here we must proceed with caution. Kant claims that "an *erring* conscience is an absurdity." He goes on to write:

> For at times one can indeed be mistaken in one's objective judgement as to whether something is one's duty or not; but judging subjectively, I cannot be mistaken as to whether I have compared it to my practical reason (here in its role as judge) for the sake of that judgement,

for then I would not have made a practical judgement at all, in which case there would be neither truth nor error. (DV 6:401)

I have been referring vaguely to the "engagement" of conscience as an activity one can deliberately undertake in order now to distinguish *inputs* into the activity of engaging conscience from the more narrowly conceived *acts* of conscience itself. This distinction will help us understand in what sense error can and cannot enter in engagements of conscience.

Errors associated with engagements of conscience are of two types, which Kant identifies in the lecture notes as errors of fact and errors of morality. Errors of fact occur when, for example, one mischaracterizes the nature of one's deed by failing to recognize a morally relevant detail. Suppose, for instance, that I am ruminating over my interactions with my students in a class I've just finished teaching. Suppose I saw someone in the class frown as I was answering another student's question. It now occurs to me that perhaps there was something wrong with my interaction. Suppose further that upon thinking over this interaction, I fail to recognize that my *manner* was condescending, and so there really was something morally amiss in how I conducted myself. Perhaps I misremember the interaction, or perhaps (worse) I have a blind spot when it comes to correctly discerning such information about myself. If I make this kind of factual error, then even if I correctly believe that it is wrong to be condescending toward others, I fail to bring my action under a moral law that pertains to this case. This mistake further leads to an act of conscience in which I acquit myself of wrongdoing, and so my act of judgment is objectively mistaken. However, Kant would not describe this as an error whose source is conscience; rather it is one of memory or perhaps understanding in describing one's action.

Errors of morality occur when one has false moral beliefs, including ones about one's moral accountability. In one place in the lecture notes, we find the remark that "In regard to his natural obligations, nobody can be in error; for the natural moral laws cannot be unknown to anyone, in that they lie in reason for all" (Col 27:255). However, even if this is true of normally functioning adults regarding basic moral laws, there can be errors in moral judgment in cases where there are competing grounds of obligation. In such "hard" cases of the sort featured in the casuistical questions (and assuming there is a fact of the matter about which ground is strongest) one can be mistaken about whether, for example, donating to a charity in lieu of repaying a debt on time is morally permissible. Again, Kant considers such moral errors to be errors of the understanding. In the *Religion*, for instance, Kant writes, "[n]ow it is understanding, not conscience, which judges whether an action is in general right or wrong" (6:186).[4] So, errors of fact and of morality are not attributable to conscience. The implication is that factual beliefs about one's actions (and circumstances) as well as moral beliefs about what morality requires are inputs into acts of conscience. Errors of both sort may be either culpable or nonculpable.

So, what, then, does conscience refer to and why can't it be in error? Considering (again, just for simplicity) engagements of retrospective conscience, we have already noted that conscience serves as an internal judge either acquitting or condemning some past action. However, engagements of deliberative conscience need to be carried out with due care—conscientiously. If I raise a question about the morality of some past action, but hastily and without due care conclude I did nothing wrong, either I did not really engage my conscience at all, or if I did, I did not engage it properly. I am at fault in either case. Thus, engaging conscience to its fullest extent involves at least the following steps[5]:

1. Carefully considering the nature of one's actions for purposes of moral evaluation.
2. Recalling any relevant moral laws that may apply.
3. Determining whether the action falls under any of the moral laws brought to mind.
4. For cases in which there are competing grounds of obligation (and thus multiple moral laws that seem to apply), judging which

---

[4] Understanding judges *in general*—at the level of basic moral rules which kinds of action are right or wrong. However, Kant also claims that it is reason (and not conscience) that judges whether "actions as cases . . . stand under the law" (R 6:186). This latter claim perhaps is meant to include hard cases in which one needs to bring one's action under that moral law that in fact grounds an obligation.

[5] There are additional elements of a well-functioning conscience, such as sincerity, that are taken up under the companion duty of self-scrutiny.

grounds are strongest and thus which moral law does in fact apply to the action under consideration.
5. Judging whether one has violated the relevant law, and thereby
6. Either acquitting oneself from wrongdoing or condemning oneself for wrongdoing.

Because acquittal signifies that one is not deserving of punishment while condemnation signifies the opposite,

7. This judgment may then trigger (respectively) either feelings of relief, or feelings of guilt or remorse (directed at the deed) and/or feelings of shame (directed toward one's character).

The feelings of guilt and shame can subsequently figure in helping one to avoid similar actions in the future. In this way, acts of conscience contribute to one's moral self-improvement.

It seems to be Kant's view (going back to the indented quote earlier) that one cannot be mistaken about having gone through this process as one engages in it. Consider steps 5, 6, and 7, which are constitutive of *acts* of conscience and seem to be the focus of Kant's claim about the absurdity of an erring conscience. At least at the time of reaching a judgment about the morality of one's action (and either acquitting or condemning), one apparently cannot be mistaken with respect to: (*i*) whether one is genuinely engaged in the activity of judging the rightness or wrongness of the action under consideration, (*ii*) for the self-conscious *purpose* of reaching a moral verdict, and (*iii*) whether and how one's conscience judges the matter. This seems to be what he means when he writes "I cannot be mistaken as to whether I have compared it [the action, M.T.] to my practical reason (here in its role as judge) for the sake of that judgment, for then I would not have made a practical judgment at all, in which case there would be neither truth nor error" (DV 6:401). Of course, even if true, it is unexceptional. Consider a seemingly analogous but nonmoral case. While I am consciously engaged in the activity of adding a column of numbers in my head with the aim of reaching a correct sum, I presumably can't be mistaken about what I think I'm doing (adding), or about what I take to be my purpose (to determine a correct sum), or about the sum I in fact reach (whether or not it is objectively correct). If the two cases are relevantly similar with respect to the issue of error, then the assumption seems to be that error is ruled out because one can be infallibly aware of such mental activities in question as one is consciously engaged in them.

Still, it is worth asking whether one really can be mistaken about whether one is engaged in an exercise of conscience, where the question concerns what is psychologically possible. The lecture notes suggest that one can be mistaken about this. Kant remarks that sometimes people confuse considerations of prudence with those of conscience. The former is "an analogue" of the latter, but entirely distinct from it. For instance:

> Many people have an analogue of conscience, which they take to be conscience itself, and the repentance often displayed on a sick-bed is not remorse for their behavior in regard to morality, but because they have acted so imprudently that, now that they are to appear before the judge, they will not be able to stand upright. (Col 27:352)

This passage says one can be mistaken about whether one is consulting conscience; that false belief about what one is doing is psychologically possible. Presumably, such issues will turn on questions about the reliability of introspection, at least with respect to cognition of one's occurrent, conscious mental states.[6]

Our fourth question is: What are the duties of conscience and how are they justified? Oddly, although the title of Section 13 mentions the duty to be one's own innate judge, there is no mention in its eight paragraphs of what this duty is. Here, again, we need to consult the remarks on conscience from the introduction, where Kant writes that the duty "is only to cultivate one's conscience, to sharpen one's

---

[6] Kant does express some reservations about the reliability of introspection. See, e.g. Anth 7:143; MFNS 4:471. One possible reply open to Kant is that whenever conscience (not prudence) condemns, one feels guilt or shame, which has a different phenomenal quality than merely feeling foolish at having been imprudent, so that the judgment of conscience in condemning is unmistakable. See CprR 5:37 on the phenomenal difference in reactions to one's losing at play (chagrin) compared to cheating at play (self-contempt).

attentiveness to the voice of the inner judge and to employ every means (hence the duty is only indirect) to make sure he is properly heard" (DV 6:401). The duty is *only* to cultivate, since all morally account-able human beings by nature have a conscience. Moreover, the duty is multifaceted, involving: (*i*) the duty to repeatedly consult one's con-science, (*ii*) the duty of due diligence in its exercise, and (*iii*) the duty to heed its verdicts. Complying with all three figure in the virtue of *conscientiousness*. The first duty is suggested in the Vigilantius lecture notes where it is recommended that to become a conscientious person "a repeated *awakening* of conscience is needed, i.e., the frequent ev-ocation of the consciousness of his deeds" (27:617). Complying with this duty requires, then, "using every means to make sure he is prop-erly heard" (DV 6:401) Proper choice of means is a matter assigned to "ethical ascetics," that part of the Method devoted to practicing virtue. The duty of due diligence involves being scrupulous in determining the morally relevant features of one's actions for purposes of accurately assessing them by the moral law.[7] The duty to heed one's conscience involves sharpening "one's attentiveness to the voice of the inner judge" (ibid.), taking its verdict to be authoritative in determining what to do going forward.

From all this, it follows that the vice associated with the virtue of conscientiousness—*unconscientiousness*—can be manifested in var-ious ways, given the plurality of duties of conscience. Principled op-position to the demands of engaging conscience and to heeding its verdicts are manifestations of the vice of *unconscientiousness*. There is room for mere lack of conscientiousness, because despite one's re-solve to be conscientious, one might suffer occasional weakness of will. Perhaps to recall some past event is so painful that it is buried deep in one's subconscious and one cannot (without therapeutic help) bring it to memory.

Turning for a moment to the justification of these duties, Kant does not offer a direct argument for them as he does for some of the other duties (e.g. suicide, lying). He thought that conscientiousness and its

---

[7] In various places Kant insists the one must be "subjectively certain" of the nature of one's actions in exercising conscience. See Vig 27:616, Rel 6:185–186, MPT 8:268, and NF 18:179–180.

companion, self-scrutiny, are crucial elements of striving to acquire an overall virtuous disposition. Thus, justification of the duties of conscience is (or can be) grounded in how they contribute to the highest moral end of moral self-perfection—their justification thus appeals to Kant's normative moral teleology. That cultivation of conscience and self-scrutiny is (or can be) justified in this contributory way is perhaps why, in the introduction to DV, Kant classifies it as an indirect duty—a duty in the service of the direct duty of moral self-perfection.[8] However, if the particular ethical virtues are the "matter" of an overall virtuous disposition, then conscientiousness and self-scrutiny are partly constitutive of such a disposition. Thus, complying with these companion duties both contribute causally to the acquisition of a virtuous disposition and as virtues are partly constitutive of it.

Our fifth and final question is about conscience and blameworthiness. Here, let us focus on matters of due diligence (although failure to either consult or follow the verdicts of conscience is typically blameworthy). Because conscience is not infallible in the verdicts it reaches about the objective rightness or wrongness of one's actions, it can at best serve as a reliable guide to what is objectively right or wrong. Kant claims that "if someone is conscious of having acted in accordance with his conscience, then nothing more can be required of him as far as guilt or innocence is concerned" (DV 6:401). However, there is a difference between diligently and with due care consulting one's conscience, and not consulting it in these ways. Thus, besides errors of fact and errors of moral principle, one might fail to consult conscience in a conscientious way. That is, even if one can't be mistaken about having consciously considered whether some deed is morally permitted and whether one has rendered a verdict, one might do so in a careless manner due to lack of sincerity and impartiality in judging one's deeds. In such cases, it would seem that contrary to Kant's proclamation, there can be cases in which consulting conscience and judging that one's deed was not wrong is nevertheless blameworthy even though this would not make the deed itself blameworthy. Such cases highlight

---

[8] A duty to care for one's own happiness is also an indirect duty as we've seen, as is the duty of sympathetic participation featured in duties of love toward others to be taken up in the next chapter.

192 THE DOCTRINE OF ELEMENTS

the need for impartiality and sincerity in consulting one's conscience which in turn concerns additional matters relating to the cultivation of conscience—the subject of the following duty of self-scrutiny.

Section II: On the first command of all duties to oneself

If one's chief moral vocation is to strive for moral self-perfection—perfection in complying with the requirements of duty and perfection in the aligning of one's motivation with duty—then what one must do first is engage in a regimen of moral self-scrutiny.[9] This sort of moral cognition of oneself, if it is to be accurate, requires both impartiality in comparing oneself with the moral law and sincerity in appraising one's moral character. The reason why the duty of self-scrutiny represents the "first command" of all positive duties to oneself is that only by first acknowledging one's propensity to evil—something to be overcome through one's efforts—can one hope to remove "hindrances within (an evil will dwelling in him) and then developing the original predisposition of a good will within him that can never be lost" (DV 6:441). Through impartial and sincere self-scrutiny one thereby contributes to the cultivation of one's conscience.

Kant mentions two important moral benefits that come from moral self-scrutiny. First, it eliminates (or at least combats) any "*fanatical contempt*" (DV 6:441) one might have for oneself as a member of the human race which, Kant says, is an inherently contradictory attitude to have. This is because (and to elaborate a bit on Kant's remarks) one can only find a human being contemptible if one assumes that they can be held morally accountable. But moral accountability assumes the noble "predisposition to the good we have in us" (ibid.)—moral personality—in virtue of which any human being is worthy of respect. Thus, one could not consistently have contempt for the human race as if it (or its members) were not owed any respect. The actions of an individual human being may make him a fitting object of contempt

[9] In Vigilantius see 27:608.

and thus contemptible,[10] but the "humanity in him," i.e. his moral personality, demands respect. Moral cognition of oneself, then, involves understanding that thorough self-contempt is irrational. The second moral benefit of moral self-scrutiny is combatting a kind of false egoistic self-esteem or self-satisfaction one might take, for example, in merely having benevolent wishes toward others that never translate into deeds. So, the kind of moral self-scrutiny that is a crucial stepping-stone toward and a continuing element of striving for moral self-perfection involves avoidance of self-contempt on one hand and false moral self-satisfaction on the other.

The duty to cultivate one's conscience and the duty of self-scrutiny, then, are both in the service of the two components of the duty of moral self-perfection: to strive to comply with the letter of the moral law through honest conscientious appraisal of one's deeds and to strive to comply with the spirit of the law that must begin with a sincere and impartial appraisal of one's motivation and character generally.

The companion duties of conscience and self-scrutiny are included in Book I, "Perfect Duties to Oneself." What I take to be the core duty of conscience—due diligence, which includes being sincere and impartial—is narrow along various dimensions: it is owed to oneself, it is specific with regard to what it demands (sincere and impartial scrutiny of one's actions), one is to exert every effort to be careful in such moral self-appraisal, and the duty is to consult one's conscience on all occasions that call for moral self-evaluation. The duty of conscience, including self-scrutiny, thus demands perfect, exceptionless compliance. This is confirmed in Vigilantius:

> Professor Kant rejects the division into a broad and narrow conscience.
>
> Since conscience involves an examination of our moral conduct that cannot, in duty, be omitted, it is impossible to suppose that anyone might leave anything out here, or could push exactitude too far. It is a strict duty . . . . (27:618)

---

[10] Whether contempt is a fitting reaction to someone is one thing; whether contempt is a morally permissible attitude to take up is another. To conflate the two is to commit what D'Arms and Jacobson 2000 call "the moralistic fallacy."

Thus, on those occasions in which one does engage conscience, one must strive to be impartial, sincere, and scrupulous in determining accurately the morally relevant aspects of one's action. In paragraph 6 of his treatment of the duty of conscience, Kant dismisses the idea of a broad or "wide conscience" that would overlook some moral infractions as if they were matters of mere trifling with details of minor significance, or as if a "true transgression [were, M.T.] judged a petty offense" (DV 6:440) at the digression of conscience. Conscience, on Kant's view, speaks involuntarily and decisively.[11]

❧❧

An "episodic section" concludes Book I, of Part I of the duties to one-self which we'll consider after discussing Kant's treatment of the imperfect duties to oneself that comprises Book II of the duties to oneself. Book II

12.2. The imperfect duties to oneself (with regard to his end)

Book II, which completes the discussion of duties to oneself, features two sections, the first on natural perfection and the second on moral perfection. We can be parsimonious in our treatment of these sections, since the fundamental duty of self-perfection was treated in chapter 7, and chapter 8 dealt extensively with moral self-perfection.

Section I: Natural self-perfection

The first section is entitled, "On the duty to oneself in developing and increasing one's *natural perfection*, i.e. for pragmatic purposes." It concerns the development of the following natural powers:

---

[11] Although engaging in a process (described earlier) of determining whether one had violated the moral law is (or can be) something one does deliberately, the "voice" of conscience in passing its judgment is involuntary.

- *Powers of spirit* that can be exercised only through reason (e.g. mathematics, metaphysics of nature, logic).
- *Powers of soul* that concern the use of one's understanding as well as the capacities of memory and imagination through which "learning [and, M.T.] taste . . . are founded" (6:445).
- *Powers of the body* the maintenance of which helps enable one to realize one's various ends.

In the first paragraph, Kant repeats his claims from the introduction to DV that developing one's naturally given powers is not merely a matter of prudence so that one may effectively achieve certain personal ends. Nor is Kant's argument merely that developing one's natural powers contributes to one's ability to strive effectively toward fulfilling the two fundamental obligatory ends. (Although, such an instrumentalist argument is available to Kant.) Rather, because one has freedom, and in particular the power to set ends on the basis of freely adopted principles, it is up to the individual to determine how to use such capacities. Kant takes this to mean that one owes the use of these natural powers not merely to instinct but also to one's freedom or, perhaps more perspicuously, to one's moral personality (humanity). The upshot is that one has this duty in order "for pragmatic purposes to be a human being suitable to the end of his existence" (DV 6:445) i.e. to be *worthy* of one's humanity.

A perhaps slightly more perspicuous version of this argument is found in Section VIII of the introduction. There, Kant says that natural perfection is the "*cultivation* of all *capacities* in general, for advancement of ends presented by reason" (DV 6: 391). A few lines later he argues:

> The capacity to set oneself an end at all is what characterizes humanity (as distinguished from animality). Thus the end of humanity in our own person also involves the rational will, and hence the duty to render a service to humanity through culture in general, to obtain or advance the *capacity* for carrying out all sorts of possible ends, in so far as this is to be found in the human being himself, i.e. a duty to cultivate the crude predispositions of his nature, whereby the animal

first elevates itself into the human being; hence it involves a duty in itself. (DV 6:392)

Living up to one's nature as a rational being and thus making oneself worthy of one's rational powers is what explains why one has this duty apart from the possible positive consequences of cultivating such powers.

Returning to the discussion in the Elements, in §20 Kant explains why the duty of natural self-perfection is wide and therefore imperfect in various ways. Although it is specific regarding to whom this duty is owed, it is open to individuals to decide how and when to cultivate these powers, which of them is more important to cultivate given one's career choices, and so on. One's duty, then, expressed most generally, is to adopt a maxim of natural self-perfection which, depending on one's natural abilities and acquired interests, serves as a basis for adopting more specific maxims (e.g. to pour time and energy into developing one's natural talent for and interest in mathematics).

Kant describes the duty of natural self-perfection as one for a "pragmatic purpose," while the duty of moral self-perfection is for a "moral purpose only." I take this difference in purpose to reflect respectively the difference between a duty to live up to one's nature as a rational being who has the capacity to freely set ends—humanity in the narrow sense contrasted with animality—compared to one's duty to live up to one's nature as a rational *and* accountable being and thus live up to one's moral personality. As an aspect of one's duty of natural self-perfection, Kant also mentions doing so in order to make oneself a useful member of the world, "since this also belongs to the worth of humanity in his own person, which he ought not thus to degrade" (DV 6:446).

Section II: Moral self-perfection

Section II is entitled, "On a human being's duty to himself in raising his MORAL perfection, i.e. for merely moral purposes." As we've learned, the duty here is to *strive* to become a virtuous person by resolving to comply with duty solely from respect for the moral law. As we've seen, a firm resolution constitutes having a good will, and the greater success one has in realizing a good will in one's actions the greater one's virtue. What gives more substance to leading a life of virtue is the acquisition of the various virtues featured in the Elements. This perfection, then, has a subjective (on the side of the subject) dimension, namely, making the resolution and then complying with it. The objective dimension of this duty (i.e. what it commands), is the following through and complying with all of one's duties from the sole motive of duty, as well as realizing one's singular moral vocation of becoming an overall virtuous person. "Be ye holy" [in motivation, M.T.] and "Be ye perfect" [in compliance, M.T.] (DV 6:446) is the motto of this duty.

It is notable that Kant never offers an explanatory derivation of this duty. In Section V of the introduction to DV, he explains that the moral command to strive for such self-perfection is "to be worthy of the humanity [moral personality, M.T.] that dwells within him" (DV 6:387). The idea seems to be that one's moral personality constitutes one's "true" self which serves as an ideal whose full realization would consist in maximizing one's internal freedom and thus maximizing one's independence from the normative and motivational force of sensible inclinations. And, of course, according to Kant, this ideal (possible for human beings with a sensible nature) grounds the duty to strive toward it, which makes a person worthy of her moral personality.

Narrow and perfect in quality, yet wide and imperfect in degree

In Section VIII of the introduction, Kant claims that "at first sight" the duty of moral self-perfection appears to be one of narrow obligation, but that owing to the human condition "the law commands only the *maxim of the action* . . . and hence not the *action itself*" (DV 6:392). In the final subsection of duties to oneself, §22, Kant qualifies his earlier claim, remarking that the duty of moral self-perfection is "*narrow* and perfect as to its quality, even though it is wide and imperfect as to its degree, and this is because of the frailty (*fragilitas*) of human nature" (DV 6:446). What does this mean and how can it be?

In chapter 7, sec. 3, I proposed the following regimentation of the narrow/wide, perfect/imperfect distinctions. The first pair concerns the so-called *quality* of the duty and refers to whether the duty (strictly speaking the law that commands the duty) requires (or prohibits) actions or, instead, requires (or prohibits) only maxims of action (general policies). The second pair concerns the required degree of compliance, i.e. how much latitude one has in complying with the duty. Narrow duties, because of their specificity, are more perfect in what they demand compared to wide duties that allow one's compliance with them to be imperfect in degree.

How, then, might we understand Kant's remark in §22? In brief, I believe the answer involves recognizing two perspectives from which one can view the duty of moral self-perfection, namely *without regard to facts about human psychology*, and taking such facts into account. These two perspectives harken back to the two ways of dividing duties from §4 of the introduction to the duties to oneself. The objective division concerns the objects of duty (their contents), however, "not with regard to the subject binding himself to duty" (DV 6:418) which is the human being. Without factoring in the kind of human frailty that Kant goes on to describe in this section, and so without regard to such facts about humans, the quality of the duty of moral self-perfection is narrow and thus perfect in obligation. However, when certain facts about human beings are brought to bear, the obligation is imperfect and so the corresponding duty is wide. Granted, this explanation does not quite match what Kant writes (that the duty is narrow and perfect in quality and wide and imperfect in degree). However, if a duty cannot be both wide and perfect or narrow and imperfect in the same sense, or from the same perspective, then the proposal on offer must be what Kant is claiming.

What, then, is it about human beings that explains why they do not have a duty to comply with duty from the sole motive of duty—a narrow duty specifying a kind of act to be performed? Kant's explanation is that human beings lack insight into their own psychologies, a kind of epistemic frailty. That is, one cannot be certain that one has performed an action complying with a duty solely from the motive of duty. As Kant rhetorically asks:

Who knows himself well enough to say, when he feels the incentive to observe duty, whether it springs entirely from the representation of the law, or whether there are not many other sensuous impulses that are predisposed towards an advantage (or towards preventing some disadvantage) and on another occasion, could just as well be serviceable to vice? (DV 6:447)

Kant's assumption here is that in order to be subject to a narrow duty of perfect obligation, which specifies an *action* to be done or omitted, one must in principle be able to determine with certainty whether one is following it. That is, when it comes to the question of legality—of whether one is following the letter of the moral law—this is something human beings can determine. But with respect to dutiful actions, one can't be certain whether one's motivation ever was or will be the pure motive of duty. This is Kant's "opacity of the will" thesis:

In fact, it is absolutely impossible by means of experience to make out with complete certainty a single case in which the maxim of an action that otherwise conforms with duty did rest solely on moral grounds and on the representation of one's duty. For at times it is indeed the case that with the acutest self-examination we find nothing whatsoever that—besides the moral ground of duty—could have been powerful enough to move us to this or that good action and so great a sacrifice; but from this it cannot be inferred with certainty that the real determining cause of the will was not actually a covert impulse of self-love under mere pretense of that idea; for which we then gladly flatter ourselves with the false presumption of a nobler motive, whereas in fact we can never, even by the most strenuous examination, get entirely behind our covert incentives, because when moral worth is at issue what counts is not the actions, which one sees, but their inner principles, which one does not see. (G 4:407)

Kant is thus tying moral accountability to facts about the limits of the human powers of introspection—something to be expected given his claim in the general introduction that in determining what moral laws require, "a metaphysics of morals . . . shall often have to take as our object the particular *nature* of human beings, which is cognized only by experience, in order to *show* in it what can be inferred from universal moral principles" (MM 6:217). However, even if one cannot be held morally accountable for acting solely from the motive of duty (in complying with duty), one can *strive* to do so. The moral law, then, only requires adopting a maxim of striving to do one's duty solely out of respect for the law. Thus, given the kind of human frailty under consideration, the duty of moral self-perfection is a wide duty—wide in quality—that permissibly allows the degree to which one is accountable for complying with the ideal to be imperfect.

Kant makes similar remarks about acquiring the various individual virtues. After all, taken individually, the strength of a virtue can only be judged "by the magnitude of the hindrances that a human being provides for himself through his inclinations" (DV 6:405). Because one cannot tell with certainty whether a virtue is strong enough to resist all possible contrary-to-duty inclinations, one cannot be certain that it has been fully realized. Thus, the duty to acquire the virtues in the sense of fully realizing them is only wide in quality and imperfect in degree.

It is notable that in the *Religion* Kant employs the quality/degree distinction in remarking on the ideal of moral perfection in relation to human beings as members of the "world of senses." But here, his point is not about the limits of human self-knowledge, but about the impossibility of realizing the ideal:

> In quality (since it must be thought as supersensibly *grounded*) this disposition can indeed be, and ought to be, holy and conformable to the archetype's [God's, M. T.] disposition. In degree, however, (in terms of its manifestation in actions) it always remains deficient and infinitely removed from that of the archetype. (R 6:75n)

That is, again, bracketing facts about human psychology, the quality of the duty of moral self-perfection is determined by appeal to an ideal (archetype) who is holy and thus morally perfect. However, given that humans are limited nonholy beings, for them, achieving moral perfection will necessarily always fall short. This quote combines, then, the two different perspectives lately mentioned, which allows Kant to in effect mix narrow quality with imperfect degree. Considering facts about human beings, then, all one can do is strive toward the ideal. Kant concludes Part I, remarking: "All duties to oneself with regard to

the end of humanity in our own person [i.e., self-perfection, M.T.] are
therefore only imperfect duties" (DV 6:447).

12.3. An amphiboly: duties *to* versus duties *with regard to*

Backtracking now to the "episodic section" (§§16–18), one question
for a metaphysics of morals concerns the scope of one's duties, so far
as this can be determined by reason alone. Scope concerns those to
whom one can be obligated. Kant has argued that there are duties
that human beings have to themselves, and he will go on to explain
the basic duties human beings have toward one another. Are there any
duties to other nonhuman beings? Kant lays down two conditions for
having duties to something: it must be a person, and it must be "given
in experience," i.e. a person who can be encountered as an embodied
rational agent with whom one might interact. The first provision rules
out having duties to inanimate nature and nonrational animals. The
second provision rules out duties to angels or God.

An amphiboly is a kind of fallacy that results from a grammat-
ical ambiguity. Talk of duty involving two beings is ambiguous between: having a duty *to* that being and having a duty *with regard* to that
being. Failure to make this distinction easily leads to the thought that
humans have duties to things other than humans. We do have duties
to treat the environment and nonhuman animals in certain ways, but
these are only duties *regarding* such beings or things; duties that are
ultimately grounded in duties we have to ourselves and others. Kant
mentions the fact that wanton destruction of what is beautiful in nature dulls one's capacity to love something in a disinterested manner
and thus just for itself.[12] Hence, such destruction violates a duty to
oneself to preserve and even cultivate one's natural capacity for love
of others. Regarding cruelty to animals, again, one has a duty to cultivate one's capacity for sympathetic feeling (as we shall see in the next
chapter). Cruelty to animals dulls this capacity and thereby can affect

---

[12] Such disinterested appreciation is a key element in Kant's theory of judgments of
aesthetic taste that he elaborates in Part I of the *Critique of the Power of Judgment*.

our relations with other human beings. Kant does not think these considerations rule out painlessly killing animals for one or another purpose (food, clothing). He does claim that the cruelty of "torturous physical experiments" (DV 6:443) on animals, especially for the sake of speculation, is a violation of a duty to oneself. Finally, what Kant says in §18 about duties regarding God is repeated later in the conclusion of the book, so we can put off elaboration until the final chapter.[13]

12.4. Kant's scheme of duties to oneself at a glance

Before concluding, let us review Kant's scheme of duties to oneself, by listing the virtues and corresponding vices for each of the duties. (See Figure 12.1.) The asterisk indicates that the virtue or vice term is explicitly mentioned by Kant. Some do not seem to have corresponding virtue or vice terms.

Not reflected in this diagram is the fact that for each of these duties one can vow to comply with it (which is partly constitutive of having good will) yet be susceptible to bouts of weakness of will, a sure sign that one has not fully realized the corresponding virtue. Room must also be made for failing to commit oneself to complying with one or another duty from the sole motive of duty, so that one tends to act from impure motives when one does comply with duty. If, as I argued in chapter 8, true vice is principled opposition to virtue so that, for example, the vice of servility is an admitted willingness to engage in false humility for the advantages it may bring, then room must be made for two types of moral failing I've described: frailty and impurity which, following Kant's discussion of the three propensities to evil in the *Religion*, do not amount to depravity and thus do not amount to true vice as a character trait.

---

[13] But what about alleged duties to future generations—many of whom one will never encounter? Perhaps, on Kant's behalf, one could say that one generation can have duties to the immediately overlapping succeeding generation. In DV, Kant does not consider duties possessed by generations or more generally by groups. Notably, though, in the *Religion*, he does discuss a "sui generis" duty (R 6:97) of the human species to strive to realize an "ethical community."

Negative Duties to Oneself	Corresponding Virtue/Vice
Qua Animal Being	
Self-disembodiment	
(Suicide and Self-Mutilation)	[No names]
Masturbation	Chastity*/Lewdness*
Drunkenness and Gluttony	Temperance/Intemperance
Qua Moral Being	
Lying	Honesty-Sincerity*/Dishonesty-Insincerity*
Avarice	Frugality/Miserliness*
Servility	True Humility*/Servility*

Positive Duties to Oneself	
Of Conscience	Conscientiousness*/ Unconscientiousness
Moral Self-Scrutiny	Scrupulousness/Unscrupulousness
Natural Self-Perfection	Industriousness/Sloth
Moral Self-Perfection	Virtuous Disposition*/Viciousness

Figure 12.1 List of duties to oneself together with corresponding virtues and vices

12.5. Concluding reflections

To wrap up my presentation of Kant's duties to oneself, let us return to what I referred to in chapter 10 as Kant's moral teleology. It was Kant's view, defended in *Critique of the Power of Judgment*, that we are not justified for the purpose of gaining theoretical knowledge of the natural world in holding that there are "natural ends"—that things in nature have intrinsic purposes. However, he also argued that for the sake of guiding scientific investigation into nature one is justified in treating natural things, especially organisms, *as if* they have intrinsic purposes. This is to appeal to natural ends for strictly heuristic purposes. In the previous chapter, I argued that Kant's references to the natural purpose of the sex organs and of communication do not serve to explain the wrongness of the vices of unnatural lust and lying, though for heuristic purposes they can serve to focus attention on certain human powers whose misuse opposes virtue. Nevertheless, as rational beings, members of an intelligible realm, we are justified in taking there to be an end or purpose to our existence. We are members of this realm in virtue of our humanity (in Kant's technical sense), that is, our "capacity to set oneself an end at all" (DV 6:392). This capacity includes inner freedom—whose full realization involves independence of our power of choice from our sensible inclinations and thus requires the kind of self-mastery constitutive of moral virtue—moral self-perfection. In Section V of DV's introduction, Kant refers to this kind of perfection as qualitative which he describes as the "harmony of a thing's characteristics with an end" (DV 6:386). Regarding the end of moral self-perfection—the greatest of perfections—the characteristics that harmonize and thus contribute to this end are the various virtues whose acquisition provide principled opposition to the various vices one is susceptible to as an animal being and as a moral being only.

In this and the previous chapter, I've presented Kant's arguments against certain types of action (and the vices that accompany them) as intrinsically wrong. This result might strike one as a grab bag of negative duties without a unifying rationale. However, viewed from the perspective of moral teleology, there is unity here. If the "greatest perfection" one is capable of is moral self-perfection which, put formally (as Kant does), is to become the kind of person who complies with duty from the sole motive of respect for the moral law, then we may view the other duties to oneself as in some sense serving or not undermining this moral end. Further, insofar as they serve this end, they thereby have moral and not just prudential significance. That is, the reason, for example, that avoidance of miserliness grounds a moral duty and not merely a prudential recommendation is that this vice hinders the kind of independence required for self-mastery. Again, because suicide destroys one's physical being and thus eliminates striving toward the end of moral self-perfection, it is morally significant, and so its avoidance is not just a matter of prudence. The same may be said of the other negative duties to oneself: the vices associated with them are hindrances, while the corresponding virtues contribute to maximizing inner freedom; one's full compliance with the moral law in both deed and motivation. As for the positive duties to oneself, principled compliance with the duties of conscientiousness, self-scrutiny, and natural self-perfection contribute positively to the end of moral self-perfection. Moreover, their contribution is not merely instrumental. Rather, coming to have the virtues associated with these positive duties is partly constitutive of fully realizing one's rational end of moral self-perfection—a quest that is intrinsically valuable. The same may be said of the virtues corresponding to negative duties to oneself. The unity of the virtues corresponding to duties to oneself consists in their mutual contribution to the supreme end of acquiring a virtuous disposition and thereby maximizing one's inner freedom.

Further Reading

- On the duty of conscience, see Hill 1998 [2002], Timmermann 2006a, Wood 2008, Esser 2013, and Kahn 2015.
- See Johnson 2011 for an extended account of Kantian self-perfection.
- Kant's view about duties regarding nonhuman animals has attracted a fair amount of attention. See, for example, O'Neill 1998, Wood 1998, Denis 2000b, Timmermann 2005, and Kain 2010.
- See Johnson 2010 for discussion of Kant's distinction between duties to others versus duties regarding others.
- For an explanation of Kant's rejection of various forms of moral perfectionism while still defending a kind of perfectionist view, see Guyer 2011 [2016]

13

Duties of Love to Other Human Beings

Part II, Chapter I, Section I

We come now to Part II of the Elements which has two chapters, a conclusion, and an appendix. The first chapter, "On duties to others, merely as human beings," represents a core set of duties that takes into consideration general features of human beings as a species of rational being. It is divided into two sections: "On the duty of love to other human beings" and "On duties of virtue toward other human beings that arise from the respect due them." The first chapter, then, features metaphysical first principles of duties to others and thus belongs to the science of ethics. In contrast, the second chapter explains that in applying first principles to life's concrete circumstances, it is necessary to consider various empirical contingencies that figure in determining what one ought or ought not to do in those circumstances. It is brief because such matters of contingent detail do not belong to a "pure" metaphysics of morals. The conclusion is about friendship, and the appendix mentions various virtues of social intercourse.

This chapter takes up the duties of love toward other human beings. Corresponding to these virtues are the vices of hatred, whose treatment I will save for the following chapter, combining discussion of them with vices opposed to the general duty to respect others. The guiding questions of this chapter include:

- What is the basis for dividing duties of love from duties of respect toward others?
- What are the duties of love and how are they justified?
- What do these duties require of human beings?

Kant's Doctrine of Virtue. Mark Timmons, Oxford University Press (2021). © Oxford University Press.
DOI: 10.1093/oso/9780190939229.003.0013

13.1 General remarks about duties of love and of respect

Chapter I begins with some introductory remarks, entitled "Division," explaining how the duties of love are distinguished from duties of respect. It is followed by "On the duty of love in particular" (§§26–28) containing further remarks about the duty of love as a basis for "Division of the duties of love" (§§29–35) which discusses the duties of beneficence, gratitude, and sympathetic participation.

Division

The "chief division" separating duties of love from duties of respect is that the former put others under obligation, while the latter do not. Acting on a maxim of beneficence in conferring a genuine benefit on another creates an obligation of gratitude on the part of the beneficiary. Following this, Kant calls attention to three further aspects of these two types of duty. *First*, in observing duties of love, one is acting meritoriously, while in observing duties of respect, one is only doing what is strictly owed to others. *Second*, while 'love' and 'respect' can refer to feelings that accompany respectively the carrying out of duties of love and respect, they also refer to maxims. I will come back in a moment to these claims about feelings and maxims.

Third, in §23, Kant claims that although the duties of love and respect can be considered separately, in practice they are "combined." For example, in observing the duty of beneficence where one helps someone in dire need, one should help in a way that preserves the needy person's self-respect. Kant's own suggestion is that one should behave as if our help is either "merely what is owed him or as a slight labor of love" (DV 6:449). In this way, one's duty of respect for others tempers *how* one goes about complying with this duty of love. Kant's remarks here suggest that there is a kind of mutual interdependence between duties of love and of respect when it comes to complying with either one. And, in §24, the theme of mutual interdependence is confirmed by an analogy Kant draws between an intelligible (ideal) world in which there is mutual love and respect among persons and the natural world in which there is mutual attraction and repulsion of physical forces in nature. I won't pause to discuss this intriguing analogy, which would require getting into Kant's *Metaphysical Foundations of Natural Science*.[1] It is worthy of note that considerations of *manner* figure importantly here and elsewhere.[2] The manner in which one carries out duties, e.g. helping others in a *way* that does not denigrate the beneficiary and helps preserve their self-esteem, is a crucial element in Kant's conception of ethics. This is one place where being emotionally attuned to the plight of others figures importantly.[3]

The treatment of the division between duties of love and respect continues in §25. Kant begins by saying that in the present context, love and respect are not to be understood as feelings. Feelings cannot as such be objects of duty; unlike actions, they are not under one's direct voluntary control, at least in the way actions are. The relevant conception of love here is "practical love"—doing good for others. As we saw in chapter 6, Kant distinguishes benevolence (*Wohlwollen*) from beneficence (*Wohltun*). The former is a matter of merely *wishing* well for others, while beneficence is *acting* (or being disposed to act, considering beneficence as a virtue) on one's benevolent wishes (active benevolence). While mere benevolence in wishes can be passive, for Kant the relevant maxim of action is one of "active, practical benevolence, making the weal and flourishing of others my *end* (being beneficent)" (DV 6:452), "in so far as [their ends, M.T.] are not immoral" (DV 6:450), and which (as active) has "being beneficent as its consequence" (DV 6:449).

Similar remarks pertain to the duty of respect owed to others. Here, respect as a feeling is not in focus, but instead the maxim of "limiting

---

[1] Sanchez Borboa [ms] contains an illuminating discussion of this analogy. As for how the duty of beneficence can constrain complying with the duty of respect, one of Sanchez Borboa's examples is telling others of one's accomplishments. Entering into sympathetic participation with one's audience (a duty of love) can properly temper *how* one conveys one's accomplishments without coming off as arrogant and thus without violating one's duty of respect toward others. Here, again, considerations of manner matter.

[2] See for example Tannenbaum 2002 on the significance of the emotions as they bear on manner in Kant's ethics.

[3] This is a theme that for reasons of space I will not develop here. It is a place where moral psychology interacts with ethics and a topic worth developing on Kant's behalf. See e.g. Tannenbaum 2002.

our self-esteem by the dignity of humanity in the person of another"
(DV 6:449)—"practical respect." Because the duties of respect toward
others that flow from this general maxim are negative duties, they are
narrow and perfect compared to duties of love, which are wide and imperfect. Negative duties, you may recall, do not leave much latitude in
how one is to comply with them, while positive duties to adopt maxims
of ends governing action do leave such latitude.

On the duty of love in particular

Sections 26–28 serve as a general introduction to duties of love. Here
we find a taxonomy of types of general attitude one might take toward
others, followed by reflections on duties of love as they relate to the
biblical injunction to love one's neighbor as oneself. The attitudes represent core elements of character types, which can be read as covering
virtue, vice, and lack of virtue associated with the duties of love.

Regarding the attitudes toward humanity, Kant identifies four types:

- The *friend of humanity*, a philanthropist, is someone who
  takes satisfaction in the well-being of human beings and so for
  whom things go well for her when things go well for all others.
  Presumably, this person not only takes satisfaction in the well-
  being of others but engages in active benevolence (beneficence).
  If her beneficence is principled, she exemplifies someone with the
  virtue of active benevolence—someone who adopts the relevant
  maxim of action and is prepared to act on it and thus engages in
  beneficent actions.
- The *enemy of humanity*, a misanthropist, is someone for whom
  things go well only when things go badly for others. This person is
  presumably someone who exemplifies one or other of the vices of
  hatred—envy, ingratitude, and especially *Schadenfreude* (taking
  malicious joy in others' misfortunes).
- The *egoist* or *self-seeker* is indifferent toward humanity so long as
  things go well for her. Insofar as this kind of person is in principle
  opposed to the maxim of beneficence, he exhibits vice. Any vice
  is an evil, though as we shall see in the next chapter, the vices of

hatred manifest a greater degree of evil than do the vices of selfish egoism.

- The *anthropophobic* is someone who, like the friend of humanity, bears no animosity toward others, and indeed wishes them well. However, like the misanthrope, he avoids others because "he can find no *delight* in them" (DV 6:450) in the sense of finding them lovable (in the affective sense of 'love'). As such, Kant labels this person an 'aesthetic misanthropist.' Presumably, he is lacking in virtue, since, in turning away from others, he has simply not adopted the maxim of beneficence (*active* benevolence).

In anticipation of handling Kant's argument for a duty of beneficence we can add to Kant's list the so-called partialist.

- The *partialist* is someone only concerned with the welfare of those within her circle, whether that be immediate family, members of one's religion, or country, or race, etc. This character is thus somewhat less egoistic than is the egoist.

Having identified types of attitude toward humanity in general, Kant proceeds in §27 to explain the basis of the *duty* of beneficence and then in 28 to address questions about its content. Both sections are difficult. They concern Kant's attempt to capture within his duty of active benevolence the biblical injunction, "love thy neighbor as thyself" (DV 6:450). Kant raises potential problems for doing this, one each in 27 and 28. Let us take a closer look.

The first of these problems poses a seeming incompatibility between (*i*) there being a universal duty for all human beings to promote the happiness of *all* (including oneself) and (*ii*) individual human beings not having a duty to promote their own happiness (as explained in Section IV of the Introduction). The second claim is, of course, a tenet of Kant's moral theory. So, the source of the tension must be the first claim. The biblical commandment, expressed in Kant's terms, clearly commands I adopt a maxim of benevolence toward all others.

But since all others except me would not be all, and hence the maxim would not have in itself the universality of a law, which is yet necessary for obligation, the law of duty of benevolence will also comprise myself as an object in the command of practical reason . . . (DV 6:451).

Thus, it appears as if the biblical commandment, translated into Kant's theory, entails that one does have a duty to promote one's own happiness. Of course, Kant denies this. It is as if the biblical commandment not only applies universally to everyone, but the duty of benevolence (its content) is owed to everyone, including oneself. He goes on to explain the resolution:

[L]egislative reason—which in its idea of humanity as such includes the whole species (thus myself along with it)—not the human being, includes, as universally legislating, according to the principle of equality, me like all others besides me in the duty of reciprocal benevolence, and *allows* you to be benevolent to yourself, on condition that you are benevolent to every other as well; for it is in this way alone that your maxim (of being beneficent) qualifies for a universal legislation, on which any law of duty is founded (DV 6:451).

Kant's resolution, I take it, is to make the universality of the law of benevolence (it applies to everyone) compatible with no one having a duty of benevolence toward themselves. Seemingly, this can be done by way of a universally applicable principle of mutual benevolence that *permits* me to be benevolent to myself on condition that I adopt a maxim of active benevolence toward all others. The result is that the principle of mutual benevolence is universally applicable, thus suitably lawlike to impose obligation on everyone (everyone is included in the content of the law), and it gives the same law to everyone. A related point is that even if there is a practical law requiring beneficence toward everyone (including oneself), there is no duty to promote one's own happiness because, as we've seen, duty entails constraint, and because we each naturally pursue our own happiness, there can be no constraint to do so.[4]

---

[4] I owe this point to Adam Cureton.

In the first of two paragraphs comprising §28, Kant refers to "the benevolence in love of all humanity" which, he observes "is indeed the greatest in its *extent*, but smallest in its *degree*" (DV 6:451). Regarding extent, this love includes *all* other human beings (maximal extent), though one's level of concern is (or can be) minimal; a matter of not being completely indifferent toward the welfare of others (minimal degree). This, then, rules out being a selfish person (self-seeker) who is indifferent toward the fate of other human beings, as well as the anthropophobic who wishes well but intentionally refrains from active beneficence. Someone nonindifferent is presumably a friend of humanity.

In the second paragraph, and regarding the issue of degree, if the maxim of beneficence (active benevolence) is supposed to capture the spirit of the biblical injunction, one might doubt whether giving preference to some over others in one's beneficence is permitted. After all, to love all others *just as* you love yourself might seem to rule out such preferential treatment, allowing no difference in degree. In response, Kant explains that the maxim of active practical benevolence allows, and sometime requires, giving preference to those who are close to oneself, such as family and friends. This maxim, after all, is not one of mere well-wishing benevolence; it requires adopting permissible ends of others. Of course, it is not possible to literally adopt the particular ends of all other living human beings. Furthermore, one's strongest obligation of beneficence is likely to be toward family and friends, whose specific ends one can come to know and adopt as one's own, in the sense of helping them to realize those ends. What the universal maxim of active benevolence requires, then, is that one be open in principle to helping those in need who are not close in the way family and friends are—this goes beyond an attitude of minimal nonindifference toward all others (mere well-wishing). However, one is permitted and sometimes required to prioritize who one benefits and thus vary one's degree of commitment to others. As we shall see in chapter 15, close friendships involve a high degree of mutual benevolence between friends.

One significant question this issue of variation in degree raises is how exactly one is to justify such prioritization. Kant doesn't say. On his behalf one could say there are various duties one has that serve to constrain one's otherwise wide-open duty of benevolence, for example, duties of gratitude toward one's parents and other benefactors. Moreover, if there is a duty to enter into friendships, then this too can serve to justify some prioritization. Such questions, of course, are matters of casuistry and so not a proper part of a metaphysics of morals.

13.2 Division of duties of love

A. On the duty of beneficence

After some remarks on the duty to properly care for one's own well-being and repeating the benevolence/beneficence distinction (reminding readers in §29 that the duty is one of beneficence and not mere well-wishing), in 30 Kant offers a derivation (justification) of the duty of beneficence.[5] It is like the one in the Introduction (Sec. VIII) which we skipped over at the time. However, I believe the earlier one includes something crucial that is left out of the argument here. To explain, let us first concentrate on the argument in 30.

Kant begins by noting that it is not obvious that one has a *duty* of beneficence; one's duties of virtue to others could be restricted to negative duties of respect. So, the duty requires justification. Of course, to justify a principle of duty, Kant must explain why, based on the CI, there is a categorical requirement to do or refrain from adopting and acting on whatever maxim is under consideration. The explanation takes the form of a derivation in which Kant appeals to the universal law formulation of the CI. The intended upshot of the derivation is: "To be beneficent, i.e. to advance the happiness of others *in need*, according to one's means, without hoping for something in return, is every human being's duty" (DV 6:453, my emphasis). Until now, Kant has not qualified the duty to promote the happiness of others by referring to others' needs. This, however, is significant if the reference is to genuine needs of human beings, such as food, clothing, shelter, and so forth. Other's

---

[5] See Collins "Of Duties Towards Other People" 27:413–422, and Vigilantius 27:496.

genuine needs might give one reason to help them, while, for example, their needing assistance with hobbies may not. In any case, Kant's argument is strongest when focused on genuine human needs.

To help articulate Kant's argument (my reconstruction of it), here is a proposed non-self-interested maxim of ends that will figure in it:

> BENEFICENCE: When I am well off, and in a position to help others, I will take their needs *as such* as a reason to help them and will (at least occasionally) act for this reason.

The derivation (to follow) for the claim that adopting and acting on BENEFICENCE is a duty has two parts. First [steps 1–4], Kant argues that a maxim of exclusive self-interest or nonbeneficence is contrary to duty. From this result, he apparently infers 5—that one has a positive duty to adopt a maxim of "general interest" or beneficence. Here is the passage in full (bracketed numbers added):

> For [1] every human being who finds himself in need wishes to be helped by others. [2a] But if he were to make known his maxim of being unwilling to assist others in turn when they are in need, i.e. [2b] to make it a universal permissive law, then [3] everyone would likewise deny him assistance when he is in need himself, or at least would be warranted to deny it. [4] The maxim of self-interest would thus conflict with itself if it were made a universal law, i.e., it is contrary to duty. [5] The maxim in the general interest, of being beneficent towards those in need, is consequently a universal duty of human beings; and this is because [6] they are to be looked upon as fellow human beings, i.e., rational beings with needs, united by Nature in one dwelling place for assisting one another (DV 6:453).

The universal law formulation of the CI commands that one act only on maxims that one can consistently will at the same time to become a universal law of nature; here Kant refers to universal "permissive" law.[6] That is, one is to consider whether one can

---

[6] Notice that here Kant's test requires one to ask whether one could consistently will that everyone well-off be *permitted* to refuse to help others in need, which leaves room for the well-off to help others anyway. In other places (e.g. G 4:423) the test

consistently will one's maxim while at the same time will that it be-come a permissive law governing the behavior of similarly situated others. If not, then adopting and acting on the maxim is morally wrong. As Kant explains in the *Groundwork* (4:424) the test is meant to reveal whether one is making an unjustified exception of oneself and thereby taking advantage of others. Let us formulate a maxim of selfishness that reflects the thinking of a prudentially rational egoist:

> SELFISH: Although I am well-off and able to help others in need, be-cause I nevertheless prefer not to help, I will refuse to help unless, of course, I judge that it would be in my interest to help. I will thus not take the needs of another as itself a reason to help and in doing so I allow myself permission not to help.

The test is to consider whether one can consistently will this maxim while at the same time will its universalized counterpart:

> UNIVERSAL: Whenever anyone is well-off and able to help others in need yet prefers not to help, they will refuse to help unless, of course, they judge it to be in their self-interest to help. Everyone will thus not take the needs others as itself a reason to help. (An example of a per-missive law to refuse help.)

With SELFISH and UNIVERSAL in mind, here is a partial and some-what liberal reconstruction of Kant's argument—partial, because it leaves out something in 2a and leaves out 6 entirely for reasons I'll explain in a moment. It is liberal because if SELFISH is the maxim being tested, then claim 1 should be suitably revised to match it. (The bracketed numbers relate the following argument to the preceding passage.)

---

requires one to consider whether one could consistently will that everyone well-off *adopt and act* on a maxim of always refusing help to others, not just be permitted to so act. Whether the "universal availability" or the "universal conformity" versions of the test make a difference to its plausibility is a matter of some scholarly debate. See, for example, Pogge 1989.

An argument for a duty of beneficence

1. Every human being who finds himself in need wishes [wills] to be helped by others, even if others in a position to help judge that it is not in their interest to do so [1].
2. If one wills SELFISH as a universal law, i.e. wills UNIVERSAL [2b], an implication is that one wills not to be helped by others when one is in need whenever it is not in their self-interest to do so—that others *not* take one's needs as providing non-self-interested reasons to help [3].
3. However, the implication mentioned in [3] is inconsistent with [1].

Thus,

4. Adopting and acting on the selfish maxim is morally wrong [4].

Thus,

5. One has a duty to adopt and act on a maxim of common interest, i.e. BENEFICENCE [5].

This reconstruction does not include all of 2a because the argument need not rely on one's maxim *being made known*, as demonstrated by the reconstruction. Indeed, 2a by itself suggests a mere publicity test: can one will one's maxim and at the same time consistently make known one's maxim? If this were Kant's test for whether acting on a maxim is permissible, then many intuitively permissible maxims would turn out to be impermissible. If police were to make public an intended raid on a sex-slave operation, their plan would be foiled. It does not follow that their intended raid is morally impermissible.[7] So, 2a, insofar as it differs from 3, can be put aside. My reconstruction does not include 6 because it isn't clear what exactly it claims and how it can be used to support 5.

---

[7] I am not saying that publicity never figures in Kant's tests; it does in his *Groundwork* argument against lying promises at 4:430.

However, there are two looming problems. *First*, premise 1 is often challenged. Why can't there be "lone wolf" individuals who would rather fail in their attempt to realize an end than be helped by anyone else?[8] Indeed, the lone wolf I have in mind refuses help even to satisfy her needs. Kant apparently intends his argument to apply to all human beings, including the lone wolf. *Second*, part 2 of the argument seems to assume that if one rejects a maxim of self-ishness [4] one is thereby committed to a maxim of beneficence [5]. After all, in 5 Kant writes that adopting a maxim of common in-terest "is consequently" a duty. If read this way, the problem is that there appears to be a logical gap between the prohibition of a selfish maxim and a requirement to adopt a maxim of beneficence. That is, rejecting a maxim of not helping does not logically commit one to a maxim or policy of helping. I might just willy-nilly help others if I feel like it—I am not in principle opposed to helping, but I've also not made it my policy to help (mere lack of virtue). Then, too, I might adopt a maxim of only taking the needs of my family, or my country, or some other select group as providing me with non-self-interested reasons to help select others.

In the spirit of charity, let us consider whether the argument might be improved to overcome these problems. Note, first, that the lone wolf example requires reading premise 1 as a mere descriptive claim: that *as a matter of fact* every human being wishes (is willing) to receive help, even in cases where it is not in the interest of others to do so. The lone wolf case challenges this claim. However, alternatively, the claim may be understood as a claim about nonmoral rationality. In the second *Critique*, Kant writes: "To be happy is necessarily the demand of every rational but finite being and therefore an unavoidable determining ground of its faculty of desire" (CprR 5:25). Suppose it is part of the nature of finite, rational beings to will their own happiness on pain of irrationality. Together with the fact that a human being is not fully self-sufficient and sometimes will need the help of others to achieve her happiness-related ends (including needs), it follows from the principle of means/ends rationality that one is rationally committed to wishing

---

[8] This objection goes back at least as far as Sidgwick 1907: 389n.

for and accepting help from others when in need. Indeed, arguably, one is committed to taking one's needs as such as providing reasons for others to help—this is indicated in the Introduction version of the argument for a duty of beneficence when Kant remarks that "we thus make ourselves an end for others" (DV 6:393). Suppose, for instance, while hiking through the Scottish Highlands you incautiously step into a bog and are now slowing sinking; without help death is imminent. Thankfully, I come along and you call for my help, which I can easily do. You take the fact that you need help to be a reason for me to help, regardless of whether it is in my self-interest to do so. Suppose we now generalize and claim that a prudentially rational person takes her needs *as such* to provide others with reasons to help her. This is meant to reflect the remark, lately quoted, from the Introduction version of the argument, which, I think, adds to the version under consideration. Let us, then, replace premise 1 with the following:

> 1*. Every human being who finds herself in need is rationally committed to wishing for and accepting help from others, even in cases where it is not in the self-interest of others to help. More specifically, every human being takes her needs as such to provide reasons for others to help meet those needs and (at least occasionally) to act for such reasons—it is in this way that we "thus make ourselves an end for others" (DV 6:394).[9]

We can now generate the desired volitional inconsistency. To will UNIVERSAL as law (per Kant's test) entails willing that others do *not* take one's needs as such to give them reason to help. But as a prudentially rational person, one is committed to taking one's own needs as such to provide others with reasons to help meet those needs. Thus, according to the CI test, SELFISH is morally impermissible—claim 4. Of course, I have not attempted to defend 1* though it strikes me as a plausible constraint on prudential rationality.

---

[9] Of course, this alleged commitment requires various qualifications. For instance, even if one takes one's needs to provide non-self-interested reason for others (in a position to help) to help meet those needs, others may have stronger competing moral or prudential reasons to refuse help.

This leaves the problem of directly inferring a duty to adopt a maxim of general beneficence from the prohibition of a maxim of self-ishness. The problem was supposed to be that because a maxim of self-ishness and a maxim of beneficence are contraries, not contradictories, rejecting the former does not logically commit one to accepting the latter. This challenge is harder than the previous one to overcome. Two related tactics for doing so come to mind. *First*, against the "willy-nilly" person one might argue that to have character at all requires being principled, as Kant claims in the *Anthropology* (7:291–295), and that impartial reason commands that one acquire (or strive for) moral character, thus ruling out not being principled with respect to helping others. And *second*, against accepting a maxim of partial beneficence, the obvious thing to do is apply the universality test to any such maxim. If all such partialist maxims fail the test, then one may conclude that the only acceptable maxim of beneficence is one of impartial benef-icence. Of course, there are too many partialist maxims to consider, taking them one by one and subjecting them to Kant's test. However, if a representative of this class of maxims fails, then it is perhaps plausible to generalize this result to all the others, leaving BENEFICENCE as the sole impartially justified maxim of practical love. Consider, then, the following partialist maxim based on our earlier addition to Kant's list of personality types:

PARTIALIST: Although I am well-off, and able to help others in need, because I nevertheless prefer to help only those members of my im-mediate family, I will refuse to help non-family, unless, of course, I judge that it would be in my (or my family's) interest to help non-family. I will thus not take the needs of non-family members as such to provide reasons for me to help them.

Standing in the shoes of the partialist, could one will that this maxim serve as a universal permissive law? The test comes down to whether one can consistently will that non–family members refuse to take the needs of my family (including me, of course) as providing (non-self-interested) reasons for them to help. If a case can be made for claiming that prudential rationality on behalf of my family commits me to wishing that non–family members take the needs of my family as such as reasons to help, then PARTIALIST is ruled out. If all such partialist maxims fail Kant's test, it leaves BENEFICENCE as the only impartially justified principle of practical love. Thus, perhaps the path from 4 to 5 in the cited argument is an iterated use of Kant's universality test. Whether this does provide a plausible solution to the "gap" problem, I leave open.

Following the argument for the duty of beneficence, in §31 Kant makes several cautionary remarks about this duty. *First,* regarding those who are rich with abundant means to help others, their acts of beneficence are not particularly meritorious, even though such acts put recipients under an obligation of gratitude. After all, it is typically no large sacrifice on the part of the rich with abundant means to contribute to the welfare of those in need. *Second,* for an act of giving to be received as genuine gratitude, one must not appear to intend to put the beneficiary under an obligation, which demeans the beneficiary—an example of the need to temper one's beneficence with respect for the self-esteem of the beneficiary. *Third,* considering this last point, it is better, if possible, to practice one's beneficence in secrecy. *Finally,* Kant remarks that practicing the virtue of beneficence realizes greater moral merit for the benefactor—he is "morally rich"—when his means are limited and he is "strong enough to silently take on himself the ills that he spares the other" (DV 6:453).

Casuistical questions

The discussion of beneficence ends with some casuistical questions. For instance, just as the duty to help preserve the self-esteem of beneficiaries constrains how one carries out the duty of beneficence, so also one's indirect duty to oneself to avoid poverty constrains how much to sacrifice for the sake of others. How are the limits of beneficence to be determined? To answer on Kant's behalf: there is no set rule to follow; good judgment considering one's circumstances is required, characteristic of a wide, imperfect duty. Relatedly, Kant asks how much moral worth is realized by a benefactor who gives "with a cold hand" (DV 6:454).

Kant also considers a case in which the master of an estate, who has a kind of authority over the hereditary subjects of the estate, paternalistically imposes her own conception of happiness on those subjects. Even if she does what *she thinks* is best for them, does depriving them of the freedom to decide such matters for themselves deprive her of the title of genuine benefactor? Alternatively, suppose the subjects were to submit to the unjust imposition; would they be "throwing away [their, M.T.] humanity in the greatest degree" (ibid.)? If so, would the care by the master count as genuine beneficence? Perhaps the merit of such beneficence can be "so great as to outweigh the right of human beings" (ibid.). Kant here seems to answer all these questions by remarking that one cannot genuinely benefit other persons by *imposing* on them one's own conception of happiness (children and the mentally disturbed being exceptions), even in cases in which recipients reluctantly agree to the "benefit." Given the value Kant puts on freedom of individuals, this is an important point for Kant because paternalism interferes with or usurps the freedom of its target.

Kant concludes by asking whether, given the circumstances of social injustice that are largely responsible for inequality of wealth, those wealthy enough to help those in need should view themselves as acting beneficently, particularly if they "gladly brag" about it as something meritorious.

B. On the duty of gratitude

Kant begins with a general description of what gratitude consists in, namely, honoring or revering a person because of a benefit received from them (DV 6:454).[10] He then makes a few observations about the duty of gratitude before remarking on its special status (§32) and content (§33).

---

[10] It is likely a mistake (perhaps by the typesetter) that Section 31, belonging to the discussion of beneficence, includes the first paragraph on the duty of gratitude. There is little in Collins and Vigilantius about gratitude as a duty of love, but much about ingratitude as a vice of hatred.

First, Kant claims that a judgment of gratitude on the part of the beneficiary is connected to a feeling of respect for one's benefactor, while the benefactor, having conferred a benefit gratuitously, stands in a relation of practical love to the beneficiary. *Second*, there is a difference between "active" and "affective" gratitude. The former involves expressing or demonstrating one's gratitude. But even mere heartfelt benevolence "without physical consequences" (DV 6:455) deserves to be considered a duty of virtue, the proper response to which is affective gratitude—being genuinely appreciative and perhaps expressing it toward the benevolent person.[11] Kant gives no example of this kind of case, but suppose a distant relative expresses a willingness to help financially with your education, not as a loan but just because they see you need the help. Even if you decline, the heartfelt benevolent gesture surely deserves your appreciativeness or what Kant is calling affective gratitude.

In §32, Kant makes clear that gratitude is a duty and not just a matter of prudence whereby one expresses gratitude merely as a means for receiving further benefits. He writes that gratitude is a "direct necessitation by the moral law, i.e. one's duty" (DV 6:455). Kant does not explicitly argue for this claim, as he does for other duties of virtue. However, he has already explained that duties of love directly impose obligations on recipients: in response to genuine beneficence, gratitude is owed to one's benefactor.

Interestingly, Kant claims that gratitude is to be considered a "sacred" duty and thus has a status unlike all other "ordinary" duties. What does this claim amount to? It is somewhat hard to tell. Here is the passage (bracketed numbers inserted):

> Gratitude must also be viewed in particular as a *sacred* duty, [1] i.e. as one the violation of which can (as a scandalous example) annihilate the moral incentive of being beneficent in the principle itself. For [2] sacred is the moral object with regard to which obligation cannot be

---

[11] Is Kant violating his claim that feelings cannot be commanded because they are not within our voluntary control and thus there are no duties to have them? (Thanks to Adam Cureton for raising this worry.) What Kant might say is that one can have a duty to *cultivate* such feelings even if, once cultivated, one experiences them spontaneously.

discharged completely by any act that conforms with it (when the one who is obligated always remains obligated still) (DV 6:455).

The "i.e." in 1 might suggest that the negative example that ingratitude sets is what makes gratitude sacred. Display of vices other than ingratitude perhaps can have the same effect. Ridiculing someone for their beneficence toward others might tend to discourage further beneficence, but it does not have the power to "annihilate the moral incentive" to gratitude as does ingratitude (which is one of the vices of hatred taken up in the next chapter). Acts of genuine beneficence characteristically initiate a special relation with the beneficiary—one of practical love. Ingratitude, particularly what Kant calls aggravated ingratitude in which the beneficiary comes to hate her benefactor, returns hate for expressions of practical love. It thereby has the peculiar power to destroy or significantly weaken the moral incentive to beneficence. As such, the duty of gratitude takes on a special status that Kant is calling "sacred" in the sense that it helps safeguard incentives to beneficence.

Sentence 2 seems to indicate something different about the sacredness of this duty, namely, that gratitude cannot be completely discharged. Yet how can there be duties that cannot be completely discharged? Kant, in many places, appeals to the thesis that "ought" implies "can"; that if one morally ought to do something, then it is something one can do. If one cannot discharge a duty, how can it be a duty in the first place? To respond, Kant explains that because the benefactor initiated the benefactor/beneficiary relationship, she has a "preeminence of merit" (DV 6:455), namely of being first in benevolence. So, the benefactor's action was meritorious in a way that the beneficiary's gratitude ordinarily cannot match. Of course, even if for this reason one cannot completely discharge a duty of gratitude (unlike repaying a loan and like our duty of moral self-perfection), one can comply with the duty to some extent by expressing or demonstrating one's gratitude. Thus, there is no violation of the "ought/can" dictum insofar as compliance is concerned. However, it remains unclear in what way the undischargability makes the duty of gratitude sacred or how it relates to gratitude's special status in helping to safeguard the incentive to beneficence.

In §33, Kant considers the content of the duty of gratitude, mentioning extent and degree. Extent concerns the scope of those to whom one ought to express gratitude, while intensity (or degree) pertains to what would count as an adequate expression of gratitude. Regarding extent, there are one's known benefactors. However, one's grateful disposition should extend to one's predecessors, "even those who cannot be named with certainty" (DV 6:455). Regarding degree, what and how much one should do for one's benefactor depends on various factors, including (*i*) the size of the benefit conferred, and (*ii*) how unselfishly it was given. Thus, the greater the benefit, the more one should do by way of expressing one's gratitude. Merely saying "thank you" to a person who saved your life is not normally an adequate expression of gratitude, at least in cases in which one has an opportunity to do more for the person. Again, the greater the level of genuine non-self-interested care expressed by the benefactor in bestowing the benefit, the greater one's appreciation should be, reflected in buying or doing something appropriate in response, or at least being disposed to do so. Kant mentions rendering to the benefactor "*equal* services" (DV 6:456) as the least one should do, where equality is to be understood as doing something for the benefactor (if possible) that is equal in prudential value to the benefit bestowed. Concerning intensity, there can be cases of under-gratitude (doing too little) and over-gratitude (doing too much). Fitting gratitude is a delicate matter.

The dimensions of extent and intensity reveal how the duty of gratitude is narrow and perfect in some ways (to whom one owes gratitude) yet wide and imperfect in other ways. In cases in which one knows the identity of the benefactor, the duty is specific concerning who one is obligated to. Also, as just noted, one is to do something for one's benefactor that is in some sense equal to the benefit received. Still, there is latitude regarding what to do and when; it is wide and imperfect along these dimensions.

Kant ends his discussion of gratitude with a remark about how one should view being a beneficiary. Because a beneficiary "stands a step lower than his patron" (DV 6:456) in owing respect to a beneficiary who does not owe such respect in return, there is a tendency to resentment. To inoculate oneself against resentment Kant suggests that the proper way to receive the benefactor's kindness is to see oneself as having an opportunity to cultivate one's love of humanity. And so, although the feeling associated with gratitude is respect, properly practiced it is as a chance to develop or increase one's own benevolent disposition toward human beings and is thereby associated with love as a feeling.

Before moving forward, it is worth considering gratitude and sincerity. If expressions of gratitude are sincere, don't they have to express *feelings* of gratefulness? Of course, feelings are not within one's direct voluntary control. So, if one has a duty to express gratitude on some occasion, yet lacks the relevant grateful feelings, isn't one obligated then to be insincere? No, for three reasons. *First*, sincerely *judging* that someone deserves one's gratitude does not require one to have grateful feelings as one makes the judgment. *Second,* nor does acting on one's judgment, thereby complying with the duty, although we might sometimes be required to hide our ungrateful feelings or pretend as if we do not have them. *Third*, Kant can say that the *virtue* of gratitude, as an acquired character trait, is most fully realized when one has cultivated feelings of gratitude that serve as the emotional core of the virtue. The cultivation of feelings brings us to the third duty of love.

C. *The duty of sympathetic participation*

This third duty of love is to recruit one's natural sympathetic feelings for others (fellow feelings) for a moral purpose.[12] A *fundamental* moral purpose is that of fully developing the virtue of "active and rational benevolence" (DV 6:456). Therefore, Kant classifies the duty of sympathetic participation as "indirect"—it can be viewed as furthering this more fundamental duty of beneficence. However, there is some complexity here, though to bring it out, one must fill out Kant's laconic remarks in these passages.

First, Kant distinguishes natural sympathy from principled sympathy. In an early writing, Kant describes sympathy as a "beautiful and

---

[12]   See Collins 27:421–422 and Vigilantius 27:677–678.

lovable feeling" which "indicates a kindly participation in the fate of other people." However, he goes on to say that "this kindly passion is nevertheless weak and always blind. For suppose that this sentiment moves you to help someone in need with your expenditure, but that you are indebted to someone else and by this means you make it impossible for yourself to fulfill the strict duty of justice . . ." (Obs 2:215–216). Thus, acting out of sympathy is only contingently related to complying with one's moral obligations, and can lead one to do what is wrong. Yet, "Nature has placed [it, M.T.] in us to do what the representation of duty by itself would not accomplish" (DV 6:457). Of course, such motivation should only be provisional while one learns to constrain such feelings by the moral law.

Second, while in the service of active rational benevolence, this duty is arguably distinctive because it adds to, and is partly constitutive of, benevolence as a fully developed virtue. Otherwise, it doesn't deserve a place of its own among the duties of love. What it adds is what Kant calls "humaneness"—a response to the weal or woe of others as a way of sharing in others' fate.[13] One way in which one naturally displays humaneness is through emotional contagion, as when one enters a room full of cheerful people and their cheer rubs off so that one participates in the group's positive feeling. This kind of sympathetic participation is passive and thus unfree. Another source of humaneness is active and located in "the *capacity* and *will* to *communicate* with one another with regard to one's *feelings* . . ." (DV 6:456). The duty of humaneness (sympathetic participation) is to develop this capacity.

Third, although Kant is not explicit about the matter, having and expressing one's sympathetic feelings, particularly toward those who are enduring hardships, is a way of communicating a sense of *moral equality* with them, regardless of the kinds of circumstance that tend to divide human beings, such as social position. It is a human way of communicating, because, as Kant says, human beings are here

---

[13] 'Humaneness' is distinct from 'humanity' in Kant's technical vocabulary. "To be humane is to interest oneself in the fate of other men; inhumanity is to take no interest in what happens to them" (Col 27:419). See also Vigilantius 27:592 where Kant is explicit about the humaneness/humanity distinction.

considered as rational beings with an animal (sensible) nature, and one mode of communication is by expressing one's feelings.

Fourth, the duty of sympathetic participation requires one to adopt the end (maxim of action) of having one's capacity for fellow-feeling be governed by moral principles—an end that is partly constitutive of active rational benevolence as a fully developed virtue. As an end to be promoted, the duty is wide and imperfect. *Fifth*, developing this virtue is achieved in concrete steps such as seeking out those who have suffered misfortune. Kant mentions visiting "places where poor people who lack the most basic necessities are to be found . . . and not to shun sickrooms or debtors' prisons" (DV 6:457). In these times, different steps can be taken including viewing documentary films about poverty, visiting websites, and so on.[14] Of course, there is more to recruiting fellow feelings than just exposing oneself to the plight of others. For one thing, part of the point of bringing such natural capacities under the control of moral principles is so that one becomes skillful regarding how and when to allow such feelings to play any role in motivating beneficent action.[15] Such matters of detail belong to Method which takes up the practice of virtue.

Sixth, and finally, to share in others' feelings in complying with the duty, at least with respect to another's sadness, does not require literally having the same or similar feelings as someone else. "[I]t cannot possibly be one's duty to increase the ills in the world, nor hence to be beneficent *from pity*" (DV 6:457). Moreover, Kant thinks that doing good from compassion does (or can) express a kind of pity for the other as if they were "unworthy" of happiness. He refers to this as a kind of insulting beneficence. Here is another instance in which carrying out the duty of beneficence is to be tempered by the duty to help preserve the self-esteem of others. Thus, the duty to "share" in others' feelings is simply to respond in ways, which, in the case of someone in need and thus likely upset, sad, depressed, or whatever, is to help them if one can.

[14] Though perhaps recruitment of one's natural sympathetic feelings is more effective if one interacts personally with others, as Kant's examples suggest.

[15] For elaboration, on Kant's behalf, of some of the finer details of the process or this kind of recruitment, see Fahmy 2009.

Casuistical questions

Finally, in the first of two paragraphs that make up the section on casuistry, Kant raises the question of whether benevolence is really to be considered a duty.[16] Perhaps it would be better for the well-being of human beings if there were only duties of right while benevolence were considered morally indifferent. Kant's reply is that the world would be missing a "great moral adornment" (DV 6:458). The rather cryptic reason he gives is that in order "to present the world as a beautiful moral whole in its entire perfection" (and apart from how it bears on human happiness), love of humanity (*Menchenliebe*) is required. Perhaps Kant's switching from talk of *Wohlwollen* to talk of *Menchenliebe* is that the latter is intended to refer to the so-called duty of humanity, a label Kant uses in §34 for the duty of sympathy. Another thought is that perhaps his remark here should be related to §24 and Kant's remark that mutual love is part of how a "moral intelligible world" is to be conceived together with mutual respect. The former "admonishes" moral beings to come closer, the latter to keep a distance. This passage in 24 comes just after Kant explains that preserving the self-esteem of those who are in need must temper how one confers a benefit upon them. However, a problem with this proposal is that Kant's response to the question about benevolence that he raises at 458 does not seem to be about keeping respect from driving moral agents away from each other.

Finally, Kant returns to his claim that gratitude involves a kind of inequality between benefactor and beneficiary—the source of its undischargability. He asks whether this is not a source of ingratitude, one of the vices of hatred that we take up in the next chapter.

13.3 Concluding reflections

In concluding, it is worth comparing Kant's conception of sympathy with the contemporary distinction between empathy and sympathy,

---

[16] He raises this same question about the duty of beneficence at DV 6:452.

for purposes of clarification. One common way of distinguishing these is to say that in empathizing with someone, one shares in whatever feeling they are having, whether the feeling is positive or negative (e.g. joy or sadness). Sympathy, by contrast, is typically characterized as "an affective response that consists in feeling sorrow or concern for the distressed or needy other (rather than feeling the same emotion)" (Eisenberg 2004: 678). If I see that you are greatly embarrassed by a remark someone makes, I sympathize with you if I feel concern for you; I need not simulate your embarrassment. This contrast between empathy and sympathy is a rough one, because philosophers and psychologists often recognize more than one species of each. For instance, empathic responses include spontaneous emotional contagion mentioned earlier as well as consciously trying to imagine what someone else is feeling and thereby coming to feel something similar.[17] Empathy and sympathy are species of fellow-feeling.

It is anachronistic to employ the empathy/sympathy terminology in interpreting Kant. One reason is that the term *Einfühlung* (translated into English as 'empathy') was not introduced until 1873. Another reason is that Kant's conception of *Teilnemung* (rendered into English as 'sympathy') seems to differ from how the term is understood in contemporary work. Nevertheless, in the spirit of trying to understand Kant's moral psychology, one can use the empathy/sympathy distinction and ask how Kant's conception of sympathy is related to this distinction. Here are a few observations.

First, Kant recognizes sympathetic *joy* (rejoicing with others) as well as sadness. These days, it is odd to say that one sympathizes with one's neighbor who is overjoyed at having just won the lottery. As reflected in the quote from Eisenberg, 'sympathy' is reserved for the kind of fellow-feeling prompted by someone else's state of need or suffering. So, Kant's conception of sympathy is broader than how it is now conceived. *Second*, Kant's conception of unfree receptivity to the feelings of joy and sadness of others describes emotional contagion, which is a kind of empathy. Of course, if one uses 'sympathy' to cover

---

[17] Arguably, these two species of empathy work through different mental mechanisms. Emotional contagion works by mimicry, while the more effortful variety works by mental simulation. (Thanks to Max Kramer for discussion of this point.)

the field of fellow-feeling, it is being used in a much broader way than we find in current usage.

Finally, a word about Kant's apparent dismissal of pity (*Mitleid*), also translated as 'compassion'. In the *Anthropology*, Kant characterizes compassion as an affect. As we learned in chapter 8, sec. 6, affects are occurrent feelings which, like a flash of anger, suspend the mind's composure, while passions are inflamed desires that take root in one's psychology. He goes on to say that "the wisdom of nature has implanted in us the predisposition to compassion in order to handle the reigns *provisionally,* until reason has achieved the necessary strength" (Anth 7:253). The necessary strength in question is the acquired ability to respond to the plight of others based on a firm maxim of benevolence tempered by respect so that one avoids feeling mere pity for victims of suffering and need. Compassion, then, is a natural human feeling that is (or can be) instrumentally morally valuable, but it is to be constrained by maxims grounded in the moral law.

Further reading

- On the duty of love in Kant, see Schönecker 2013.
- On gratitude, see Smit and Timmons 2011 [2017a], and Moran 2016.
- On sympathetic participation, see Denis 2000a, Fahmy 2009, and Thomason 2017.

14

The Vices of Hatred and of Disrespect

Part II, Chapter I, Section I (continued), and Chapter II

The previous chapter left off just before Kant turns from the duties of love to the corresponding vices of hatred. The treatment of these vices completes Section I of the first of two chapters in Part II of the Elements. It is followed by Section II on the duties of respect toward others, all of which are negative and concern the vices of disrespect. This chapter covers both these species of vice. It also covers the second chapter of Part II, which is a brief one-paragraph set of remarks about the application of the duties of virtue considering the varying circumstances of human beings.

Given this chapter's focus, let us review some points about vice, mentioned in previous chapters. *First*, talk of vice can refer to a particular action, as when one tells a lie—something a person may do without having the character trait of dishonesty. Of course, Kant's main concern in DV is moral character, and so with virtue and vices as traits of character. *Second*, as we've learned, Kant distinguishes vice from mere lack of virtue. Returning for a moment to Section VII of the introduction to DV, Kant remarks that strength of resolution in complying with one's duties (specifically the imperfect ones) is properly called virtue; "one's weakness . . . is not so much *vice* . . . as rather mere *lack of virtue*, shortage of moral strength. . . . Every action contrary to duty is called a *transgression*. . . . But if it is intentional and has become a matter of principle, it actually constitutes that which is called *vice* . . ." (DV 6:390, Latin terminology omitted). And again, later in the introduction, Kant contrasts lack of virtue with vice, relating them respectively to affects and passions. He writes that lack of virtue "can very well coexist with the best will" (DV 6: 408) characteristic of action driven by affect (e.g. anger). By contrast, when a propensity to an affect becomes a passion (e.g. hatred), one thereby takes up "evil (as intentional) into its maxim; and then it is *aggravated* evil, i.e. a true *vice*" (DV 6:408). With these

Kant's Doctrine of Virtue. Mark Timmons, Oxford University Press (2021). © Oxford University Press.
DOI: 10.1093/oso/9780190939229.003.0014

points in mind, here are the guiding questions pertaining to the vices of hatred, saving the vices of disrespect until Section 2.

- What are the vices of hatred?
- What is their source?

14.1 The vices of hatred

Section 36 is entitled "On the vices of hatred of humanity, which are directly (*contrarie*) opposed to the love of humanity" and features brief discussions of envy, ingratitude, and *Schadenfreude*. Not only do these vices violate one's duties of virtue toward others, but because they are "secretive and veiled" (DV 6:458) they violate a duty to oneself. Kant does not mention any particular duty to oneself one violates; however, a likely candidate is the duty of sincerity discussed along with lying. Working in secret against the well-being of others requires insincerity (or being prepared to be so) in one's interaction with the target of one's envy, ingratitude, or *Schadenfreude*, adding to the viciousness of the vice. All three vices pertain to one's own self-esteem (earlier discussed in 10.4 in relation to the vice of servility).

Envy

As a character trait, envy disposes one "to perceive the weal of others as painful [i.e. to be pained at their good fortune or general well-being, M. T.], even though it does not infringe on one's own ..." (DV 6:458).[1] The others are typically one's peers with whom one compares oneself. Envy "proper" (aggravated envy) refers to instances in which one *acts* out of envy in harming or attempting to harm someone. Envy that does not manifest in outward harm toward others is experienced as a kind of resentment. Kant also remarks that *movements* of envy are

---

[1] See Collins, the section "Of Jealousy, and the Envy and Ill-Feeling that Result" at 27:436–444, and in Vigilantius the section "Envy, Ingratitude and *Schadenfreude*" at 27:691–698.

ubiquitously present in human beings where "movements" perhaps refers to the impulse to compare oneself with others regarding one's own well-being, which is the psychological source of this battery of vices (addressing our second question). The Vigilantius notes refers to this impulse as rivalry and explains that maxims associated with the vices of hatred,

> take the ground of their origin from a property of human nature native to man, which not only makes us intrinsically guiltless, but also determines us to an admirable purpose: namely, the instinct of antagonism or rivalry, i.e., the inclination to work against the perfection of others, or to surpass them by ever-increasingly promoting our own cultivation, in agreement with the laws of morality. This is shown in appearance by the fact that we constantly compare ourselves with other men, and feel a chagrin on discovering their good points, whether it be their dutiful conduct, their honor, or their well-being. (Vig 27:692)

Interpersonal comparisons of well-being are morally unproblematic when they prompt one (within the bounds of morality) to improve one's condition. For instance, I view the welfare-contributing habits of my neighbor as something that I currently lack and wish to have, and her example inspires me to emulate her. This is a friendly sort of rivalry through which I raise myself up in some way, although even this sort might not be entirely beyond rational reproach because the standard we use to estimate how well off we are is not by "its inner worth but only by comparison with the weal of others" (DV 6:458). The bad sort is where I view the other's prosperity as a threat to my self-esteem, and rather than attempt to raise myself up to their level, I disapprove, and perhaps try to deprive them of whatever good they have that is a source of my distress. Notably, envy, according to Kant, is only an "indirectly malevolent" disposition, because such self-other comparisons at the basis of envy concern the good of proper self-esteem. The problem is that the envious person mistakenly takes the lowering of a rival's well-being as a way to protect or promote his own self-esteem. Understood in this way, envy is intrinsically related to the good of self-esteem. By contrast, the vice of *Schadenfreude* (i.e. taking malicious joy in the woe of others), as we shall see, is *directly* opposed to the well-being of others.

Ingratitude

Here, Kant contrasts ingratitude "proper" (aggravated ingratitude) with mere unappreciativeness.[2] The latter (as a vice) is a disposition (and thus a character trait) which inclines one to refrain from expressing gratitude toward one's benefactor.[3] This can be done by just avoiding the benefactor. It is when this disposition includes hatred that it becomes aggravated. Notice that the aggravated/unappreciativeness contrast, as Kant describes it, is not the same as the aggravated/resentment distinction between two kinds of envy. Aggravated envy involves outwardly acting on one's envious feelings; aggravated ingratitude is described in terms of hatred, which need not break out into action.[4]

What Kant goes on to explain (albeit very briefly) is that the (or a) main source of ingratitude is misunderstanding one's duty to oneself— the duty, in Kant's words, of "not to need or to invite the beneficence of others" (DV 6:459). Of course, sometimes one does need the help of others. Thus, it is when one needs others' beneficence only because one has mismanaged one's own affairs that one violates a duty to oneself—presumably a duty of frugality discussed in the lecture notes.[5] Again, the source of ingratitude as a vice is feeling somehow inferior to one's benefactor in owing him more than he owes us and viewing this as a threat to one's self-esteem, because we thereby tend to see ourselves as having an inferior status in the system of duties that we can never get out of. But as Kant remarks in his discussion of the virtue of

[2] See Collins 27:441–443 and in Vigilantius the section "Envy, Ingratitude and *Schadenfreude*" at 27:691–698.

[3] Another form of unappreciativeness is what is often called "non-gratitude"—a failure to be sensitive to the beneficence of others, manifesting a mere lack of virtue, rather than a vice directly opposed to expressing gratitude.

[4] Between the propensity to envy and aggravated envy, there are cases of *wishing* that others experience their weal as painful, having an *inclination* to *act* out of envy toward someone in particular, and forming an *intention* to do so. This range of attitudes allows Kant to distinguish degrees of vice. On this point, see Smit and Timmons 2015.

[5] This duty is described as moderation or abstinence in the possession of material goods (Col 27:406; Vig 27:696). It is a species of the more general duty of self-mastery.

gratitude, in a person who has a proper sense of self-esteem, gratitude represents an opportunity to unite gratitude with "love of humanity" (DV 6:456). Thus, aggravated ingratitude in response to practical love manifested in heartfelt beneficence—returning hate for love—stands love of human beings "on its head" (DV 6:459). Presumably, this remark reflects one of the reasons Kant identifies gratitude as a sacred duty: as explained in the previous chapter (sec. 2): ingratitude has the capacity to "annihilate the moral incentive to being beneficent in the principle itself" (DV 6:455).

Schadenfreude

Schadenfreude or malicious pleasure as a character trait is directly opposed to sympathy for others and is thus a vice.[6] When one acts on it to harm others it is *Schadenfreude* "proper" (aggravated). Again, like envy and ingratitude, its source is woven into human nature via the instinct of rivalry. Specifically, Kant mentions a law of contrast by which one feels one's own well-being more strongly when comparing ourselves to others less fortunate. One likewise feels their own good conduct more strongly when one compares herself to the public moral downfall of others. There is nothing inherently wrong or vicious about such comparisons. However, taking an immediate delight in the misfortune of others or even wishing for it is "secret hatred of humanity" (DV 6:460) and thus directly opposed to love of and sympathetic participation with others. This kind of person was identified earlier (in §26, see chap. 13.1) as an enemy of humanity. Kant speculates that often what triggers *Schadenfreude* is the haughtiness of others over their well-being and/or their self-conceit over their good conduct, especially when such advantages are due mostly to luck—luck in one's prosperity, rather than its owing to hard work, and luck in not having one's character tested by having to confront serious temptation.

   Schadenfreude can take various forms. Kant singles out a desire for vengeance as its "sweetest form" which, he notes, is often accompanied

---

[6] In Collins, see the section "On Enmity" at 27:430–432, and in Vigilantius see "Envy, Ingratitude and *Schadenfreude*" at 27:691–698.

by the illusion that one has a right of justice to make harming someone an end regardless of whether doing so would be to one's advantage. One thus has a duty to avoid such hostility, both in attitude and in action. Nor should one "call upon the judge of the world [God, M.T.] to take revenge" partly because the caller himself "is saddled enough with his own guilt to be greatly in need of forgiveness" (DV 6:461) and partly because no punishment (even meted out by God) may be imposed out of hatred.[7] After these remarks the passage continues:

> That is why *conciliatoriness* (placabilitas) is a human duty; and it must not be confused with *meek toleration* of wrongs . . . , the renouncing of rigorous means (rigorosa) for preventing the recurrence of being wronged by others. For that would be throwing away one's rights under the feet of others, and violating a human being's duty to himself (ibid.).

Meek toleration of one's rights being violated is itself a violation of the duty to avoid servility. What isn't clear is whether the duty of conciliatoriness refers to a duty of forgiveness or whether it refers merely to avoiding the hostility that comes with *Schadenfreude* and, in particular, with the desire for vengeance. In the sentence preceding the quote, Kant mentions everyone's great need of forgiveness,[8] yet the quote is separated from the preceding text by a dash, suggesting perhaps that Kant is here referring to the negative duty he has just explained—the duty to avoid a desire for vengeance. If avoiding or at least forswearing hostile feelings toward others is sufficient for complying with a duty of forgiveness (and thus assuming it doesn't entail a positive duty to outwardly express forgiveness to someone), then perhaps talk of forgiveness is equivalent to talk of conciliatoriness. Unfortunately, Kant nowhere discusses (or is reported as discussing) a duty of forgiveness.

The discussion of vice ends with a section entitled "Remark," in which Kant briefly (and rather obscurely) reflects on two views one

---

[7] Indeed, the rights of (human) punishment for crimes belongs to the state, not individuals seeking revenge—a topic treated in DR.

[8] The German term here is *Versöhnlichkeit* which Gregor translates as 'forgiveness', while Timmermann and Grenberg translate it as 'conciliation'.

might have of human nature based on experience and given its susceptibility to the vices. The first juxtaposes so-called diabolical vices with their counterpart angelic virtues. Elsewhere, the vices of hatred are called diabolical (see R 6:27) and contrasted with the brutish vices (see later). Kant understands the intended contrast to be between ideas of maximum vice and maximum virtue. He does not give examples, but perhaps he has in mind, for example, a perfect ideal of a beneficent person contrasted with a thoroughly malicious counterpart. The point of this contrast (gathering from what Kant says) is its use for determining whether human beings are to be "assigned" either to heaven or to hell—presumably as they approach in their character either angels or devils. (From the first sentence in this passage, I take Kant to be referring to the human species rather than individual members.) Kant rejects this way of classifying human beings, remarking that the "juxtaposition . . . is an exaggeration" (DV 6:461), presumably because human beings as a species are not properly thought of as devils or angels, assigned to hell or heaven. In chapter 8, we considered Kant's thesis of radical evil from the *Religion*. Although the human species is characterized by a propensity (in Kant's technical sense) to subordinate morality to self-love, this does not make a comparison with devils apt. Nor, of course, are human beings by nature angelic.

The second view is taken from Albrecht von Haller (Swiss scientist and literary figure, 1708–1777) who apparently described humans as a hybrid "of angels and of brutes" (ibid.) thus being by nature something intermediate between angel and devil. One of Kant's complaints is that this conception, which attempts to combine "heterogeneous" components, leads to no determinate classification. However, his more substantial criticism comes in the Remark's final sentence. Kant apparently takes Haller as attributing to the human species a predisposition to the brutish vices and so commenting on this view he writes: "though human beings do—alas!—also fall into *brutish* vices, [this, M.T.] does not justify ascribing to them a predisposition to these vices *that belong to their species*, any more than the deformity of some trees in a forest is grounds for making them a special *kind* of plant" (ibid.). The brutish vices discussed in DV include those associated with negative duties to oneself as an animal being (self-disembodiment, lustful self-defilement, gluttony and drunkenness) and are referred to here

238 THE DOCTRINE OF ELEMENTS

(given Haller's angels/brutes remark.) Kant denies that these vices are predispositions (in the technical sense of 'predisposition' discussed in chap. 8) because to do so would contradict his thesis from the *Religion* that as intelligible beings humans have a predisposition to the good, and that vices result from the misuse of one's freedom of choice. He would say that same about all vices.

14.2   On duties of respect toward others and the vices of disrespect

Chapter I, Section II of duties to others is entitled, "On duties of virtue toward other human beings that arise from the respect due them," and composed of eight Sections. In the five of them that precede discussion of the vices of disrespect, Kant discusses a variety of respect-related topics, the most important of which address these questions:

- What is the basis for the respect owed to every human being?
- What is the nature of contempt for human beings?
- Is contempt for human beings ever justified?
- What are the vices of disrespect?
- What is their source?

Modesty versus self-gratification (egotism) and self-conceit

Human beings by nature have a desire to be loved as well as respected by others.[9] If we understand the desire to be loved as the desire and expectation to receive help from others, then one way of overstepping one's legitimate expectation is to expect more from others than one is willing to contribute to their welfare. Those who do so are guilty of *self-gratification*—a kind of moral egotism.[10] And if we understand the

---

[9] See in Collins, "Of the Two Drives of Nature, and the Duties Relating to Them" (27:407–412), the two drives being love and respect.

[10] The person of self-gratification (*Eigenliebe*) should be compared to the self-seeker (*Selbstsüchtiger*) mentioned at DV: 6:450 and described in the previous chapter (sec. 2).

desire to be respected as the desire that others recognize one's dignity as a person, then one is overstepping one's legitimate expectation if one exalts oneself over others by demanding more respect from them than one is willing to grant them as human beings with a capacity to be virtuous. Those who do so are guilty of *self-conceit*.

The attitudes involved in self-gratification and self-conceit are opposed to what Kant calls "modesty." Modesty is a matter of willfully restricting one's demands and expectations of others concerning both love and respect. Persons indulging in self-gratification fail to respect the fact that other human beings are beings of need and whose self-interest *as such* is not of lesser importance than one's own. Those guilty of self-conceit fail to recognize the self-esteem that others ought to preserve for themselves. Both are forms of immodesty.

The duty of respect for others

The second paragraph of §38 explains the basis of the duty of respect toward others and is worth quoting in two parts (brackets inserted), with commentary on both.

> [1] Humanity itself is a dignity. For [2] a human being cannot be used merely as a means by any human being (neither by others nor even by himself), but must always be used at the same time as an end; and [3] precisely therein consists his dignity (personality), by which he elevates himself above all other beings in the world that are not human beings and can yet be used, and hence above all things.

Claim 2 of course, is a statement of the formula of humanity of the CI. What is worthy of note is that this formula expresses what one's dignity consists in. That is, dignity is not being conceived as an intrinsically valuable state or status which is (*i*) independent of and prior to the moral law and (*ii*) serves to justify the moral law. That is, Kant's

---

The former demands or expects more beneficence from others than she is willing to give them. The latter is indifferent to the welfare of others and seems to be identical to what Kant refers to as a 'moral egoist' in the *Anthropology* at 7:130.

moral theory is not a version of consequentialism, which, as a generic type of theory (there are many species) is distinguished by these two claims. Nor is it any other view that makes the good (even partly) prior to the right.[11] Rather, Kant's view is that human beings have an *inherent dignity*, an elevated status compared to nonrational beings, *in virtue of* being subject to the CI whose metaphysical ground is one's freedom (autonomy). In the cited passage Kant refers to humanity and to (moral) personality which, in this context, refer to the same *capacity* for being motivated by respect for the law (namely, autonomy).[12] While the first part of the passage rehearses basic elements of Kant's metaethical views, the remainder completes the argument.

> [4] But just as he cannot give himself away for any price (which would conflict with the duty of self-esteem), so [5] neither can he act contrary to the equally necessary self-esteem of others, as human beings, i.e., [6] he is obligated to acknowledge practically the dignity of humanity in every other human being, and hence [7] there rests on him a duty that refers to the respect that must by necessity be shown to every other human being.

Claim 4 refers to one's duty to oneself not to "give himself away"—the duty to avoid servility in standing up for one's dignity (which is to express moral self-esteem or true noble pride). The passage then points out that all others have this same duty. And just as one's duty of true noble pride demands that you preserve your standing as a person with dignity, so too you are obligated to recognize others' equal standing. Kant would say the same sort of thing about one's attitudes even if not outwardly exhibited.

Although Kant does not invoke the formula of universal law in this argument, the flavor of it is like his use of that formula in arguing for a duty of beneficence. That is, just as someone takes her ends as a reason for select others to help in achieving those ends, similarly, in light of the duty of proper self-esteem, she in effect demands that others treat her

[11] For an extended defense of this claim, see Sensen 2011.
[12] Though, as noted in chap. 7, sec. 1, 'humanity' is sometimes used in a narrower sense that contrasts with both animality and moral personality.

in ways that recognize her dignity as a human being and do nothing to threaten her self-esteem (that is, the esteem she does or should have for herself). In the case of those guilty of self-gratification who take their own ends as reasons for others to help them (though are unwilling to reciprocate), such people cannot consistently will their maxim become universal law. Thus, a *policy* (maxim) of not helping others is wrong. Somewhat similarly, the conceited person who demands a level of respect from others that he is not willing to return is acting on a maxim that he cannot consistently will everyone to adopt and act on. Thus, the maxim on which the self-conceited person acts in either expressing their arrogance, defaming, or ridiculing others is wrong. Of course, in the case of beneficence, the duty is wide and imperfect—to adopt the maxim of promoting the happiness of others—while the duty of respect toward others is a narrow, perfect negative duty.

Stephen Darwall, in an influential paper from 1977, distinguishes two kinds of respect: recognition respect and appraisal respect. The former, as it pertains to persons, involves responding to persons as having equal moral standing simply in virtue of their moral personality (in Kant's technical sense), i.e. the capacity to freely act for reasons whose source is the moral law. This capacity confers dignity in equal measure on all persons. So, the kind of respect Kant is concerned with here is recognition respect. Appraisal respect is something earned by those who distinguish themselves in some way and thus responds to merit. As a response to someone's morally meritorious behavior it is perhaps best conceived as moral *admiration* for the person, an attitude Kant distinguishes from (recognition) respect. (See for example, CprR 5:76–77).

Besides the recognition/appraisal distinction, we should also distinguish mere "outward respect" for others from "inner respect." The former refers to behavior of the sort that outwardly complies with a duty to others, regardless of one's inner attitude in such compliance. For instance, one might donate to charity, but only because doing so makes one look good in the opinion of others while in truth having little care or even respect for the beneficiaries. In so doing, one is not outwardly doing anything wrong, yet one's maxim is not strictly one of beneficence (helping others "without hoping for something in return," DV 6:453) nor, of course, does one's action have any moral worth.

Kant's concern in DV is, of course, not with mere outward behavior that superficially resembles acting benevolently. Duties to others where the concern is just with outward behavior is treated in *The Doctrine of Right*. DV, as explained in chapter 6, is mostly concerned with one's inner life; with maxims of choice rather than mere outward "external" actions of, for example, politeness.

Contempt

In §37 Kant describes contempt as "judging an entity to be one that has no worth" (DV 6:463). There is a difference between *treatment* that expresses one's judgment of contempt for others and *regarding* others with contempt, where the latter need not be manifested in how one treats others. Kant is here claiming that regarding others *as such* with contempt, in the sense of internally thinking of them as having no worth and thus not deserving of respect, is contrary to one's duty. *All* human beings, in virtue of their inherent dignity (a predisposition to the good as moral personality), are worthy of some degree of basic respect, in both treatment and attitude. In §39 Kant writes that even regarding a vicious person, I cannot withdraw respect from him "at least in his quality as a human being, even though by his deeds he makes himself unworthy of it" (DV 6:463). So, for example, Kant condemns disgraceful punishments that are presumably prompted by contempt "such as quartering, having someone torn to pieces by dogs, cutting off noses and ears" (ibid.) as examples of treatment inconsistent with respect owed to even a vicious criminal even though the criminal, by his evil actions, makes his phenomenal self unworthy of his own humanity or rational nature. Indeed, in having an innate predisposition to good, a person is always capable of moral improvement.

In the "Remark" added to these comments, Kant also condemns attitudes and actions that simply express disrespect for another person's "logical use of his reason" (DV 6:463) by, for example, calling out their errors in dismissive fashion. Of course, one can offer criticism, but one should do so with an aim of improving them. This is an example of how one's duty of love toward others can combine with respect for them; a theme from the opening passage (§23) of duties toward others.

Kant does point out that at times having *feelings* of contempt or of little esteem for others is "inevitable" (DV 6:463), presumably as a spontaneous reaction to their bad deeds and taken as evidence of a seriously flawed character. Spontaneous feelings of contempt—feelings that one perhaps cannot control—are not subject to moral appraisal, though one might be morally responsible for being the kind of person who overreacts and feels contempt for all sorts of behavior that is not contemptible. Indeed, Kant refers to some attitudes and behavior as contemptible (DV 6:420; 429)—behavior *worthy* of contempt. If some behavior is worthy of contempt, is it morally wrong to have such a reaction? Now, here we need to draw an important distinction between the question of whether contempt (or any attitude directed toward persons) is *fitting* on the one hand, and whether it is *morally apt* (permitted if not required) on the other. This distinction is commonplace in contemporary discussions of the emotions.[13] Consider moral blame. The attitude of blame presents its target as having violated a moral duty without justification or excuse. This attitude directed toward someone is fitting if it is true that the target has violated a moral duty without justification or excuse. But it is a further question whether (and under what conditions) taking up the attitude of blame is morally apt (where 'apt' can mean either permitted or obligatory). Perhaps we morally ought *not* to blame others, despite it being fitting to do so, because it expresses a kind of moral superiority that we are not justified in having, given human frailty. So, questions of fit should be distinguished from questions of moral aptness.

For Kant, contempt for someone presents them as not deserving of respect owed to persons as such. But all persons as such are deserving of a basic level of respect; so, it seems that on Kant's view contempt for a person as a whole is never fitting even if contempt for the actions or character of others is sometimes fitting. If it is never fitting, then since fittingness is a condition of moral permissibility, contempt is wrong. Here, it is noteworthy that some contemporary philosophers defend the moral aptness of contempt in some cases, indeed, arguing that it

---

[13] See D'Arms and Jacobson's influential 2000 article.

is compatible with a Kantian respect for persons. We will revisit this topic in the chapter's final section.

Respectable behavior versus scandal

In §4 of the introduction to the duties to oneself, Kant writes that "love of honor" is the virtue opposed to all the vices associated with duties to oneself. In the *Anthropology* he makes the more sweeping claim that "love of honor is the constant companion of virtue" (Anth 7:258). Here, in §40, Kant writes that love of one's honor is a claim-right that one cannot forfeit. Of course, a virtue itself, as a character trait, is not a right, as Kant's remark seems to suggest. Rather, exercising one's right to demand respect from others grounds love of honor as a virtue— that is, as a complex disposition to revere one's dignity and to defend it against attacks. Kant writes that the outward manifestation of love of one's own honor is *respectability* (external comportment with the moral law), the breach of which is *scandal,* something one must avoid. However, Kant cautions that *taking* the behavior of others as scandalous needs to be properly directed so that one guards against taking merely unusual behavior as scandalous. Nor should one mistake mere custom for something demanded by the moral law—"a tyranny of popular morals . . . contrary to a human being's duty to himself" (DV 6:464). And finally, blind imitation of others who set some sort of example is contrary to one's duty to oneself because it opposes the very spirit of becoming virtuous that requires a kind of ongoing vigilance, including a kind of thoughtfulness that resists blind imitation.

Omitting duties of love versus omitting duties of respect

The distinction between mere lack of virtue and vice figures in here. Omitting to be beneficent, at least on occasions where one could help others without undue cost, is (or can be) mere lack of virtue. Perhaps one was too self-absorbed to notice the need for another's help. By contrast, "omission of duty that springs from the *respect* owed to every human being as such is *vice*" (DV 6:464). Kant's reason is that no one is wronged by omitting to act beneficently, but another person is wronged if one intentionally detracts from their self-esteem. Kant rather cryptically adds that "what does not only not add anything to morality but even eliminates the worth of the added benefit that would otherwise accrue to the subject, is *vice*" (ibid.). He might be thinking of cases in which someone outwardly helps others, which could have been a genuine benefit to them, yet his seeming beneficence is undermined by having conferred the benefit in a demeaning manner. This example again illustrates Kant's claim from §23 that observing the duty of respect should temper benefitting others if one is to express genuine beneficence.

Kant concludes this section by remarking that, unlike the duties of love in which others do not have a right to one's beneficence, others do have a right to one's respect, although this right, unlike those discussed in *The Doctrine of Right*, is not derived from the Universal Principle of Right. And this right is properly exercised (at least in outward behavior) by refraining from various types of action. Hence, the duties of respect are presented as duties of omission, among which there are those of arrogance, defamation, and ridicule.

14.3 On vices that violate respect for other human beings

Kant now uses the first three letters of the alphabet along with the name of the vice to organize his discussion of this battery of vices in §§42–44.

A. Arrogance

Arrogance refers to "the inclination to always swim *on top*" where one expects others "to esteem themselves but little in comparison with us" (DV 6:465).[14] Since others have a right to be recognized and treated as persons with dignity, arrogance is, in an extended sense, unjust.

---

[14] See Collins 27:457–458 and Vigilantius 27:708–709.

Arrogance, then, is opposed to the proper pride (self-esteem) others should have for themselves, while servility is also opposed to the proper pride (self-esteem) one should have for oneself.

Kant makes several interesting observations about arrogant people. *First*, such "honour cravers" who think they can elevate themselves over others by, for example, excessive bragging about their accomplishments (real or invented), prompt others to look upon them as buffoons.[15] This is because "the more someone who is arrogant shows himself to be striving for others' respect, the more everyone refuses it to him" (DV 6:465). *Second*, it often goes unnoticed that an arrogant person is "*self-abasing*" (DV 6:466). That is, in demanding that others think little of themselves in comparison with him, an arrogant person is someone who would not find it hard to grovel and waive all rights to respect from others were his fortune to change. In other words, an arrogant person likely also harbors a nascent servility.

B. Backbiting

Backbiting or talking ill of someone (defamation) is "the immediate inclination, aimed at no particular purpose, to spread a rumor disadvantageous to the respect for others" (DV 6:466).[16] While arrogance involves elevating oneself over others, defamation involves lowering the image of those defamed in the eyes of others.[17] Of course, spreading false claims or rumors about the behavior of others is a form of lying or untruthfulness that violates respect for others. However, even calling attention to someone's actual scandalous behavior *with no particular aim in view*—behavior of the target that expresses a lack of respect for oneself or others—is wrong because it detracts from their self-esteem. Backbiting, whether what is spread about someone is true or false, also encourages a contempt for human beings generally. If expressing contempt for someone is wrong, then so is encouraging others to be

[15] See remarks in the *Anthropology* at 7:203 and 210 for additional remarks about arrogance.

[16] See Collins 27:436, "Of the slanderer."

[17] Kant says that he is only referring to defamation with no end in mind, but as we shall see, he also condemns such behavior when one's aim is self-aggrandizement.

contemptuous, whether their contempt is directed toward an individual or toward human beings generally.

While one might defame others with no particular purpose in mind, Kant also mentions taking pleasure in exposing the faults of others with the aim of making oneself appear as good as, or at least not worse than the person being defamed. Doing so is a case of treating another person merely as a means for promoting one's own image.

Complying with the duty of virtue of respect for others, then, requires that one keep negative judgments about others to oneself, in cases in which not doing so would be defamatory. Kant also warns about "spying on the morals of others" as a kind of offensive inquisitiveness that should be avoided. Exposing the faults of others and being offensively inquisitive about their morality, then, are things to avoid in complying with the virtue of modesty. Furthermore, from what Kant says in this section, one more fully embodies the virtue of modesty if one is willing to "cast the veil of love of humanity" (DV 6:466) over the faults of others. So, the virtue of modesty, while it is primarily a negative duty (in this case to avoid the vice of defamation), also bids one to positive action.

C. Derision

Derision is mocking others fueled by taking fiendish joy in another's faults (*Schadenfreude*), if not motivated by outright malice or wickedness.[18] As a negative character trait, it is "the propensity to expose others to ridicule, to make the faults of another [whether real or fabricated, M.T.] the immediate object of one's merriment" (DV 6:467). Kant contrasts ridicule with the sort of well-meaning joking and banter among friends who make light fun of someone's peculiarities for the amusement of others. The morally significant difference between banter and ridicule is motive. Ridicule, unlike banter and joking, is at bottom motivated by the desire to deprive the target of the respect she is owed by others, as a person. The propensity (as a character trait) to

---

[18] See Collins 27:458 and Vigilantius 27:709.

engage in ridicule thus motivated is the vice of "*bitter* mockfulness" (ibid.). Because (as Kant is conceiving this kind of person) the mocker takes diabolical or fiendish joy in what he does, this vice is "therefore an *even more* serious violation of one's duty of respect toward other human beings" (DV 6:467, my emphasis). Presumably, the comparison here is with the two other vices of contempt, which characteristically are not accompanied by such joy.

Interestingly, Kant remarks that in defending oneself against ridicule, one may respond by "contemptuous rebuttal" (ibid.), assuming that the content of the mockery is not something in which "reason necessarily takes a moral interest." Otherwise one is to either meet the mockery with silence or defend oneself with "dignity and seriousness" (bid.). Kant gives no examples to illustrate the difference he has in mind between cases that reason necessarily takes a moral interest and those it does not. Presumably, being ridiculed for one's scrupulous moral behavior does merit moral interest, while being ridiculed for an article of clothing usually does not.

This present section ends with a "Remark" in which Kant elaborates the reason why these duties are fundamentally negative. The duties of respect for others concern what all persons are *owed* simply as persons. One does not strictly owe it to others to positively benefit them. Nor does one owe it to others to show them high positive esteem. Positive moral esteem (appraisal respect) is a fitting response to the meritorious behavior of others; not all others deserve it. But respect for the predisposition to (moral) personality is something all persons necessarily have and constitutes their dignity as persons. Recognition respect is the attitude that recognizes this dignity.

Recall from §25 that Kant contrasts the primary duty of love with that of respect, and says of the latter, "the duty of respect for my neighbor is contained in the maxim not to degrade another human being merely as a means to my ends (not to demand the other should throw himself away in order to be subservient to my end)" (DV 6:450). I think it is clear from Kant's remarks about instances of defamation done with no particular purpose in view that not all violations of the CI involve using someone merely as a means to one's own ends, at least in the sense of somehow promoting one's own welfare. Kant's humanity formula, then, should not be read as saying that all wrong actions use others merely as means to promote one's self-interest. Some wrongs fail to respect others as ends in themselves without treating them merely as means.

Following his discussion of the duties toward others is Chapter II, "On ethical duties of human beings towards one another with regard to their *condition*" (DV 468), in which Kant addresses two looming questions:

- How do particular facts about human beings and their varying circumstances (e.g. age, rank, and health) figure in the application of the principles of a metaphysics of morals (featured in the Elements) to individual cases?
- Should a metaphysics of morals include additional rules that reflect the application of the a priori principles of ethics to cases considering such varying conditions?

14.4 Duties to others regarding their condition

In response to the first question, Chapter II explains that in applying the duties of virtue (virtue rules) to cases, one must consider morally relevant details of circumstances.[19] For example, one sometimes needs to consider any differences in "estate, age, sex, state of health, affluence or poverty" (DV 6:469) of those one affects. One thereby acts on "special rules" of application that take into consideration the morally relevant circumstances of others. Kant gives no examples in DV, but it is easy to come up with some. For instance, the duty of beneficence in contexts of helping someone who is in the process of dying might yield a rule of application that directs one to aid in making this ailing person as comfortable as possible until they die. What counts as making that person comfortable will depend on facts about them, what resources are at one's disposal, and perhaps other things that cannot be specified in advance. Sensitivity to the particularities of circumstance is thus paramount in applying general rules, requiring good judgment.

---

[19] See Collins 27:461–470, "Of special duties to particular kinds of people," "Of duties to the virtuous and vicious," and "Of duties in regard to differences in age."

Another example is determining what would count as a fitting way to thank a benefactor, which will depend on such factors as the size of the benefit, the level of inconvenience the benefactor had to bear in conferring the benefit, and what the benefactor might welcome as a demonstration of one's gratitude.

Finally, in answer to our second question about the place of special rules of application that include within them circumstantial details suited to application, Kant's view is that they cannot be organized a priori into a complete system of rules and so cannot take their place within a science of metaphysics. They thus lie outside the purview of a systematic metaphysics of morals developed from a priori grounds, and thus can only "be appended to the system" (DV 6:469).

14.5 Kant's scheme of duties toward others at a glance

Let us now briefly review Kant's scheme of basic duties toward others and the virtues and vices associated with them. In all cases, the duty (as an action type) and the associated character trait share the same label. Some character traits have no name in English and there is one master virtue associated with duties of respect. (See Figure 14.1.)
Again, because one can pledge never to engage in any of these acts of disrespect yet on occasion be guilty of weakness of will, one will exhibit mere lack of virtue (a failure of strength).

Positive Duties to Others	Corresponding Virtue/Vice
Beneficence	Benevolence/Envy
Gratitude	Gratitude/Ingratitude
Sympathetic Participation	Sympathy/*Schadenfreude*

Negative Duties to Others	Corresponding Virtue/Vice
Arrogance	Modesty/Arrogance
Backbiting	[No names]
Derision	[No names]

Figure 14.1 List of duties of love and respect toward others together with corresponding virtues and vices

14.6 Concluding reflection

Let us consider in more detail what Kant says about contempt—both as an attitude and as outward contemptuous behavior. He says that judging someone to be worthless as a person is contempt. He also says that "[t]o regard others with *contempt* . . . , i.e. to deny them the respect a human beings is owed as such, *is in any case* contrary to duty" (DV 6:463, my emphasis). He follows this remark noting that sometimes one can't help looking down on some in comparison with others, although outwardly expressing contempt is still an offense. He also claims that in some cases a morally legitimate response to insulting mockery is with a jocular, even if derisive, brushing aside the insult with contempt. Perhaps one can accomplish this brushing aside without harboring contempt for the mocker. However, one might ask whether having and/or expressing genuine contempt is always a violation of a duty to others. Do people ever deserve contempt from others? As noted earlier, this question should be disambiguated: Is it ever fitting to have contempt for others? Is it ever morally apt (permitted if not obligatory) to have contempt for others?

Kant distinguishes contempt from hate. As negative attitudes toward others, both are generally (if not always) "global" in the sense that they are directed toward someone's whole person.[20] However, hate is opposed to love, and it is normally elicited by something about another's person that one strongly dislikes. Hatred is aggressive; it motivates one to "pursue and destroy" (Anth 7:271). By contrast, contempt is directed toward a person's perceived "inner worth" and motivates one to distance oneself from its object. Hatred is Kant's prime example of a passion that has become a vice. Although in the *Anthropology* Kant does not list contempt as one of the passions, presumably, someone who is generally contemptuous of human beings has a passion that is also a vice. Alongside contempt as a character trait, consider instances of being contemptuous of someone for their behavior. The question for moral theory is whether having this attitude toward certain individuals

---

[20] In this way hate and contempt as global, person-focused attitudes are fitting responses to someone's "bad*being*" while indignation and resentment are fitting action-focused responses to someone's wrong-*doing*.

is always *morally* wrong, even if it is an otherwise fitting response to their behavior.

Arguably, it isn't. Consider individuals who are grossly arrogant. I'm thinking of people who are braggarts, who never take responsibility for their immoral deeds, who belittle others who disagree with them—anyone who deserves to be called a "conceited ass" (as Kant says).[21] Specifically, I'm thinking of anyone like this who holds political office. One's aim in expressing contempt might be to influence others to avoid the person in question and people like them. For arrogant people who hold political office, the aim is likely to dissuade others from supporting them in elections. However, the more interesting question is whether contempt, properly directed, is (or can be) noninstrumentally valuable or good, which I will not address here.

Finally, I quoted Kant as condemning all contempt. However, there is one remark in DV that perhaps mitigates such condemnation. In discussing the duty of self-scrutiny, Kant writes, "only through the glorious predisposition to the good we have in us, which makes the human being worthy of respect, is it possible that he finds the human being who acts contrary to it (himself, but not the humanity in him) contemptible" (DV 6:441). The distinction between the individual human being and their humanity gives Kant a way of holding that although a human being's predisposition to the good (i.e. their moral personality) makes them deserving of a basic level of respect, yet individuals who are outwardly, and without apparent shame, grossly arrogant deserve the contempt of others, and that others are morally justified in having and expressing their contempt. The idea would be that it is possible and morally justified to have contempt for someone's conduct and acquired character, yet at the same time respect that element (or "seed") within them that is capable of virtue. This would imply that contempt for others, when justified, need not be a global attitude directed toward the whole person. Arguably, there is such a thing as "respectful contempt."[22]

---

[21] 'Conceited ass' is Gregor's translation of the German *Narrheit* which Timmermann and Grenberg have as 'buffoonery'. Translation aside, the former is more fitting for the individual I have in mind.

[22] Here, I am thinking of Hilary Putnam's reported reaction to Robert Nozick's views on social issues, which Putnam describes as one of respectful contempt, "respect

Further reading

- For further discussion of the psychology of the vices of hatred (referred to in Vigilantius as the devilish vices), see Smit and Timmons 2015 [Timmons 2017a].
- For an overview of the duties of respect, see Sensen 2013.
- On love of honor as a virtue in Kant, see Denis 2014.
- Mason 2003 and Bell 2011 defend the moral propriety of contempt, subject to certain conditions. Bell argues that Kant's view is compatible with having contempt for others.

for the intellectual virtues [of Nozick]; contempt for [his] intellectual and emotional weaknesses" (1981:166).

15

Friendship

Conclusion of the Elements

"On the most intimate union of love and respect in friendship" is a fitting conclusion to the doctrine of duties to others. As the title indicates, Kant conceives friendship as combining mutual love and respect. In the two Sections that comprise this discussion, Kant first considers friendship as an unattainable ideal (§46) before sketching in 47 a humanly possible kind of moral friendship. Following the conclusion is a short appendix about the moral significance of certain social graces. Kant's remarks about friendship raise these questions:

- What is the ideal of friendship and why is it not humanly possible?
- What kind of moral friendship, then, is humanly possible?
- Why are such friendships rare?
- Is there a duty to enter a moral friendship?

15.1 The ideal

An *ideal* for Kant is that of an individual—an exemplar—which corresponds to an a priori *idea* of perfection not derived from experience.[1] Friendship as an ideal "(considered in its perfection) is the union of two persons through equal reciprocal love and respect" (DV 6:469). Kant describes the ideal as combining "sympathetic participation and communication in the weal of each united through a morally good will" (ibid.) Like the ideal of moral perfection, which humans can

---

[1] In the *Critique of Pure Reason* (A567–568/B595–596) Kant distinguishes between idea (*Idee*) and ideal (*Ideal*). These are technical terms in Kant. An idea is a concept of complete perfection, such as the concept of God. An ideal is "an individual thing" that realizes a corresponding idea.

Kant's Doctrine of Virtue. Mark Timmons, Oxford University Press (2021). © Oxford University Press.
DOI: 10.1093/oso/9780190939229.003.0015

only approximate without ever achieving, one can only strive to approximate the ideal of friendship.

Kant explains why the ideal cannot be humanly realized in the following rather cryptic passage (brackets inserted).

> For [1] how can a human being, in his relations with his neighbor, work out the *equality* of one of the requisite parts of just the same duty (e.g. of reciprocal benevolence) within one with just that same disposition within the other; or, more difficult still, [2] which relation the feeling arising from one duty has towards the other (e.g. from benevolence, to that from respect) in one and the same person; and whether, [3] if one of them is more ardent in *love*, he does not precisely because of this suffer the loss of some of the *respect* of the other, so that subjectively love and high esteem towards each other will hardly be brought into the proportion of equality that, after all, is required for friendship (DV 6:469–470)

Kant's first point is that for either element of the complex disposition of love and respect constituting friendship, one is not able to determine *with certainty* (and thus work out) the precise measure of equality of love and respect for the other. For example, to determine one's appropriate level of sympathetic participation and communication with someone else so that it is *precisely equal* to theirs would require that I know what their level of love for me is. But this would require the God-like power of scrutinizing the mental states of others. The same point holds concerning a proper level of respect to have for the other. Specifically, I would need to know the level of respect of the other person and whether she felt or believed herself to be somehow elevated above me or beneath me—again, something I cannot reliably know.

Kant's second point refers to feelings arising from the duties of love and respect. You may recall from his opening remarks about duties toward others (see chap. 13), Kant mentions feelings that naturally accompany the maxims of love and respect. His second point in the cited passage (itself obscure) may be that for each party to an ideal relationship the relation between their feelings of love and respect must be in a state of *equilibrium* so that one's feelings of love are tempered by feelings of respect, otherwise one is likely to be guilty of "obtruding [one's, M.T.] goodwill, by rash communication, and by unrestrained love" (Vig 27:685). Similarly, one's feelings of respect should not hinder one from sympathetic participation toward the friend. After all, as Kant observes, love "can be considered as attraction" (DV 6:470) and thus tends to move one toward greater intimacy with the danger of becoming too familiar, while respect motivates keeping one's distance from the other.[2] But how can one determine just how to bring these feelings into such equilibrium, even supposing that one has sufficient control of them? Finally, the third point (related to the second): if my love for my friend is stronger than the friend's is for me, I am in danger of losing the equal respect of the friend, thus undermining equality of respect or esteem. But how can I know how much is too much?

In the third paragraph, Kant tells us that ideal friendship requires *purity* and *completeness* without explicitly defining these characteristics. However, with help from the lecture notes together with other remarks in these passages about the challenges of friendship (including the earlier quote), here is how we might understand them.

> *Purity*: a friendship is ideally pure when it rests firmly on moral principles of love and respect.
>
> *Completeness*: a friendship is ideally complete when parties (*i*) share a *precise* measure of equal love and respect for the other, thus requiring "a precisely determinate maxim" (DV 6:472) of love and respect. Furthermore, in an ideal friendship, as with any ideal, the "measure is always the maximum" (Col 27:423) and thus (*ii*) the *degree* to which each party loves and respects the other is unreserved.

We can use these ideal characteristics to evaluate humanly possible friendships. For instance (moving now to the fourth paragraph), the duty of benevolence requires pointing out a friend's faults. But doing so is sometimes hard, contrary to one's feeling of love since following through with this duty risks causing the friend to feel in some respect

---

[2] Another reading of this second claim is that one cannot be certain that one's feelings of love and respect for the other are *precisely equal*, which perhaps fits better with the focus on *equality* in the quoted passage. But what does it even mean to say that one's feelings of love and respect are equal? Whatever it is, why is it part of an ideal?

inferior, disrupting the balance of mutual respect friends should have for one another—compromising completeness. Another risk is striking a proper balance between one's confidence that a friend is poised to help you yet at the same time sparing one's friend the burden of having to help in order not to disrupt equal respect (i.e. overburdening one's friends with one's own needs). To ask too much is to risk undermining the friend's respect and also puts one in the position of owing gratitude and thus "a step lower" in relation to one's friend—further challenges to the equality in completeness. Kant concludes §46 remarking that friendships based merely on reciprocal advantage or on mere feeling and thus lacking purity cannot safeguard the stability of the friendship that requires basing it on "principles or rules that prevent overfamiliarity and limit demands of mutual love by respect" (DV 6:471).

15.2 Moral friendship

Section 47 discusses a kind of friendship that is humanly possible, namely, a "merely moral friendship [that] is not just an ideal but (like the black swan) actually exists every now and then in its perfection" (DV 6:472).[3] "*Moral friendship* . . . is the complete confidence of two persons in disclosing their secret judgments and feelings to each other, so far as it is consistent with respect towards each other" (DV 6:471). Unlike the description of ideal friendship, there is no mention here of love (either as feeling or maxim) or of equality. Yet we know from the previous section that the duty of friendship is for each person in the relationship to strive for equality of love and respect with her friend. Why does Kant describe moral friendship in this way?

The answer is that he thinks moral friendship answers to a deep need that human beings have to share thoughts and feelings with others, so that "he is not completely alone with his thoughts, as in a prison" (DV 6:472), and thus able to enjoy a unique kind of freedom of expression. Such private thoughts and feelings about, for example, one's associates, religion, and government are ones that might be used against a person,

---

[3] See Collins 27:422–430, "On Friendship," and Vigilantius 27:675–686 for far richer discussions of friendship than we find in the passages we are considering.

thus a reason to conceal them from others. What one needs, then, is a *trusted* close friend who will not indiscreetly reveal those thoughts and feelings to others, at least without one's permission. Nevertheless, to preserve the respect your friend has for you, you must be careful in how much you reveal. Close friends need not, and perhaps should not, reveal to each other all their most secret personal thoughts, feelings, and faults. Besides offending one's friend by such information and risking loss of respect, there is the plain fact that friends sometimes fall out of friendship even to the point of becoming enemies. Of course, there is far less risk of this happening in a friendship that is genuinely moral (one of purity) compared to other types of friendship. Still, for both moral and prudential reasons, one needs to be guarded in revealing one's secrets if one is to maintain an approximation of equality of love and respect that the best friendships exemplify and thus maximal, *unreserved* confiding in others is to be avoided.

Kant makes additional observations about true moral friendship which, together with the just-cited remarks, help explain why it is rare. For instance, a stable moral friendship is more likely if friends share the same moral outlook on many issues of importance, that "though men may be as benevolent to one another as possible, they still do not long remain friends if they differ from each other in their *principia*, or in the operative force of their faculty of judgment" (Vig 27:683–684). However, "identity of thought is not required . . . on the contrary, it is difference, rather, which establishes friendship, for in that case the one supplies what the other lacks" (Col 27:429). Here it is interesting to note that one of Kant's close friends (perhaps the closest) was Joseph Green (1736–1798), a British merchant. Kant's longtime association with Green is perhaps why the Collins lectures have him saying "a scholar may well have a friendship of taste with a merchant or soldier, and so long as the scholar is no pedant, and the merchant no blockhead, then each can entertain the other on his own subject" (Col 27:426). Although Kant is here referring to a friendship of taste—i.e. one based on some mutual interest such as chess—the point holds for any friendship.

To sum up: the kind of humanly possible moral friendship Kant has in mind involves a special bond between two individuals, something that requires time to cultivate and maintain. Friends should strive for stability, grounded in moral principles of mutual benevolence and respect, i.e. purity. It must also include mutual equal feelings of love and respect between friends (equality). And, finally, given human nature, one must guard one's love and respect, so it is *reserved* mutual equal love and respect that represent the core of humanly possible moral friendship—reserved in *degree*. No human friendship can realize the maximum of purity and completeness; we can only use it to evaluate humanly possible friendships.

Let us close by remarking on the "duty of friendship" referred to in the first paragraph of 46. Certainly, there are duties *within* a friendship, the main one being that the friends strive to realize the ideal. As lately noted, it is like the duty of moral self-perfection which bids us to strive toward the ideal without requiring complete achievement of it. But is there a duty to *make* friends, keeping in mind that we are talking about moral friendship, a special bond between individuals? The Vigilantius notes has Kant remarking that insofar as a true friendship involves mutual liking (and not just well-wishing) arising naturally from "the esteem the other has acquired through his characteristics, and the acknowledgment of his worth" (27:676), one cannot be commanded to have a friendship. However, this claim is consistent with having a positive imperfect duty to *seek* a close moral friendship by at least being open to it, especially given that it combines striving for self-perfection (in seeking the unique freedom of expression that comes with it) together with striving for a most perfect union of love and respect with another. In any case, Kant does make clear that one has a duty to oneself not to isolate oneself from others. This, indeed, is the first claim he makes in the appendix.

15.3 Appendix: On the virtues of social intercourse

In concluding the Elements, Kant adds a brief appendix arguing that one has a duty to do what one can to "let virtue be joined by the graces" (DV 6:473). He mentions the outward behaviors of conversability, courtesy, hospitality, and gentleness. These are not themselves virtues; rather Kant classifies them as graces or social manners which, as he puts it, "promote the disposition of virtue by making virtue at least *well-liked*" (DV 6:474). The thought is that being well mannered is not the same as having a virtuous disposition or having any of the virtues. However, as Kant remarks in the *Anthropology*, while good social manners only represent an appearance of moral goodness, it also involves having "the inclination to place a value even on the semblance of moral goodness" (Anth 7:244).

Finally, given that one should practice such manners toward humanity generally, Kant ends with the question whether one may keep company with vicious people. He worries that doing so communicates that one is willing to trade off the value of virtue for something one expects from the vicious. He claims that one ought to avoid such associations and break them off if they already exist.

15.4 Concluding Reflection

One likely reaction to Kant's conception of moral friendship is that it leaves out the affection and fellow feeling that make friendships so enjoyable. Granted, he does not wax poetic in his description and praise of moral friendship. However, he clearly recognized this element when he reportedly said: "The sweet delight in the enjoyment of friendship is afforded only by the harmony of judgment, i.e., that the feelings and thoughts of the parties derived from the same *principia*" (Vig 27: 683). And after all, Kant's discussion of friendship occurs within a book on the metaphysical principles of ethics in which one would expect him to be describing the grounds of true moral friendship and not its pleasures.

Kant had many friends during his long life; he was quite social. In his biography, Manfred Kuehn describes Kant's daily routines during his time as a professor that were typical of professors in Germany at that time. Kuehn writes, "The only thing that was perhaps not typical about Kant's life was the great role that socializing with his friends assumed in it. Kant was a very gregarious and social being . . ." (Kuehn 2001: 273). For someone who did as much socializing as he did, the feelings that make friendships so appealing, the "sweet delight in the enjoyment of friendship"—was apparent to Kant.

Further reading

- Those interested in Kant's views on friendship should begin by consulting the Collins lecture notes of 1784–1785 and the later Vigilantius notes of 1793, where one finds much more on friendship than in any of Kant's published writings.
- See Baron 2013 for a close reading of Sections 46 and 47.

PART V

THE DOCTRINE
OF METHODS OF ETHICS
AND CONCLUSION

16

Moral Education and Practice

The Ethical Doctrine of Method (Part II of DV) discusses teaching ethics and the cultivation of virtue. Following the Methods, the book's conclusion explains why religion as a doctrine of duties to God is excluded from the science of ethics. We begin with remarks about the concept of and need for a doctrine of methods.

16.1 What is a doctrine of methods for ethics?

Ethics, as part of a doctrine of morals, is a *practical* science; it aims at the improvement of human conduct and character. A doctrine of methods is therefore a necessary complement to the doctrine of elements. Kant describes these methods as indicating "the way in which one can provide the laws of pure practical reason with *access* to the human mind and *influence* on its maxims, that is, the way in which one can make objectively practical reason *subjectively* practical as well" (CprR 5:151). For the law to gain access one must have a basic mastery of moral concepts and principles. This could be accomplished yet have little or no influence on the learner's maxims and thus on her overall quality of will. So, the second task is to stimulate the learner toward realizing a life of virtue.

The Methods addresses these tasks by proposing various well-thought-out procedures to employ that will properly serve the learner. More than one method will be needed, since a method that works well for young children will differ from methods that work for adolescents and adults.[1] Obviously, anthropology will

---

[1] In Collins, Kant identifies three stages of education: "for childhood, for youth, and for manhood" (Col. 27:469). He recommends that education for youth (adolescents) begin around the age of ten, "for by then he is already capable of reflection" (ibid.).

Kant's Doctrine of Virtue. Mark Timmons, Oxford University Press (2021). © Oxford University Press.
DOI: 10.1093/oso/9780190939229.003.0016

importantly figure in devising a proper method of instruction for the intended audience. For instance, most adults will already understand moral concepts and have a grasp of basic moral principles; what they most need is a change in character. The important thing is that the teaching of ethics and the cultivation of virtue should not be haphazard; it must proceed according to a plan tailored to a specific audience.

16.2 Teaching ethics

The doctrine of method begins by reminding readers that it is part of the concept of virtue that it must be *acquired*. Kant then rehearses virtue's basic ingredients. As explained in chapter 8, becoming an overall virtuous person involves acquiring sufficient strength of will to comply with one's resolution to discharge all of one's duties and do so solely out of respect for the moral law. This resolution constitutes the core of a good will. "Be perfect" (in complying with all of one's duties) and "Be holy" (in doing so solely from respect for the moral law) are the mottos of someone striving for moral self-perfection.

Kant remarks that this resolution must be made "completely all at once" (DV 6:477) in the sense that it is a single act—an explicit vow one makes to oneself. The content of this vow must be *complete* by pledging to comply with *all* of one's duties, striving in *every* case to do so *solely* from respect for the moral law. Of course, having made this resolution is compatible with failing on occasion to comply with it, either by failing at duty or by doing one's duty but not from the sole motive of respect. So, becoming a virtuous person requires strengthening one's resolve by cultivating those virtues that give content to virtue as strength. Accomplishing this requires practice "trying to combat the inner enemy within the human being" (DV 6:477), particularly any passions that have become vices. If, then, the ultimate goal of moral education is to methodically draw the student to the point where he or she freely embarks upon a life of virtue—takes an "interest" in morality (DV 6:484)—how can this be accomplished?

At a minimum, and elaborating on Kant's behalf, proper moral education will include the following steps:

(1) Mastering such basic ethical concepts as duty, moral worth, and virtue.

Because, as Kant writes, "*principles* must be built on concepts" (CprR 5:157), mastering ethical concepts provides the basis for:

(2) Gaining knowledge of basic moral principles and the various virtue rules of the sort featured in the Elements.

Because there is an important difference in the strength of duties, moral education requires:

(3) Appreciating the difference between strict (narrow/perfect) and meritorious (wide/imperfect) duties.[2]

Additionally, because the virtue rules are to be used in practice, moral understanding requires:

(4) Developing the skill of applying virtue rules to concrete cases; a matter of moral judgment, particularly with respect to wide imperfect (meritorious) duties.

Accomplishing this much should yield an *understanding* of what morality requires in the way of action. However, such knowledge and skill are not sufficient to bring about in the learner the kind of personal commitment constitutive of a good will that is essential to virtue—the ultimate goal of moral education. As we know, what Kant refers to as the *morality* of action depends on one's character including the motives from which one does what is morally right (legal). And, of course, mastering the concept of moral worth involves:

(5) Understanding the difference between moral and nonmoral motivation and what constitutes virtuous character.

---

[2] This step is explicitly mentioned in the methodology part of the second *Critique* at 5:159.

However, understanding this difference does not automatically result in the learner having a good will. Moral education requires more.
As we shall see, dwelling on the *capacity for* and *significance of* having
such a character also figures importantly in Kant's conception of the
psychology of virtue acquisition. First, though, let us consider Kant's
remarks on methods of teaching ethics.

16.3 Methods of teaching

Kant briefly describes various methods of teaching in §50. One
method is where a teacher simply lectures to an audience that merely
listens. This is to present a doctrine "acroamatically." Another method
is "erotetic," in which the teacher interacts with students either through
dialogue that engages the student's reasoning capacity, or by a catechism method that appeals more to a student's memory. The erotetic
method featuring dialogue is where the teacher presents cases for the
student's consideration intended to elicit responses about the concepts
and principles of ethics. The student then asks questions to resolve
any unclarity and to further probe concepts and principles being
presented. As a result of student questioning, the teacher learns how to
ask better questions. This method is appropriate for students who are
beyond the beginner stage of moral education. However, moral education of young pupils must begin with the catechism method. One kind
of moral catechism is a manual composed of questions and answers
that the student commits to memory. But a catechism can also refer to
oral instruction. So, one method of teaching is to have the pupil study
the questions and answers written down in a manual, and then for
the teacher to question the pupil in order to see whether the pupil has
committed the answers to memory. This method, which relies heavily
on memorization, is "mechanical-catethetical" (Ped 9:477). However,
a more Socratic version of the catechism method is for the teacher
to elicit from the pupil's reasoning certain concepts, principles, and
doctrines of ethics by judicious questioning.[3]

---

[3] In *On Pedagogy*, Kant writes: "The Socratic method should be the rule for the
cathethical method" (Ped 9:477). So, presumably, this method differs from the dialogic

However, before illustrating how a moral catechism might be conceived, Kant first remarks on the use of examples in teaching ethics (§52). Any method will employ actual or hypothetical examples of both good and bad conduct and character. Examples have their use in early moral education as a means for helping students begin to cultivate virtue and avoid vice by demonstrating that action on a maxim of virtue is a real possibility. A particularly striking example of exemplary behavior from history is the case of Henry Norris who was threatened by Henry VIII's people to either make false accusations against the latter's spouse, Anne Boleyn, or be executed. Norris refused to lie and was consequently executed. (Kant alludes to this case in the second *Critique* (5:155–156) as he develops a hypothetical example like it.) What this example helps make vivid is the *real* possibility of standing firm on one's moral convictions even in the face of death.

Kant warns that an example, even one of exemplary conduct, should not be used as a "model but only as a proof that what conforms with duty is feasible" (DV 6:480). What is it to use exemplary conduct as a model, and what is wrong with it? Consider, for instance, a teacher correcting a pupil by pointing to another child and saying, "take an example from that good (orderly, diligent) boy!" (ibid.). There are two looming problems with such comparisons. First, as we know from chapter 14 on the vices of hatred and contempt, such interpersonal comparisons risk causing mere resentment in the pupil being corrected. Second, it isn't the "good boy's" example that serves as a model of conduct and character; rather it is the moral law and the standards it sets. If comparisons are to be made, it should be to the moral law.

Another bad use of examples, mentioned in the second *Critique*, is holding up as moral examples sages, saints, and heroes, often featured, writes Kant, in "our sentimental writings." Such figures are described as performing "*noble* (supermeritorious) actions" (CprR 5:155). One problem is that such examples do not feature "common and everyday obligation" which, compared to the actions of superheroes, can seem "insignificant and petty" (ibid.). But they aren't. A related worry is that

method in that it does not involve the pupil challenging the instructor and is thus suitable for teaching the neophyte.

a learner might want to imitate the superhero prompted merely by the emotional enthusiasm stirred up by the example. Here is Kant:

> It is altogether contra-purposive to set before children, as a model, actions as noble, magnanimous, meritorious, thinking that one can captivate them by inspiring enthusiasm for such actions. . . . But even with the instructed and experienced part of humankind this supposed incentive has, if not a prejudicial effect on the heart, at least no genuine moral one, though this is what one wanted to bring about by means of it. (CprR 5:157)

Such examples, then, are counterproductive both for children and even for the "instructed and experienced."

Following these remarks about the use of examples, Kant provides a fragment of a moral catechism followed by brief commentary.

16.4 Fragment of a moral catechism

The fragment includes eight segments in which one or more question is raised by the teacher and either the pupil is silent, and the teacher gives the answer, or, as the segments progress, an answer is elicited from the student. What is methodical about the catechism and corresponding instruction is that the questions are ordered according to "common human reason" (DV 6:479).

The fragment begins with "What is your greatest, indeed your entire, longing in life?" (DV 4:480). The pupil is silent and so the teacher nudges the process along by suggesting an answer: "That for you *everything* should *always* go according to your wish and will" (ibid.) From there, the instructor's further questioning leads the student to appreciate the distinction between being happy and *deserving* to be happy. It is notable that the teacher begins with questions that invites the pupil to start from her own personal perspective. After getting the pupil to recognize that he (the pupil) wishes for his own happiness, the teacher then asks him to imagine being able to control "all happiness (that is possible in the world)" (DV 6:480). Further questioning about distributing happiness to those who are either lazy, drunkards, swindlers, or violent individuals leads the pupil to the concept of being *worthy* of happiness—a moral concept. With that concept now in focus, the teacher prompts the pupil to ask whether he himself is worthy of happiness, which then leads to the concept of duty and finally to an articulation by the teacher of the condition under which one is worthy of happiness: "So, a human being's observance of his duty is the universal and sole condition of the worthiness to be happy, and the former and the latter are one and the same" (DV 6:482). The student has now become explicitly aware of a fundamental principle that connects worthiness to be happy with duty. In the final two segments, the teacher has the student reflect on how a person of good will might hope for the happiness they deserve. The fragment ends with the teacher suggesting that perhaps this hope should be based on the supposition that there is a God with the power to ensure that virtue is met with deserved happiness. In response, the student elaborates this proposal, having come far from his initial silence.

Again, nothing in this fragment reveals much about the psychology of how a learner can eventually come to *have* a good will and make progress toward acquiring the strength to act accordingly. The fragment partly addresses the task of how concepts and principles of ethics can gain *access* to the understanding, but what about *influence* on the will? Kant allows that pointing to the advantages of virtue and the disadvantages of vice can figure in moral education as "leading strings" (CprR 5:152) to help the student steer toward virtue. However, these leading strings must be left behind. But what takes their place?

In his comment on the fragment (which concludes the section on teaching ethics), Kant makes two observations that partly address this question. He recommends that the catechism method include casuistical questions to help students sharpen their powers of moral judgment. His point is that the sharper a student's judgment about some subject matter, the more he or she is likely to "love" (as Kant says) the subject. When the subject is morality it is likely to stimulate a student's interest in morality—in being a person of good moral conduct and character.

The second observation is that at the end of formal moral instruction: if the student is brought to understand that he has the power to overcome all inclinations (even a strong aversion to his own death) then he is poised to contemplate the question: "what within you is it that may dare to enter into combat with all the forces of nature in you and around you, and to vanquish them if they come into conflict with your moral principles?" (DV 6:483). Kant remarks that even though one is not able to understand this power—one's autonomy—cognizing that one has it naturally leads to an experience of "an elevation of the soul" (ibid.). This feeling (hopefully) inspires one to hold duty sacred, "the more it is challenged" (ibid.). This holding sacred can lead one to resolve to comply with duty out of respect for the moral law, and it can strengthen the resolve one already has. With this observation, we should add to our list of recommended steps the significance of:

(6) Contemplating the power one possesses to overcome all contrary-to-duty inclinations and the dignity this power confers on one's very being.

In the introduction to DV at the very end of Section X, Kant remarks that the way to acquire the strength needed to overcome "all sensible counteracting impulses" on a path to virtue is "by contemplating . . . the dignity of the pure law of reason in us . . . and at the same time by *practice*" (DV 6:397). We have just seen how contemplation can play a role in becoming virtuous. So, consider a person who comes to have a good will (a proper moral resolve) based partly upon contemplating one's power to overcome opposing sensible impulses. The task then is to strengthen one's resolve or strengthen it further. But how? This is where practicing virtue—ethical ascetics—enters the picture.

16.5 Practicing virtue

Section II of Methods is called "Ethical Ascetics" (§53), which refers to a regimen of self-discipline whose aim is to develop a virtuous disposition. It is not to be confused with "monkish ascetics" that involves pointless self-denial by imposing hash punishments on oneself to atone for sins. In chapter 8, we saw that according to Kant in order to become virtuous one must gain control over any passions or affects that would hinder complying with one's duties out of respect for the moral law. (In this section, Kant refers to this practice as "ethical gymnastics.") In chapter 12, we saw that the duties to cultivate one's conscience and to engage in self-scrutiny are also critical in striving toward moral self-improvement and thus virtue. In this section on ethical ascetics, Kant makes further observations about the proper state of mind of someone who is successfully putting into practice their good will by striving to comply with all of their duties out of due respect for the moral law. There are proper frames of mind—being both *valiant* and *cheerful*—which is characteristic of the truly virtuous person. Pursuit of a valiant frame of mind is captured by the Stoic motto: learn to put up with life's misfortunes and do without "superfluous pleasures." This Stoic advice is a matter of maintaining a kind of moral health. However, Kant insists that something more positive be added in an Epicurean spirit, namely, an "ever-cheerful heart" (DV 6:485). The thought is that in practicing virtue one should strive to do so in a positive, cheerful frame of mind. "What is not done with pleasure but merely as a chore, . . . has no inner worth for the one who thereby obeys his duty . . ." (DV 6:484).

One might wonder how to go about acquiring or maintaining the recommended frames of mind. Kant's answer is that combatting natural impulses that oppose duty and doing so successfully—ethical gymnastics—"makes one robust and, in the consciousness of one's regained freedom, cheerful" (DV 6:485). We can now add another component of moral education that involves:

(7) Acquiring a valiant and cheerful frame of mind in practicing virtue resulting from ethical gymnastics.[4]

Kant concludes the section by noting that the practice of virtue, involving as it does the sort of discipline gained through ethical

---

[4] Insofar as doing this is compatible with Kant's claim that duties involve constraint, he must be thinking that recognizing that one has a duty is to some extent painful, hence the need for constraint, yet one can be determined to carry out one's duty in a positive frame of mind. Thanks to Adam Cureton for prompting this remark.

gymnastics, and thereby practicing virtue with a cheerful heart, makes one's striving for moral self-perfection all the more meritorious.

In §51, Kant insists that the catechism be "purely moral" and not include any questions about religious doctrine. It *can* be purely moral, featuring only moral concepts and principles, as illustrated in the Elements. It *should* be purely moral for reasons that Kant makes explicit in the conclusion of *The Doctrine of Virtue*.

♋♋

16.6 Conclusion to *The Doctrine of Virtue*: Why the science of ethics does not include religion

The conclusion to the entire *Doctrine of Virtue* is entitled "Religious doctrine as the doctrine of duties to God lies outside the bounds of pure moral philosophy." In it, Kant explains why, in expounding a theory of ethics, he has not followed the usual practice of bringing religion (conceived as duties to God) into ethics. Kant allows that duties to God are part of a complete doctrine of morals. What he denies is that duties to God are part of the *science* of pure moral philosophy. In explaining his position, he appeals to the distinction between duties *to* God and duties *with regard to* God that he introduced earlier in the Episodic Section (§§16–18). As you may recall, there Kant argues that human beings only have duties to other human beings. Regarding inorganic matter and organic beings including plants and nonhuman animals, one only has duties regarding these things. His claim is that to have a duty *to* something, it must be something that (*i*) is encountered in one's experience, and (*ii*) is capable of holding one accountable for one's deeds. Things we encounter in our experience (other than human beings) do not satisfy the second condition. God, if God exits, does not satisfy the first.

However, there is a role for the *idea* of God in one's moral life. This was mentioned in the Episodic Section and is elaborated here by distinguishing the "formal aspect" of all religion from its "material aspect."

In its formal aspect, religion is defined as the "totality of all duties *as* . . . divine commands" (DV 6:487). And this, Kant says, does belong to a science of morals. How so? Kant's thought is that when religion is conceived in this formal way, one abstracts from the question whether God exists. Rather, using our *idea* of God as a divine being who has the authority to issue categorical obligations to human beings, we can make the idea of such obligations intuitive for ourselves. In conceiving of one's duties as though they were commands of God, one is in effect considering one's reason, which issues universal moral laws, as the "spokesman" for God or as God itself. The point of doing so is to help strengthen one's moral incentive. However, this should not be taken as the proposal to take love or fear of God as one's moral incentive. As Kant insists, the only true moral incentive is respect for the authority of the moral law.

The material aspect of religion is the "totality of duties *to* . . . God, i.e. the services to be provided for him" (DV 6:478). This would be to consider specific duties to God as divine commands that are *not* derived from reason as universal laws. Rather, they would have to be discovered empirically through revelation. More precisely, such duties could not be derived from the CI together with the sorts of empirical knowledge of the nature of human beings (anthropology) needed to derive duties from reason. In any case, as we know from chapter 2, it is not possible, according to Kant's epistemology, to know whether God exists. And even though we are permitted to postulate God's existence in order to conceive the realization of the highest, most complete good, this does not permit one to include duties to God as part of the science of ethics.

In a "concluding remark" Kant attempts to bolster his claim that religion as a doctrine of duties to God is not part of the science of ethics. The gist of the remark is that it is seemingly incomprehensible how to reconcile God's right in ensuring punitive justice for humankind with God's end of creating human beings out of love for them. Kant's reasoning (which for reasons of space I will skip over) leads him to conclude that "what sort of relation obtains between God and human beings completely exceeds the bounds of ethics and is absolutely incomprehensible for us" (DV 6:491). Following the conclusion is a table that lists the parts, books, chapters, and main sections that compose the body of the *Doctrine of Virtue*.

16.7 Concluding reflections

We began this chapter quoting Kant, who says that there are two main tasks in developing a theory of moral education:

Access: how the pure laws of morality can gain access to the mind, and
Influence: how those laws can influence one's choice of maxims.

The access question is partly addressed through moral catechism, suitable for children of the right age and ability, which includes judicious use of hypothetical and actual examples. The more challenging task is to explain how the laws of morality can influence one's choice of maxims. A person must somehow leave behind thoughts of any personal advantage in complying with the moral law and replace those "leading strings" with a recognition of the authority of the moral law and the dignity of virtue as a proper basis for conduct and character. Coming to have a good will and cultivating virtue is an exercise of free will, and not a mechanical process that guarantees success, which highlights the importance of devising techniques for strengthening one's moral resolve, including contemplating the dignity of the moral law and practicing virtue.

To bring Kant's theory of moral education into full focus, one needs to consult the Methodology of Pure Practical Reason from the second *Critique*, as well as *On Pedagogy*. There are also remarks in the *Anthropology* and some of Kant's essays, including Section I of "On the common saying: That may be correct in theory, but it is of no use in practice" (TP 8:278–289). So, I've only been able to present a partial account of Kant's views on moral education and practice.

Further Reading

- In addition to Kant's writings on education just mentioned, those interested in his views on moral education should consult the essays in *Kant and Education: Interpretations and Commentary*, K. Roth and C. W. Suprenant, eds., 2012.
- See Guyer 2012 [2016] on the multiple uses of examples in Kant's ethical theory.
- Those interested in Kant's concluding remarks about religion, God, and moral science should dig into Kant's 1793 *Religion within the Limits of Reason Alone.*

Concluding Reflections on *The Doctrine of Virtue*

Kant's *Doctrine of Virtue* has gained increasing attention in the past few decades and serves to correct an otherwise lopsided picture one might have of Kant's moral philosophy from just reading the *Groundwork of the Metaphysics of Morals* or the second *Critique*. My inspiration for writing this guide has been to help portray (at least some of) the rich and nuanced character of Kant's substantive normative ethical theory. I will close by calling attention to what I see as some of the most salient features of Kant's normative ethical theory as articulated in DV, followed by remarks situating the theory in relation to others.

At a general level of description, then, here are the theory's features I have in mind.

- DV's primary focus is moral character rather than external action.
- The theory offers a formal conception of virtue as a global character trait combining moral resolve with an acquired strength of will to comply with one's resolve.
- It is conceived by Kant as a doctrine of ends one has a moral obligation to adopt.
- The theory offers a system of duties derivable from a single principle, most prominently the formula of humanity.
- The system is structured by the fundamental ends of moral self-perfection and the happiness of others.
- It highlights the significance of duties to oneself.
- It also highlights the interdependence of love and respect in treating others as ends in themselves and the importance of *manner* in morals.
- The system of virtues and vices associated with these duties collectively provide "substance" to the formal conception of virtue.

- The theory finds a place for moral feeling, conscience, love of one's neighbor, and respect as self-esteem as presuppositions of being subject to moral requirements, as well as a place for such feelings as appreciativeness associated with gratitude and fellow-feeling more generally (suitably morally constrained of course).
- Its treatment of casuistical questions and the emphasis on the importance of taking account of varying circumstances in moral deliberation and choice highlights the importance of moral judgment—a skill-like capacity of applying midlevel moral rules to concrete cases.

These elements help situate Kant's normative ethical theory among contemporary theories in ethics. *First*, Kant's is not a version of divine command theory. Yet, Kant did hold that ethics leads by way of the concept of the highest good to religion and, in particular, to the idea that moral imperatives are properly conceived as commands of God—themes developed most fully in his 1793 *Religion within the Boundaries of Mere Reason*. However, Kant denied that God (and religion generally) is needed to explain the source and authority of the moral law, and he denied that they are needed to explain moral motivation. (See especially R 6:3.) Because Kant does not prioritize the good over the right, his view differs from natural law theory as, say, developed by Aquinas (sometimes referred to as a 'teleological ethic'), yet teleology does play a role in his ethics as explained in chapter 10, sec. 3 and chapter 12, sec. 4. As noted in chapter 10, sec. 5, Kant denies that the value of consequences explains why some actions are obligatory and others are wrong—another implication of denying the priority of value (or good) over duty. Yet, consequences figure importantly in *The Doctrine of Right* with its focus on protecting external freedom (which is not to say that Kant is a consequentialist in his legal and political theorizing). And, for example, when judging how to benefit others, one needs to consider how the intended beneficiaries will likely be affected and thus what the consequences of one's actions are likely to be. While DV is primarily concerned with motivation and character, Kant's normative ethics is not a version of so-called virtue ethics that would attempt to explain the deontic status of actions by appealing to considerations of virtue, taking virtue to be explanatorily prior to duty. (On this point, see Robert Johnson 2008.) Robert Adams (2006) usefully distinguishes virtue ethics from ethics of virtue (or character) that aims to explain what makes a character trait a virtue or a vice and what constitutes being a person of overall virtue. Kant's ethical theory, of course, addresses questions pertaining to an ethics of character.

Kant's theory is often classified as a version of deontology.[1] However, except for being opposed to all forms of consequentialism, I am not aware of a positive characterization of this species of theory that covers all views considered to be within this camp. Regardless, Kant's theory does not amount to a stark list of rules that merely demand outward compliance; its emphasis on motivation, attitude, and manner makes this much clear. On the issue of structure, it is useful to compare Kant's theory to W. D. Ross's (1930) ethics of prima facie duty, which counts as a version of deontology if any view does. Ross defended a pluralist account of the structure of the deontic realm denying there to be a single principle of morality that is: (i) more fundamental than a system of midlevel prima facie duties, (ii) determinate enough to figure in derivations of midlevel duties, (iii) complete enough to justify the full range of commonly recognized duties, (iv) while also yielding plausible explanations of the deontic status of actions. And even if we are likely to disagree with certain aspects of Kant's ethics—including, for example, his views on sexual morality and his apparent rigorism—we can ask whether a Kantian ethic might accomplish what Ross thought was improbable if not impossible—a project that has its contemporary advocates.[2]

⚛ ⚛

Considering the past decade or so of Kant scholarship, we see a flourish of interest in Kant's moral psychology as it impacts his ethics, including work on the various virtues and vices that compose his ethical system. There is also excellent work on the relation between Kant's ethics and religion and the relation between the doctrines of right and virtue, just

[1] This classification has been challenged by some contemporary scholars who prefer to read Kant as committed to some version of consequentialist or teleological theory, perhaps despite himself. For a concise overview of this matter, see Johnson and Cureton 2019, sec. 13.

[2] Including, for example, Robert Audi 2004, Barbara Herman 2007, and Thomas E. Hill, Jr. 2000, 2002, 2012.

to mention two topics where I believe advances have been made in our understanding of Kant. Many issues remain to be explored, including, for example, how Kant's ethics might handle forgiveness, which Kant did not discuss. Normative ethics includes both theory and application, and we find a growing literature addressing contemporary moral problems fruitfully employing the resources of Kant's ethics. Scholarship on Kant's ethics continues to flourish, as does its influence on contemporary moral theorizing.

Contrasts between *The Doctrine of Right* and *The Doctrine of Virtue*

1. Type of lawgiving distinguished by incentive (chapter 5, sec. 5)
   DR: Allows for external incentives, including coercion by the state.
   DV: Requires internal incentives, most generally respect for the moral law.
2. Type of freedom involved (chapter 6, sec. 2)
   DR: External freedom in relation to others.
   DV: Inner freedom (moral self-mastery over inclinations).
3. Type of law (chapter 5, sec. 5)
   DR: Laws enacted by a state.
   DV: Laws one gives to oneself, grounded in the moral law.
4. Type of obligation (chapter 5, sec. 5)
   DR: Juridical.
   DV: Ethical.
5. Type of duty (chapter 5, sec. 5.5)
   DR: Concerns external actions only.
   DV: Includes duties to adopt ends and corresponding maxims of action.
6. Proper starting points of inquiry (chapter 6, sec. 3)
   DR: Given those personal ends one adopts, one is to act on maxims of action as means to those ends consistent with the external freedom of others in accordance with universal law.
   DV: Establishes ends that one has a duty to promote and on their basis grounds maxims "with regard to ends we *ought* to set ourselves" (DV 6:382).
7. Relation of duties to enforceable rights (chapter 6, sec. 6.3)
   DR: Duties to others correlated with enforceable rights.
   DV: Duties to others not correlated with enforceable rights.
8. Nature of the duty and corresponding compliance with obligation (chapter 7, sec. 3)
   DR: Narrow duties requiring perfect compliance.
   DV: Both narrow duties requiring perfect compliance and wide duties requiring only imperfect compliance.
9. Status of the two fundamental principles of the doctrine of morals (chapter 9, sec. 2)
   DR: The universal principle of right is analytic a priori.
   DV: The supreme principle of the virtue is synthetic a priori.

Guide to Terminology

Each entry includes references to places in this text where the term is explained.

Affect An occurrent feeling which, on Kant's definition, is a state of "surprise through sensation, by means of which the mind's composure ... is suspended" (Anth 7:252), e.g. anger triggered by an insulting remark. See also *passion*. (Chapter 8, sec. 6)

A posteriori Cognition that depends on sense experience, including introspection. (Chapter 3, sec. 2)

A priori Cognition that is independent of sense experience, grounded in reason. (Chapter 3, sec. 2)

Analytic proposition A proposition whose truth is a matter of the meanings of the proposition's constituent terms. See also *synthetic proposition*. (Chapter 3, sec. 2)

Animality Aspects of human nature pertaining to their animal nature. In *Religion*, Kant recognizes the predisposition to animality as one of the predispositions to good. See also *humanity, moral personality*. (Chapter 8, sec. 1)

Anthropology A systematic doctrine of "knowledge of the human being" (Anth 7:119), representing the empirical part of a doctrine of morals. (Chapter 3, sec. 5)

Autocracy of the will The *developed* capacity of the will of a nonholy rational agent to make the moral law her sole and sufficient motive of choice and action in cases where "duty calls." (Chapter 6, sec. 3)

Autonomy of the will The capacity to give oneself the moral law and by doing so to act solely on the basis of one's recognition of its authority. This is Kant's positive conception of freedom of the will. See also *heteronomy of the will*. (Chapter 2, sec. 2)

Beneficence, duty of A wide duty of love toward others that commands one to adopt a maxim of *active benevolence*, i.e. to promote the happiness of others in need, according to one's means, without hope of receiving something in return. See also *benevolence*. (Chapter 13, sec. 2)

Benevolence As mere well-wishing it is passively taking satisfaction in the happiness of others. Active benevolence in its most generic form involves adopting a maxim of actively promoting the happiness of others. In its more specific form, the maxim is concerned with the needs of others and is identical to the maxim of beneficence. See also *beneficence, duty of.* (Chapter. 7, sec. 4 and Chapter 13, sec. 1)

Choice The faculty of desire when "joined with one's consciousness of the ability to bring about its object by one's action is called *choice*" (*Willkür*). See also *will*. (Chapter 4, sec.1)

Cognition Representation of an object or state of affairs. Theoretical cognitions purport to represent how things are (or have been or will be), practical cognitions purport to represent how things ought to be (or ought to have been) through the use of one's freedom. (Chapter 3, sec. 1)

Comply with duty Actions that accord with the *letter* of the law prescribing duty, without regard for one's motive in doing so. As I use this expression it is equivalent to Kant's usage of "acting in conformity with duty." See also *legality versus morality*. (Chapter 5, sec. 4)

Dignity of humanity A status possessed by all human beings in virtue of having autonomy and by which one is raised above all other nonautonomous beings. (Chapter 5, sec. 2 and Chapter 14, sec. 2)

Duties of commission Positive duties that require performing some action or adopting some maxim of action. See also *duties of omission*. (Chapter 5, sec. 1)

Duties of ethics All duties that belong to the doctrine of virtue, thus equivalent to duties of virtue; not to be confused with Kant's concept of an ethical duty. See also *duties of virtue, ethical duties*. (Chapter 5, sec. 5)

Duties of omission Negative duties to refrain from some action. See also *duties of commission*. (Chapter 5, sec. 1)

Duties of right Duties pertaining to the doctrine of right that comprises Kant legal and political philosophy. (Chapter 5, secs. 5 and 6)

Duties of virtue Duties that are the proper subject matter of ethics (as a division of moral philosophy distinct from the doctrine of right) and thus belong to the doctrine of virtue. (Chapter 5, secs. 4 and 5 and Chapter 6, sec. 3).

Duty An action (including omissions) that one is morally obligated to perform. Thus, the "content" or "matter" of an obligation. (Chapter 5, sec. 1)

End An end of action, at it figures in explaining actions, is the purpose (aim, goal) for which one performs the action. Of course, one can perform a single act for multiple purposes at a time, and one's purposes are often "nested." Kant tells us that all intentional action involves some end or other (MM 6:385). He also refers to ends as the "matter" of choice. Kant distinguishes two sorts of end: subjective and objective. See also *objective end, subjective end*. (Chapter 6, secs. 2, 3, and 4)

End in itself A being whose existence has an absolute (nonrelative) worth in virtue of having moral personality. See also *moral personality*. (Chapter 5, sec. 2)

Ethical action See *virtuous action*.

Ethical duties Duties associated with ethical (internal) lawgiving. Duties of virtue are "directly" ethical since the only incentive associated with them is the motive of duty. Duties of right are in the first instance subject to juridical (external) lawgiving whose associated incentives allow for motives other than duty. Yet, they are also subject to internal lawgiving and so "indirectly ethical" duties. See also *ethical lawgiving, juridical lawgiving*. (Chapter 5, sec. 5, and Chapter 6, sec. 4)

Ethical lawgiving Lawgiving that makes an action a duty that also makes duty (respect for law) the proper incentive (motive) for compliance. See also *lawgiving, juridical lawgiving*. (Chapter 5, sec. 5)

Ethical obligation Obligations characteristic of ethical lawgiving. See also *ethical lawgiving, juridical obligation, obligation*. (Chapter 5, sec. 5)

External action A publicly observable action that requires outward bodily movement, such as paying a bill or helping someone in need. See also *internal action*. (Chapter 5, sec. 5)

External duty An obligation to perform an external action. (Chapter 5, sec. 5)

External freedom Freedom of external action from interference by others or other external impediments. See also *external action, inner freedom*. (Chapter 5, sec. 6 and Chapter 6, sec. 2)

Faculty of desire "The faculty to be, by means of one's representations, the cause of the objects of these representations. The faculty of a being to act in accordance with its representations is called *life*" (MM 6:211). The faculty of desire in human beings is their "will," in the broad sense of including both practical reason (the legislative element) and choice (the executive element). See also *will*. (Chapter 4, sec 1)

Feeling (as a fundamental faculty of the mind) The capacity to have experiences of pleasure and displeasure. See also *moral feeling*. (Chapter 4, sec. 1)

Feelings (nonmoral and moral) Particular feelings. Nonmoral feelings have their source in a human being's sensuous nature. Moral feelings have their source in reason itself. Besides the feeling of respect (which is central to Kant's conception of moral motivation), he mentions such moral feelings as disgust, guilt, horror, and shame. (Chapter 4, secs. 1, 3, and 4)

Freedom See *external freedom* and *inner freedom*.

Happiness Roughly, taking pleasure in the realization of one's inclinations. (Chapter 3, sec. 5)

Heteronomy of the will Acting for nonmoral reasons—reasons that are grounded in one's sensible nature. To refrain from lying because it is not in one's long-term self-interest is an exercise of heteronomy of the will. (Chapter 2, sec. 2)

Homo noumena Human beings considered as members of the intelligible realm. So considered, human beings are taken to have autonomy, and thus considered as persons to whom actions are imputable. (Chapter 2, sec. 2)

Homo phenomena Human beings considered as members of the sensible realm. So considered, human beings are understood as merely natural beings. (Chapter 2, sec. 2)

Humanity This technical term, as it figures in the formula of humanity version of the CI, refers to one's moral freedom, that is, the *capacity* to comply with duty from the sole motive of duty. In this sense it is equivalent to one's moral personality. However, in the *Religion*, Kant contrasts humanity with both animality and moral personality. In this context, it is the mere capacity to set ends, which is compatible with only being able to adopt ends based in sensible inclination. See also *animality, moral personality*. (Chapter 5, sec. 2 and Chapter 8, sec. 1)

Imperfect obligation/duty See *wide obligation/duty*.

Impulse A generic term referring to such empirical motivational states as desires, aversions, inclinations, that is, "sensuous" motivational states. (Chapter 4, sec. 1)

Incentive "The subjective determining ground of the will" (CprR 5:72–73) that refers to a motivating reason—a consideration that one takes to be a reason for choice, the "taking up" of which (can or does) plays a causal role in explaining choice and action. This is to consider an incentive as a psychological state. However, talk of an incentive can also refer to whatever consideration or fact is a normative reason for an individual (the "object" of the incentive qua psychological state). The fact that by performing a particular action one would thereby suffer harm is a reason for one to refrain from the action—an incentive *not* to perform the action. Such a reason would be the "object" of an incentive as a psychological state—its intentional content; what the psychological state is about or directed toward. (Chapter 4, sec. 3)

Incentive, moral "Respect for the moral law is . . . the undoubted moral incentive, and this feeling is also directed to no object except on this basis" (CprR 5:78). When Kant refers to respect (qua moral feeling) as an incentive, I take him to be foregrounding the motivational role of normative reasons grounded in the moral law as they figure in one's psychology. The "object" of such a psychological (motivational) state is a particular moral reason or perhaps the moral law itself (in one of its guises). (Chapter 4, secs. 3 and 4, and Chapter 5, sec. 5)

Incentive, nonmoral A nonmoral consideration (such as potential financial gain) that can be taken up by an agent as a normative reason for action and thus serve as a motivating reason for acting. (Chapter 4, sec. 3)

Inclination In some places, Kant glosses this as "sensible habitual desire" (Anth 7:251; also MS 6:212). Inclinations (including desires and aversions) are part of our sensible, empirical nature. Inclinations are *acquired* on the basis of past experience; the basis of an inclination is what Kant refers to as a "propensity." This is "inclination" in the narrower sense of the term. "Inclination" in the broad sense refers to *all* of those motivational elements that are grounded in one's sensuous nature. See also *propensity.* (Chapter 4, secs. 1 and 3)

Innate dignity of humanity See *dignity of humanity.*

Inner freedom The capacity of self-constraint involving self-legislation necessary for there being duties of virtue. See also *external freedom, duties of virtue.* (Chapter 6, sec. 2)

Interest "An interest is that by which reason becomes practical, i.e., becomes a cause determining the will" (G 4:460n. see also, CJ 5:204). "From the concept of an incentive arises that of an *interest,* which can never be attributed to any being unless it also has reason . . ." (CprR 5:79). Nonmoral interests for Kant are grounded in what one takes to be their own happiness. See also *moral interest*. (Chapter 4, sec. 3)

Internal action A private mental action that does not require bodily movement, such as the act of deciding (adopting a maxim of ends) to go to law school. (Chapter 5, sec. 5)

Internal duty A duty to perform an internal action. See also *internal action*. (Chapter 5, sec. 5)

Juridical lawgiving Lawgiving that makes an action a duty associated with incentives drawn from inclinations and aversions (including state coercion). This type of lawgiving is characteristic of coercible duties of right (justice) treated in DR. See also *lawgiving, ethical lawgiving*. (Chapter 5, sec. 5).

Juridical obligation Obligations that arise through juridical lawgiving. See also *obligation, ethical obligation*. (Chapter 5, sec. 5).

Law In *The Metaphysics of Morals*, this term can either refer to a law of morality or to a statutory law of a state. Moral laws, directed to nonholy rational beings, express an obligation to do or refrain from doing something (a duty). In DV, when Kant claims that some action violates 'the law,' he is claiming that it violates a law of morality; one that sets forth a duty of virtue. See also *moral law*. (Chapter 5, sec. 1)

Lawgiving The action of prescribing (or proscribing) actions involving two elements: (*i*) a law that represents an action as necessary to do (or refrain from doing), thus making the action a duty and (*ii*) an incentive that serves to connect the law representing a duty with a reason for complying with the duty that can also serve as a sufficient motive to comply. The distinction between ethical and juridical lawgiving is the basis for distinguishing DR from DV. See also *juridical lawgiving, ethical lawgiving, duties of right, duties of virtue*. (Chapter 5, sec. 5).

Legality versus morality When one complies with (conforms to) a duty, one's action is said to have legality. When one complies with a duty from the sole motive of duty, one's action is said to have morality, i.e. moral worth in addition to legality. On this usage, 'legality' is not restricted to actions that comply with the laws enacted by a state. (Chapter 5, sec. 4).

Love There are at least five (maybe more) senses of this term in DV. (1) love as sexual inclination, which Kant says is "the narrowest sense of the term" (6:426), (2) love of human beings as a general predisposition on the side of sensibility to acquire an aptitude to beneficence (6:402), (3) love as delight,

(4) love as well-wishing (passive benevolence), and (5) active practical benevolence, expressed in a maxim that one has a duty to adopt. See also *benevolence*. (Chapter 13, sec. 1)

Maxim The content of an intention on which an agent acts (or is disposed to act)—one's intention is what constitutes an action (at least partly). "A maxim is the *subjective* principle of acting. . . (G 4:441n)," in the sense that it is a principle upon which one does in fact act or, in cases of commitment to ends, a principle one intends to act on. (Chapter 4, sec. 2)

Moral feeling The "susceptibility to feel pleasure or displeasure merely from being aware that our actions are consistent with or contrary to the law of duty" (MM 6:399). Kant denies that moral feeling so understood is some sort of sense by which one can perceive or quasi-perceive moral qualities, nor is moral feeling the basis or foundation of morality. (Chapter 4, sec. 4 and Chapter 8, sec. 2)

Moral interest One "takes an immediate interest" in an action when conforming one's conduct and character to the moral law is a sufficient motive (subjective determining ground) of one's performing that action. "Only such an interest is pure" (G 4:460n), and only such an interest is a "moral interest"; also referred to as an "interest of reason" (MM 6:213). Kant identifies respect for the moral law as moral interest at G 4:402n, see also, G 4:460–462. See also *interest*. (Chapter 4, sec. 4)

Moral law Used in the singular, this term refers to *the* moral law—the supreme principle of morality, the Categorical Imperative. It is also used to refer to the body of specific laws of morality, as when one says that the moral law includes prohibitions on suicide, lying, ridicule, etc. (Chapter 2, sec. 2)

Moral merit Doing more than the moral law strictly requires is morally meritorious. On the interpretation offered in the text, complying with a wide, imperfect duty, even if not done from the sole motive of duty (e.g., an act of beneficence), is meritorious. See also *comply with duty, moral worth*. (Chapter 5, sec. 4).

Moral personality One's supersensible capacity to act independently of inclination (negative freedom) and solely out of respect for the moral law (positive freedom). In *Religion* (6:26–28), Kant distinguishes three predispositions to good in human nature: animality, humanity, and moral personality. See also *animality, humanity*. (Chapter 5, sec. 2 and Chapter 8, sec. 1)

Moral worth Actions performed from the sole motive of respect for the moral law have moral worth. Similarly, for the adoption of maxims of action. Moral worth should not be confused with moral merit. See also *moral merit*. (Chapter 5, sec. 4; Chapter 7, sec. 3)

Narrow obligation/duty An obligation whose content (the duty) is to perform or refrain from performing a specific sort of action on specific occasions (as opposed to adopting a policy) allowing no exceptions and thus requiring "perfect" compliance. Such duties are narrow in *quality*, perfect in *degree* and tend to be duties of omission. See also *duties of omission, wide obligation/duty*. (Chapter 7, sec. 3 and Chapter 12, sec. 2)

Objective end An end that "is given by reason," and hence an end that is "valid" for all rational agents, whether one adopts the end or not. See also *subjective end*. (Chapter 6, sec. 2)

Obligation A relation of 'necessitation' between a moral law representing an action as necessary (a duty) and the faculty of choice of a nonholy rational being, who may or may not comply with the law. (Chapter 5, sec. 1)

Passion An inclination (as a dispositional mental state) that "can be conquered only with difficulty or not at all" (Anth 7:251). Because passions shut out the sovereignty of reason in a principled way, they constitute vices. See also *affect, vice*. (Chapter 8, sec. 6)

Perfect obligation/duty See *narrow obligation/duty*.

Pleasure (and displeasure) Feelings that "express nothing at all in the object, but simply a relation to the subject" (MM 6:212). In the *Anthropology,* Kant remarks that one can explain these feelings "by means of the effect that the sensation produces on our state of mind" (Anth 7:230–231), i.e. by their functional role. Pleasure tends to result in one's staying in the pleasurable mental state; pain "urges me to *leave* my state" (Anth 7:231, see also, 254). (Chapter 4, sec. 1)

Practical law A principle that represents an action as necessary without taking into account whether the being to whom the law is addressed is a holy being (God) who necessarily complies with the law or a nonholy being (e.g. human beings) whose compliance with the law is contingent. (Chapter 5, sec. 1)

Practical principle This term refers to maxims (subjective practical principles) and to imperatives of practical reason (objective practical principles). See also *maxim, law*. (Chapter 4, sec. 2)

Predispositions Constituent parts of a being "required for it as well as the forms of their combination that make for such a being" (R 6:28). They are "original" if they belong with necessity to the possibility of the being; otherwise they are contingent. See also *animality, humanity, moral personality*. (Chapter 8, sec. 1)

Propensity "The subjective *possibility* of the emergence of a certain desire, which *precedes* the representation of its object" (Anth 7:265). In *Religion* Kant writes that propensity is a "predisposition to desire an enjoyment which, when the subject experiences it, arouses *inclination* to it" (R 6:29n). Some are acquired through experience, others are "natural" in the sense of innate. Hence, with respect to moral good and evil Kant refers to the "natural propensity to evil." (R 6:29). (Chapter 8, sec. 5)

Pure will A will "is called a pure will insofar as the pure understanding (which in this case is called reason) is practical through the mere representation of law" (CpuR 5:55). This includes the formal principle of hypothetical imperatives as among pure practical principles. But this formal principle of instrumental reason does not *itself* ground any reasons for action. (Chapter 5, sec. 1)

Respect Used by Kant to refer to a "peculiar" feeling, as in respect for the law, and to ways of treating others. Respect qua feeling is complex (see G 4:402n, and CprR, Chapter III), and figures in Kant's conception of moral motivation. "Respect for the law" is how Kant often refers to the "moral incentive" which, if it is the sole motivating force in complying with duty, then one's action has moral worth. See also *moral worth*. (Chapter 8, sec. 2 and Chapter 14, sec. 2)

Subjective end An end one has based on desires and aversions, having only "relative worth—worth *for the individual who has it*." Such ends are also referred to as having *conditional worth* and being *contingent and discretionary*. See also *objective end*. (Chapter 6, sec. 2)

Synthetic proposition A proposition whose truth value depends on the meanings of its constituent terms plus whether it corresponds to facts that it purports to represent. See also *analytic proposition*. (Chapter 3, sec. 2)

Vices Traits that dispose one to violate the moral law such as envy, ingratitude, and malice. Also, an action that violates the moral law may also be referred to as a vice, as in "He indulged in the vice of drunkenness." Vices are constituted by passions. See also *passion*. (Chapter 6, sec. 3 and Chapter 8, sec. 6)

Virtue As a global character trait or what Kant refers to as a "virtuous disposition," it is to resolve to comply with one's duties from the sole motive of duty (i.e. to have a good will) and to have acquired the strength of will to comply with one's resolve. (Chapter 8, sec. 4 where this concept is most fully developed.)

Virtues Acquired traits of character, grounded in respect for the moral law, that dispose one to comply with one or another duty, e.g. beneficence, gratitude, sympathetic participation. (Chapter 6, sec. 3)

Virtuous action Dutiful action (whether belonging to DR or DV) motivated solely out of respect for the moral law. (Chapter 5, sec. 5)

Wide obligation/duty An obligation whose content (duty) requires adoption of a general policy of action (a maxim of action) that is nonspecific in what it requires and therefore leaves some latitude for complying with it. Such duties are wide in *quality*; imperfect in *degree* of compliance. See also *narrow obligation/duty*. (Chapter 7, sec. 3 and Chapter 12, sec. 2)

Will In humans, a capacity of the faculty of desire to exercise freedom of choice (*Willkür*) by exercising one's practical reason ('will' in the narrow sense). See also *choice*. (Chapter 4, sec. 1)

Bibliography

Adams, R. 2006. *A Theory of Virtue: Excellence in Being for the Good* (Oxford and New York: Oxford University Press).

Allison, H. E. 1990. *Kant's Theory of Freedom* (Cambridge: Cambridge University Press).

Allison, H. E. 1993. "Kant's Doctrine of Obligatory Ends," *Jarbuch für Recht und Ethik* 1: 7–23. Reprinted in Allison, *Idealism and Freedom*: 155–168.

Allison, H. E. 1996. *Idealism and Freedom: Essays on Kant's Theoretical and Practical Philosophy* (Cambridge: Cambridge University Press).

Anderson-Gold, S., and P. Muchnik, eds. 2010. *Kant's Anatomy of Evil* (Cambridge: Cambridge University Press).

Audi, R. 2004. *The Good in the Right: A Theory of Intuition and Intrinsic Value* (Princeton, N. J.: Princeton University Press).

Audi, R. 2006. *Practical Reasoning and Ethical Decision* (New York: Routledge).

Bacin, S. 2013. "The Perfect Duty to Oneself Merely as Moral Being," in Trampota, et al., *Kant's Tugendlehre*: 245–268.

Baiasu, S., and M. Timmons, eds. 2021. *The Kantian Mind* (New York: Routledge).

Baron, M. 2013. "Friendship, Duties Regarding Specific Conditions of Persons, and the Virtues of Social Intercourse," in Trampota, et al., *Kant's Tugendlehre*: 365–382.

Baxley, A. M. 2010. *Kant's Theory of Virtue: The Value of Autocracy* (Cambridge: Cambridge University Press).

Beck, L. W. 1960. *A Commentary on Kant's* Critique of Practical Reason (Chicago, IL: University of Chicago Press).

Bell, M. 2011. *Hard Feelings: The Moral Psychology of Contempt* (Oxford and New York: Oxford University Press).

Betzler, M., ed. 2008. *Kant's Theory of Virtue* (Berlin and New York: Walter de Guyter).

Card, C. 2010. "Kant's Excluded Moral Middle," in Anderson-Gold and Muchnik, *Kant's Anatomy of Evil* 2010: 74–92.

Card, C. 2016. "Taking Pride in Being Bad," in M. Timmons, ed., *Oxford Studies in Normative Ethics* 6 (Oxford and New York: Oxford University Press): 37–55.

Darwall, S. 1977. "Two Kinds of Respect," *Ethics* 88: 36–49.

D'Arms, J., and D. Jacobson. 2000. "The Moralistic Fallacy," *Philosophy and Phenomenological Research* 61: 65–90.

Denis, L. 1999. "Kant on the Wrongness of 'Unnatural' Sex," *History of Philosophy Quarterly* 6: 225–247.

Denis, L. 2000a. "Kant's Cold Sage and the Sublimity of Apathy," *Kantian Review* 4: 48–73.

Denis, L. 2000b. "Kant's Conception of Duties Regarding Animals: Reconstruction and Reconsideration," *History of Philosophy Quarterly* 17: 405–423.

Denis, L., ed. 2010a. *Kant's Metaphysics of Morals: A Critical Guide* (Cambridge: Cambridge University Press).

Denis, L. 2010b. "Freedom, Primacy, and the Perfect Duties to Oneself," in Denis, *Kant's Metaphysics of Morals: A Critical Guide*: 179–191.

Denis, L. 2014. "Love of Honor as a Kantian Virtue," in A. Cohen, ed., *Kant on Emotion and Value* (Hampshire, UK: Palgrave and Macmillan): 191–209.

Denis, L. and O. Sensen, eds. 2015. *Kant's Lectures on Ethics: A Critical Guide* (Cambridge: Cambridge University Press).

Eisenberg, N. 2004. "Empathy and Sympathy," in M. Lewis, J. M. Haviland-Jones, eds., *Handbook of Emotions*, 2nd ed. (New York and London: The Guilford Press): 677–691.

Engstrom, S. 2002. "The Inner Freedom of Morality," in Timmons, *Kant's Metaphysics of Morals: Interpretative Essays*: 289–315.

Esser, A. M. 2013. "The Inner Court of Conscience, Moral Self-Knowledge, and the Proper Object of Duty," in Trampota, et al., *Kant's Tugendlehre*: 269–292.

Fahmy, M. S. 2009. "Active Sympathetic Participation: Reconsidering Kant's Duty of Sympathy," *Kantian Review* 14: 31–50.

Frierson, P. R. 2014. *Kant's Empirical Psychology* (Cambridge: Cambridge University Press).

Foot, P. 1972. "Morality as a System of Hypothetical Imperatives," *The Philosophical Review* 81: 305–316.

Gregor, M. J. 1963. *Laws of Freedom* (New York: Barnes & Noble, Inc.).

Grenberg, J. 2010. "What Is the Enemy of Virtue?" in Denis, *Kant's Metaphysics of Morals: A Critical Guide*: 152–169.

Griffin, J. 1986. *Well-Being* (Oxford: Oxford University Press).

Guyer, P. 2010. "Kant on Moral Feelings: From the Lectures to the *Metaphysics of Morals*," in Denis, *Kant's Metaphysics of Morals: A Critical Guide*: 130–151. Reprinted in Guyer, *Virtues of Freedom*: 235–259.

Guyer, P. 2011. "Kant's Perfectionism," in L. Jost and J. Wuerth 2011: 194–214. Reprinted in Guyer, *Virtues of Freedom*: 70–86.

Guyer, P. 2012. "Examples of Moral Possibility," in K. Roth and C. W. Surprenant, eds., *Kant and Education: Interpretations and Commentary* (New York: Routledge): 124–138. Reprinted in Guyer, *Virtues of Freedom*: 260–272.

Guyer, P. 2016. *Virtues of Freedom: Selected Essays on Kant* (Oxford and New York: Oxford University Press).

Guyer, P. Forthcoming in 2021. "Kant's Life and Work," in Baiasu and Timmons, *The Kantian Mind* (New York: Routledge).

Herman, B. 1981. "On the Value of Acting from the Motive of Duty," *Philosophical Review* 90: 359–382. Reprinted in Herman, *The Practice of Moral Judgment*: 1–22.

Herman, B. 1993. *The Practice of Moral Judgment* (Cambridge, MA: Harvard University Press).

Herman, B. 2007. "Obligatory Ends," in *Moral Literacy* (Cambridge, MA: Harvard University Press): 254–275.

Herman, B. 2019. "Being Prepared: From Motives to Duties," in M. Timmons, ed., *Oxford Studies in Normative Ethics*, vol. 9 (Oxford and New York: Oxford University Press): 9–28.

Hill, T. E., Jr. 1973. "Servility and Self-Respect," *The Monist* 51: 87-104. Reprinted in Hill, *Autonomy and Self-Respect*: 4-18.

Hill, T. E., Jr. 1991. *Autonomy and Self-Respect* (Cambridge: Cambridge University Press).

Hill, T. E., Jr. 1992. "A Kantian Perspective on Moral Rules," in J. Tomberlin, ed., *Philosophical Perspectives* 6 (Atascadero, CA: Ridgeview Publishing Co.) Reprinted in Hill, *Respect, Pluralism, and Justice*: 33–55.

Hill, T. E., Jr. 2000. *Respect, Pluralism, and Justice* (Oxford: Oxford University Press).

Hill, T. E., Jr. 1998. "Four Conceptions of Conscience," *Nomos* XL: 13–52. Reprinted in Hill, *Human Welfare and Moral Worth: Kantian Perspectives*: 277–309.

Hill, T. E., Jr. 2002. *Human Welfare and Moral Worth: Kantian Perspectives* (Oxford and New York: Oxford University Press).

Hill, T. E., Jr. 2006. "Kantian Normative Ethics," in D. Copp, ed., *Oxford Handbook of Ethical Theory* (Oxford: Oxford University Press): 26–50.

Hill, T. E., Jr. 2010. "Kant's *Tugendlehre* as Normative Ethics," in Denis, *Kant's Critique of Practical Reason: A Critical Guide*: 234–255. Reprinted in Hill, *Virtue, Rules, & Justice: Kantian Aspirations*: 160–182.

Hill, T. E., Jr. 2012. *Virtue, Rules, & Justice: Kantian Aspirations* (Oxford and New York: Oxford University Press).

Hume, D. 1739. *A Treatise of Human Nature* (Oxford: Oxford University Press, 1973).

Johnson, R. N. 1996. "Kant's Conception of Merit," *Pacific Philosophical Quarterly* 77: 310–334.

Johnson, R. N. 2010. "Duties to and Regarding Others," in Denis, *Kant's Critique of Practical Reason: A Critical Guide*: 192–209.

Johnson, R. N. 2008. "Was Kant a Virtue Ethicist?" in Beltzer, *Kant's Theory of Virtue*: 61–76.

Johnson, R. N. 2011. *Self-Improvement* (Oxford and New York: Oxford University Press).

Johnson, R. N. and A. Cureton. 2019. "Kant's Moral Theory," *The Stanford Encyclopedia of Philosophy* (Spring 2019 Edition), Edward N. Zalta, ed., URL = <https://plato.stanford.edu/archives/spr2019/entries/kant-moral/>.

Jost, L., and J. Wuerth, eds. 2011. *Perfecting Virtue: New Essays on Kantian Ethics and Virtue Ethics* (Cambridge: Cambridge University Press).

Kahn, S. 2015. "Kant's Theory of Conscience," in P. Muchnik and O. Thorndike, eds. *Re-Thinking Kant*, vol. IV: 135–155.

Kain, P. 2010. "Duties Regarding Animals," in Denis, *Kant's Critique of Practical Reason: A Critical Guide* 2010a: 210–233.

Kleingeld, P., and M. Willaschek. 2019. "Autonomy without Paradox: Kant on Self-Legislation and the Moral Law," *Philosophers' Imprint* 19: 1–18.

Korsgaard, C. 1986. "The Right to Lie: Kant on Dealing with Evil," *Philosophy and Public Affairs* 15: 325–349. Reprinted in Korsgaard, *Creating a Kingdom of Ends*: 133–158.

Korsgaard, C. 1996. *Creating a Kingdom of Ends* (New York: Cambridge University Press).

Kriegel, U., and M. Timmons. 2021 "The Phenomenology of Kantian Respect for Persons," in O. Sensen and R. Dean, eds., *Respect* (Cambridge: Cambridge University Press): 84–105.

Kuehn, M. 2001. *Kant: A Biography* (Cambridge: Cambridge University Press).

Kuehn, M. 2010. "Kant's *Metaphysics of Morals*: The History and Significance of its Deferral," in Denis, *Kant's Critique of Practical Reason: A Critical Guide* 2010a: 9–27.

Louden, R. B. 2000. *Kant's Impure Ethics* (Oxford and New York: Oxford University Press).

Mahon, J. E. 2006. "Kant and the Perfect Duty to Others Not to Lie," *British Journal for the History of Philosophy* 14: 653–685.

Mason, M. 2003. "Contempt as a Moral Attitude," *Ethics* 113: 234–272.

McCarty, R. 2009. *Kant's Theory of Action* (Oxford and New York: Oxford University Press).

Moran, K. A. 2016. "Much Obliged: Kantian Gratitude Reconsidered," *Archiv für Geschichte der Philosophie* 98: 330–363.

Muchnik, P. 2010. "An Alternative Proof of the Universal Propensity to Evil," in S. Anderson-Gold and P. Muchnik, *Kant's Anatomy of Evil*: 116–143.

O'Neill, O. 1998. "Kant on Duties Regarding Nonrational Nature," *Proceedings of the Aristotelian Society*, Supplementary Volume 72: 211–228

Papish, L. 2018. *Kant on Evil, Self-Deception, and Moral Reform* (Oxford and New York: Oxford University Press).

Pasternack, L. R. 2014. *Kant on* Religion within the Boundaries of Mere Reason (New York: Routledge).

Pogge, T. 1989. "The Categorical Imperative," in O. Hoffe, ed., *Grundlegung zur Metaphysik der Sitten: Ein Kooperativer Komentar* (Frankfurt am Main: Vittorio Klostermann): 172–192.

Potter, N. 1985. "Kant on Ends That are at the Same Time Duties," *Pacific Philosophical Quarterly* 66: 78–82.

Potter, N. 1993. "Reply to Allison," *Jahrbuch für Recht und Ethic* (*Annual Review of Law and Ethics*) 1: 391–400.

Potter, N. 2002. "Duties to Oneself, Motivational Internalism, and Self-Deception in Kant's Ethics," in M. Timmons *Kant's Metaphysics of Morals: Interpretative Essays*: 371–390.

Putnam, H. 1981. *Reason, Truth and History* (Cambridge: Cambridge University Press).

Reath, A. 1994a. "Legislating the Moral Law," *Nous* 28: 436–64. Reprinted in Reath, *Agency and Autonomy in Kant's Moral Theory: Selected Essays*: 92–120.

Reath, A. 1994b. "Agency and Imputation of Consequences in Kant's Ethics," *Jahrbuch für Recht und Ethik* 2: 259–82. Reprinted in Reath, *Agency and Autonomy in Kant's Moral Theory: Selected Essays*: 250–269.

Reath, A. 2006. *Agency and Autonomy in Kant's Moral Theory: Selected Essays* (Oxford and New York: Oxford University Press.

Reath, A., and J. Timmermann, eds. 2010. *Kant's Critique of Practical Reason: A Critical Guide* (Cambridge: Cambridge University Press).

Roth, K., and C. W. Surprenant, eds. 2014. *Kant and Education: Interpretations and Commentary* (New York and London: Routledge).

Ross, W. D. 1930. *The Right and the Good* (Oxford: Oxford University Press).

Sanchez Borboa, S. MS. "Kant and the Balance of Moral Forces."

Schönecker, D. 2013. "Duties to Others from Love," in Trampota, et al., *Kant's Tugendlehre*: 307–341.

Searle, J. 1984. *Minds, Brains, and Science* (Cambridge, MA: Harvard University Press).

Sensen, O. 2011. *Kant on Human Dignity* (Berlin/Boston: Walter de Gruyter GmbH & Co).

Sensen, O. 2013. "Duties to Others from Respect," in Trampota, et al., *Kant's Tugendlehre*: 343–364.

Sidgwick, H. 1907. *The Methods of Ethics*, 7th ed. (New York: Dover Publications, Inc.)

Smit, H. 2009. "Kant on Apriority and the Spontaneity of Cognition," in S. Newlands and L. M. Jorgensen, eds., *Metaphysics and the Good: Themes from the Philosophy of Robert Merrihew Adams* (Oxford University Press): 188–251.

Smit, H., and M. Timmons. 2011. "The Moral Significance of Gratitude in Kant's Ethics," *The Southern Journal of Philosophy* 49: 296–320. Reprinted in Timmons, *Significance and System: Essays on Kant's Ethics*: 241–267

Smit, H., and M. Timmons. 2013. "Kant's Grounding Project in the *Doctrine of Virtue*," in Baiasu and Timmons, 229–268. Reprinted in Timmons, *Significance and System: Essays on Kant's Ethics*: 175–218.

Smit, H., and M. Timmons. 2015. "Love of Honor, Emulation, and the Psychology of the Devilish Vices," in Denis and Sensen, *Kant's Lectures* on Ethics: A Critical Guide 2015. Reprinted in Timmons, *Significance and System: Essays on Kant's Ethics*: 271–292.

Tannenbaum, J. 2002. "Acting with Feeling from Duty," *Ethical Theory and Moral Practice* 5: 321–337.

Thomason, K. K. 2017. "A Good Enough Heart: Kant and the Cultivation of Emotions," *Kantian Review* 22: 441–462.

Timmermann, J. 2005. "When the Tail Wags the Dog: Animal Welfare and Indirect Duty in Kant's Ethics," *Kantian Review* 10: 128–149.

Timmermann, J. 2006a. "Kant on Conscience, 'Indirect' Duty, and Moral Error," *International Philosophical Quarterly* 26: 1–16.

Timmermann, J. 2006b. "Kantian Duties to the Self: Explained and Defended," *Philosophy* 81: 505–530.

Timmermann, J. 2013. "Duties to Oneself as Such," in Trampota, et al., *Kant's Tugendlehre*: 205–219.

Timmons, M. 1992. "Necessitation and Justification in Kant's Ethics," *Canadian Journal of Philosophy* 22: 223–261. Reprinted in Timmons 2017a, *Significance and System: Essays on Kant's Ethics*: 13–49.

Timmons, M., ed. 2002a. *Kant's* Metaphysics of Morals: *Interpretative Essays* (Oxford: Oxford University Press).

Timmons, M. 2002b. "Motive and Rightness in Kant's Ethics," in M. Timmons, *Kant's Metaphysics of Morals: Interpretative Essays*: 255–288. Reprinted in Timmons, *Significance and System: Essays on Kant's Ethics*: 139–174.

Timmons, M. 2013. "The Perfect Duty to Oneself," in A. Trampota, et al., *Kant's Tugendlehre*: 221–243. Reprinted as "Perfect Duties to Oneself as an Animal Being," in Timmons, *Significance and System: Essays on Kant's Ethics*: 219–240.

Timmons, M. 2017a. *Significance and System: Essays on Kant's Ethics* (Oxford and New York: Oxford University Press).

Timmons, M. 2017b. "The Good, the Bad, and the Badass: On the Descriptive Adequacy of Kant's Conception of Moral Evil," in Timmons, *Significance and System: Essays on Kant's Ethics*: 293–330.

Trampota, A., O. Sensen, and J. Timmermann, eds. 2013. *Kant's* Tugendlehre (Berlin and New York: Walter de Guyter).

Van Roojen, M. 2015. *Metaethics: A Contemporary Introduction* (New York: Routledge).

Wood, A. W. 1984. "Kant's Compatibilism," A. W. Wood, ed., *Self and Nature in Kant's Philosophy* (Ithaca and London: Cornell University Press): 73–101.

Wood, A. W. 1998. "Kant on Duties Regarding Nonrational Nature," *Proceedings of the Aristotelian Society*, Supplementary Volume 72: 189–210.

Wood, A. W. 2008. "Conscience," in *Kantian Ethics* (Cambridge: Cambridge University Press): 183–192.

Index